Craig Swann
Gregg Caines

XML
in Flash™

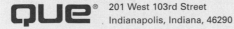 201 West 103rd Street
Indianapolis, Indiana, 46290

XML in Flash

Copyright © 2002 by Que Publishing

International Standard Book Number: 0-67232-315-x

Library of Congress Catalog Card Number: 2001096695

Printed in the United States of America

First Printing: December 2001

04   03   02   4   3   2

Trademarks

Warning and Disclaimer

Executive Editor
Jeff Schultz

Acquisitions Editor
Kate Small

Development Editor
Susan Hobbs

Managing Editor
Charlotte Clapp

Project Editor
Elizabeth Finney

Copy Editor
Lisa M. Lord

Indexer
Eric Schroeder

Proofreader
Paula Lowell

Technical Editor
Ryan Carver

Team Coordinator
Amy Patton

Media Developer
Dan Scherf

Interior Designer
Alan Clements

Cover Designer
Alan Clements

Page Layout
Mark Walchle

Contents at a Glance

Contents

Acknowledgments

I would like to first thank my family for being super supportive in every initiative I take. Without their love, guidance, and encouragement, none of this would be possible. Love you guys.

I would also like to send shout-outs to the wonderful and talented people I have had the pleasure of working with here at CRASH!: Rob Marks for his creative passion, endless nights, and ability to accept bent humor while lending graphical assistance on this book; Luminita Necula for her insight, dedication, and attention to detail; and Cam "heynow" Mead for his overall input, research support, and stress-relieving trips to the links!

I could never thank all the people who have given inspiration or provided insight or information from the Flash community. It's a wonderful thriving beast that constantly amazes me, and I am thankful for being a part of it. Of all the people I come in contact with online who have affected, inspired, or amazed me, there are those I've also had the pleasure of getting to know offline. So thanks to all of those faces and aliases I have come into contact with ever since this whole Web thing blew up—I hope this book gives back in some way.

The future is ours.

—Craig Swann

First off, I would like to acknowledge the help and support from my family and friends—in particular, my parents who have been a constant source of support and encouragement and my girlfriend, Martha, who's always been there for me and who I know always will be.

Of course, this book wouldn't be possible without the keen eyes of our editors, Kate Small, Susan "Suz" Hobbs, Elizabeth "Elf" Finncy, Lisa Lord, and Ryan Carver. They were diligent and made sure we dotted all our i's and crossed all our t's in addition to providing great input and even debugging code. This book couldn't be what it is without them.

In addition, I would like to give much respect to the Flash development community in general. I've learned a lot from them, and I hope the "open source" nature of this gives a little bit back.

—Gregg Caines

About the Authors

Craig Swann has been an active member of the Flash community since its early days and formed CRASH!MEDIA in 1997 as a way to express and explore this nonlinear and interactive digital landscape. CRASH!MEDIA is a Toronto-based Interactive Design Agency that specializes in integrating fresh ideas with cutting-edge technology. CRASH!MEDIA has worked on a wide range of Flash projects for the following companies: Coca-Cola, Intel, Alliance Atlantis, YTV, General Mills, University of Toronto, The Canadian Gemini Awards, MGI Software, and the Toronto Symphony Orchestra as well as creating Flash rich-media ads for the Excite @ Home Network, last year CRASH!MEDIA's Flash site received the Best National/International Design award at the South by Southwest Interactive Festival, and this year has received the coveted Macromedia Site of the Week Award. CRASH!MEDIA is currently extending into new wireless markets, creating wireless applications for Flash-enabled devices, including PocketPC, set-top boxes, and PDAs. When unplugged from the matrix, Craig likes to munch crullers and get his freak on.

Gregg Caines has been a freelance Web developer for a number of years, pinch-hitting for some big-name companies, including RaceFace, Durex, Aramark, and CRASH!MEDIA. His specialties are Flash, ASP, and PHP, but he enjoys tackling new languages and technologies just as much. When he's not downing colas and hacking out Web apps, he enjoys snowboarding, punk rock, and long walks on the beach.

Tell Us What You Think!

As the reader of this book, *you* are our most important critic and commentator. We value your opinion and want to know what we're doing right, what we could do better, what areas you would like to see us publish in, and any other words of wisdom you're willing to pass our way.

As an Executive Editor for Que, I welcome your comments. You can e-mail or write me directly to let me know what you did or didn't like about this book—as well as what we can do to make our books stronger.

Please note that I cannot help you with technical problems related to the topic of this book, and that due to the high volume of mail I receive, I might not be able to reply to every message.

When you write, please be sure to include this book's title and author as well as your name and phone or fax number. I will carefully review your comments and share them with the author and editors who worked on the book.

E-mail: CTFeedback@quepublishing.com

Mail: Jeff Schultz
Executive Editor
Que
201 West 103rd Street
Indianapolis, IN 46290 USA

{ Introduction }

Why Read This Book?

So, you might ask, "Why should I read this book?" Well, the answers are simple—because Flash is the premiere interactive development tool for the Internet, and because XML is the new language of the Web.

Flash is the number-one downloaded browser plug-in in Internet history—and for good reason. It's the ultimate tool for creating entertaining, engaging, and interactive content for the Web. Whether it's Web-based animations, dynamic multiuser games and environments, or the most interactive and engaging Web applications possible, there's an excellent chance that Flash is the tool behind them.

You've probably heard all the hype about XML before, so we're not going to get into that much (yet!). Our only goal is that you believe that hype. XML and its related technologies will be transforming the way information is stored, communicated, and processed. You don't want to miss out on that. If you work in the industry, you cannot afford to remain illiterate in this language. It's just not worth it because learning XML is sooooooooo easy! It's not a difficult, mysterious language.

If you are a Flash developer, you often need to have Flash to be able to communicate with the Web server or even the database—to speak the same language. Sure, Flash and the Web server or database each has its own methods of storing information, but if they are speaking the same language, they can communicate. And that's the *big* difference.

Granted, XML is just another computer language, but you'll never see it as *only* that when you realize that it's what you use to communicate your ideas. Are your ideas, content, or information boring? Of course not! So embrace XML, for when you understand the beauty in the simplicity, you are free to express and communicate with the rest of the digital world.

Who Should Read This Book?

Well, if you're reading this, there is a good chance this book is for you! Whether you are a programmer, a designer, a producer, or a manager, this is a book that every studio should have. Period. How presumptuous, huh? However, there isn't another book that covers this information so comprehensively and attempts to appeal to everyone in the development process, including managers, motion graphics designers, ActionScripters, server-side programmers, and database designers.

This book is ideal for anyone interested in getting his or her Flash movies to communicate with the server. Whether you are a Microsoft-based ASP developer or an open source developer using PHP, all examples incorporating server-side script are covered in both these languages and are relatively easy to follow and well commented. If you have never done any server-side work before, don't sweat it. We include all the files needed to run these applications. You can simply place these files on the server and customize the FLAs included on the accompanying Web site (`http://www.xmlinflash.com`) to your liking. We hope that you do try some of the server-side stuff, though. We'll start off gently so that if you are just getting into server-side development, you should be able to follow along with our examples. This certainly isn't a beginner's manual to PHP or ASP; those books already exist. We think that if you use this text while you learn about ASP and PHP, you'll see just how easy it is to make Flash talk to your server or database.

The ActionScript does require an ActionScripter of an intermediate or more advanced level. We don't expect you to know anything about the `XML`, `XMLNode`, or `XMLSocket` objects in Flash, but we do expect you to understand the basics. By "basics," we mean you should understand `for` loops and `if` statements, and you should know a bit about targeting objects with Flash 5 syntax. You should be familiar with the `movieClip` object, and you should be comfortable with editing your scripts in Expert mode.

If you come from any kind of background in which you've worked with HTML, this book will be a breeze. For the time being, think of XML as HTML, except that you can create your own tags. Unlike HTML, where you are limited to pre-defined tags, XML allows you to come up with any name you want! Well, there are a few exceptions we'll uncover, but let your mind run wild with the possibilities.

If you've ever wanted to know how you can integrate Flash into your user's browser (or standalone) with scripts, databases, and applications on the server, this book is for you!

What You Will Learn

After reading this book, you will not only have a tight grasp on the concept and role XML plays in development, but you will be able to conceptualize applications of XML in Flash. You'll learn the ins, outs, and syntax of the XML language. You'll discover the possibilities that XML offers you as a Flash developer, and if you are a server-side developer working with XML, you'll learn just how easy it is to port your data structures into a highly flexible, dynamic, and visual environment created with Flash.

You'll learn the most efficient ways to import data via XML into Flash—faster than using the standard `loadVariables()` method you might be used to. You'll learn how to efficiently work with whitespace, whether it's handled inside Flash or handled server-side through middleware such as PHP or ASP. You'll see working examples and applications that include the following:

- Flash-based XML Editor and Reader
- An interactive directory-tree read from the server directory with PHP/ASP
- A dynamic news box/weblog generated with XML and PHP/ASP
- A database-driven multiuser message board application
- Optimization techniques, both native to Flash and generated server-side
- A live socket connection that updates stock quotes
- A multiuser Web-based chat application developed in Flash with an XML socket server

Coding Conventions

Throughout this book, we will be illustrating code examples with the same general layout. All code examples are displayed in a monospace computer font and are accompanied with a header bar describing the code being demonstrated. Here is an example:

```
function factorial(n) {
  if (n == 1) {
return(n);
  } else {
return(n * factorial(n-1));
  }
}
```

Also, in certain code examples, we use **bold monospace** to indicate what the reader types in or to emphasize specific blocks of code that we are talking about.

Also, we will be using the following syntax when creating variables, objects, and functions:

```
thisIsMyCustomObjectName;
```

As you can see, we follow the convention of capitalizing only the first letter in each new word. We use no spaces, and we generally do not use underscores to separate words. This is the same syntax that Flash uses, and is a common technique used by programmers to name and label created objects and functions.

However, we do use underscores when we have an object that is represented by a movieClip. We don't want to enhance or override the movieClip object, but we do want to have it appear as though we've done that, so it makes sense in an object-oriented way.

The Web Site

In today's world of rapid-paced development cycles, it's hard to keep up. Although this book includes many advances in the arena of XML in Flash, things change. And they change fast! That's why we're providing an accompanying Web site: www.xmlinflash.com. We've included as much up-to-the-minute information and content as possible, but sure enough, the day this book goes to print, there will be some new discoveries. This is the objective of the Web site, however, to offer updates on new XML applications, information, and techniques.

We have spent considerable time developing a supporting Web site for this book—and of course it's built entirely in Flash and XML! This Web site aims to not only be a resource for Flash and XML developers, but also a close community of developers with the shared intent of creating an environment where we can all learn from one another.

The Web site has a fully functioning message board—modified from the very same example used in this book—that allows us to share ideas, new concepts, new techniques, and code optimizations with other developers. XML in Flash is still so new that there will be many advances and discoveries in the coming months, and the site aims to document them. From bugs to new player releases, this site will add to the knowledge base that has begun with this book.

We will also be updating the site with future techniques and discoveries. A full, constantly updated FAQ section, pulled from an appendix in this book, will be put together with an easy-to-use suggestion box so that discoveries from around the planet can be placed here for all to learn from.

The Web site will also contain several examples from this book so that they are available at any time for reference. Source code for several examples as well as newly created code will be available for review and download at the site. Although the accompanying Web site contains all the code used throughout this book, source code will also be available online to access.

Of course, any new undocumented features, corrections, or amendments to work offered in this book will be updated on the site.

{ Part I }

Introduction to XML in Flash

{ Chapter 1 }

An Overview of XML in Flash

Flash stormed onto the Web scene in the late 1990s as a lightweight yet powerful animation tool. It was quickly touted as the ultimate Web-based multimedia tool and the most dynamic platform for delivering interactive content. Since the inception of Flash version 5, it has become the most interactive tool for creating dynamic Web applications, thanks in part to the improved and vastly more powerful ActionScript as well as the addition of XML—eXtensible Markup Language. With the emerging opportunities of XML, you are positioned to create some of the most compelling and engaging Web applications the Net has to offer.

It's amazing how much excitement surrounds XML, and yet few people truly understand the power this new technology holds. XML has started a new revolution in content structure and data exchange for the Web. Linked with the Web's most revolutionary interactive application—Flash—you have a wonderful world of new interactive opportunities. In its own right, XML is one of the hottest and fastest growing technologies on the Net today. It is shaping the next generation of Internet applications. In this chapter, we are going to review exactly what XML is and how it applies to Flash development. One of the most common problems with learning about XML for the first time is wrapping your head around its purpose. XML has so many applications that it is important to first understand XML as a concept and not just how it can be used in a certain application.

The power of XML ultimately rests with the developer. It's much more important to understand how to apply XML in your Flash applications than to understand each and every detail of the XML specification. For this reason, the first chapter of this book will focus on giving you an understanding of what exactly XML is and how it can be used with Flash (what *you* can use it for). The chapter concludes with a high-level look at how you can use Flash and XML in your own Web development projects.

XML's single purpose is to simply contain data in a structured format. That's all. It is not a magical technology, and it is certainly not a programming language— it is merely a standardized technology that can be used universally by multiple applications and even multiple platforms/operating systems. What that data consists of is up to you. So when reading through this chapter, think about the role XML plays and how it can be leveraged for projects you might be working on. This chapter is not going to hit you over the head with complex terminology and detailed examples. We'll do that later (we're saving that until it's 3 a.m., when it's well past midnight and you're on your sixth mochaccino latte). Right now, if XML, or the idea of using it with Macromedia Flash, is new to you, this chapter gives you an overview of the technology, its implications, and its applications.

What Is XML?

As mentioned, XML is simply a file format for containing data. What makes it special is that it is a widely adopted standard, capable of existing on any platform and of being used by a massive and growing number of applications and programming languages. In fact, it's supported by some of the largest and most powerful companies in the computer industry. Major players in the industry, such as Microsoft, SUN Microsystems, and IBM, have incorporated and embraced this technology in their product lines, thus staking their future success on it. It's definitely here to stay.

In the beginning, XML was developed by an XML Working Group (originally known as the SGML Editorial Review Board) formed under the influence of the World Wide Web Consortium (W3C) in 1996. Like its cousin HTML (Hypertext Markup Language), XML is a descendant of a technology called *Standard Generalized Markup Language* (*SGML*). SGML, developed and standardized by the International Organization of Standards (ISO) in 1986, is a system for organizing and structuring data systems through tagging—much like tags in HTML. However, unlike HTML, SGML is not used for visual layout formatting, but for describing the structure of the information and its internal relationships.

SGML is a complex markup language for complex data structuring, but for the most common applications, the relatively high level of complexity is simply not necessary. XML was soon created as a simplified, stripped-down subset of SGML to handle the majority of the needs of SGML in a comparatively easy-to-use format. Because of this, XML's primary purpose—much like SGML—is the power to structure complex data in an open-standard format for use among different applications and even among different organizations.

XML is referred to as "extensible" because it is not a fixed language like HTML, which has a single set of predefined tags. In fact, XML is a meta-language that enables you to design your own customized markup language, thus allowing you to custom-design and structure XML documents for specific applications. Although it is a language, it's as much about a new way of structuring and passing data.

We're assuming that, as a Flash developer, you have a moderate amount of experience with HTML and understand the basics of tags and how they work. This experience is helpful because like HTML, XML is a markup language. For instance, you are familiar with HTML tags such as these:

```
<font>
```

or

```
<table>
```

XML is different in that it gives you complete control over naming all tags. There are some limitations and guidelines in creating these tags (covered in Chapter 2, "The Details of XML"), but for now, it's important only to grasp the concept that these tags are author-defined.

In XML you can create tags with whatever name you want; in other words, the author decides the naming structure. These names are used to classify and describe data. For instance, you can have tags called

```
<product_id>
```

or

```
<headline_story>
```

These custom tags are used to create your own content-specific data structure. You can see from these examples how "readable" XML can be, and how natural a language it is for developers, designers, and producers. For the most part, it's straight English. There are no obscure tags to memorize, as with HTML. The only tags you'll be using are ones you make yourself.

XML deals only with information, so it allows you to think in a conceptual way when working with it. For example, take a news-based Web site. The feature story is called "Flash Most Popular Plug-in in History." To visually display that caption, you might want to use HTML tags such as <u>, <font>, or <b>. However, there is no indication whatsoever as to what that information is. The tags simply document how the information should be displayed, as shown in this example:

```
<p>
<font size='4'>
  <u>Technology</u>
  <b>
    Flash Most Popular Plug-in in History
  </b>
</font>
  <br>
  by John Smith
</p>
```

By formatting your content with XML, you can see how easy it is to find and follow that content, and how simply the information's internal relationships can be represented, as shown here:

```
<section id='Technology'>
<story>
  <headline>
    Flash Most Popular Plug-in in History
  </headline>
  <author>
    John Smith
  </author>
</story>
</section>
```

This is pure information. There's no description of how the data should be presented, so it is probably not something you would want to show on a Web site. However, we have effectively removed the presentation markup (the HTML) and added new markup to denote the data's internal relationships.

Why XML?

In short, XML is a flexible, open-standard format that can be accessed by countless applications across multiple platforms. That means applications can be built faster, to be more robust and easier to maintain. The following sections discuss some of its advantages in more detail.

Content/Presentation Separation

Ultimately, the Internet is about content. It is merely a medium by which we contribute and share content. Because of this focus on content, XML holds quite a bit of promise in the online realm.

Separating the data and its structure from its presentation is a common goal among Web developers, to make Web site maintenance faster and more efficient. The same XML document can be created just once, yet presented in many different ways. The document's content can be displayed for Web pages, cell phones, PDAs, and more.

At the same time, multiple XML documents with the same structure but different information can be presented in the same way, allowing a developer to create a single interface for a variety of information. Content/presentation separation is often used in Web sites that specialize in providing content, such as `wallstreetjournal.com` or `amazon.com`. These types of Web sites draw from a data source (often a database, although XML may be better for some purposes, and some other applications can benefit from both) and put that data into a common HTML interface. That way, all the news items at `wallstreetjournal.com` are presented in the same fashion, so a simple change to the presentation method is reflected in all the articles the user views.

Obviously we're being a bit ambiguous by using a term like "presentation method," but we'll clarify it later. For now, you should simply understand that the data in an XML document can be shown in an infinite number of ways. The possibilities really are endless. Gone are the days of building different sites for different end users. XML structures the content, and XML specifies the content elements. The content is displayed by using some presentation method (maybe HTML, maybe WML, maybe Flash, maybe something entirely different) that is responsible for rendering a version specific to the platform. Whether you're using a desktop computer or a wireless handheld device, the same content can be pulled in via XML, yet be displayed entirely differently.

Standardized Format

If the XML format weren't standardized, it wouldn't be worth much more than your favorite Foghat 8-track tape in today's world of compact discs. Standards are essential for technologies that involve interoperability and communication in general.

A quick look at www.ibm.com/xml, www.sun.com/xml, www.oracle.com/xml, and www.microsoft.com/xml shows that these major players are putting quite a bit of stock into XML, which will ensure that XML is around for years to come. The fact that these fiercely competitive companies can all agree on a single technology is a testament to XML's interoperability.

The W3C (World Wide Web Consortium) encompasses the inventors and governing body for all things XML, as can be seen at www.w3.org/XML. Because it's a centralized authority on the subject, it's unlikely that any single company will be able to hijack XML (or even "embrace and extend" it) for its own purposes. The W3C is a not-for-profit organization, too, so you can be reasonably sure that W3C is working in the best interests of the Web. Its other recommendations, including HTML, PNG (Portable Network Graphics—an excellent format to use in Flash, by the way), SGML, and CSS (cascading style sheets) round out the W3C's astounding accomplishments on the Web and drive home the point that it's made up of the people who create the standards that make the World Wide Web what it is today.

Standards aren't just important because you want to be cool like everyone else, either. When everyone agrees on a standard such as XML, it becomes a heavily supported technology. Many companies are backing up the standard with a myriad of applications. This support ensures that XML can be read, edited, and used on a number of platforms and in a variety of programming languages and applications.

Commercial supporters are by no means the only supporters. Open source software (OSS) is greatly influenced by XML's power and interoperability, too. A quick search on http://www.sourceforge.net reveals an impressive number of XML projects that are either under development or have released useful applications utilizing XML for one purpose or another. Mozilla (the open source version of Netscape Navigator) has some XML support already and more is promised later, and the Apache Software Foundation (author of the wildly popular Apache Web server) has started the Apache XML project (http://xml.apache.org) to fuse a number of XML-related technologies into Apache development. With so many commercial and open source software creators working with this standard, we'll certainly see more and more XML-oriented applications every day.

Dynamic Content

When we mention *dynamic content*, we're referring to information that is generated or imported into Flash dynamically. That means the content or information does not reside within the Flash environment, but exists in a database or is generated on-the-fly by using some sort of server-side script.

XML is a textual file format, so it is easy to write with a short program instead of writing it manually. Take, for example, an XML document representing the messages of users on a Web-based bulletin board. When a user posts a new message, the XML document should certainly reflect this event. You could use one of several different programming languages or server-side technologies to automatically modify the XML document accordingly.

In this way, XML is considered to be "dynamic," meaning that the document can be written automatically, on-the-fly, whenever necessary. Part II, "Flash and Dynamic XML," will delve more deeply into these types of applications, which are some of the most exciting and impressive types of Flash applications on the Web today.

That dynamic XML can then be imported into Flash and used to alter the Flash movie accordingly enables the movie itself to be highly dynamic. You can create the SWF (ShockWaveFlash format) once using Flash, although different content is pulled in every time a user views the movie. You can get much of the same functionality of Macromedia Generator, or other server-side SWF generation tools, without the complexity or costs. It's this type of functionality that will enable you to create message boards, dynamic news boxes, and file-system browsers using Flash as the front end.

In addition, Flash allows this data to be read whenever the Flash developer wants it to be read. This is actually a very sexy feature that any Web developer can appreciate because the data in the Flash movie can be refreshed *automatically* without any user interaction. For example, a stock ticker written in Flash can get and display stock prices every five minutes or so to ensure that the prices are always relatively up to date. Everyone knows that Flash's presentation of data is dynamic, but it's this added feature that makes the data itself dynamic.

As if all this capability wasn't enough, Macromedia has added the `XMLSocket` object to Flash. With this new "socket" (which will be discussed in more detail in Part III, "Flash and the XML Socket"), a server can actually send data to a Flash movie *whenever the server wants to send it*. This is completely different from the request-and-receive method the Web normally uses. Instead of a Flash movie requesting more data from the server, the server can simply send data to the movie as the server deems necessary. This type of communication is widely referred to as *push technology* because of the way information is "pushed" to the Flash movie instead of waiting for the movie to request it. This feature has opened up a whole new world of possibilities for Flash development because it makes the client-server interaction so much closer to real time. With this new feature, it's possible to vastly improve the stock ticker example by allowing the server to send the stock prices to the Flash movie whenever they are updated. In this case, if the prices are constantly updated, the server can just continually send the new information to the movie, thereby keeping the movie perpetually up-to-date.

Stock tickers are obviously not the most exciting applications in the world, but there are other possibilities that Flash developers are just starting to realize. The latest developments have been in creating multiuser environments. Because the XMLSocket object allows such quick updating of data (compared to the other available methods), a Flash movie can represent actions of one user to another user, and in that way, the users interact. Chat applications, multiplayer games, and multiuser whiteboards have all come out of this new method of accessing data. (Chapter 11, "Creating a Multiuser Chat Application," will describe and explain the creation of one such multiplayer application.)

Machine-Readable

XML markup is what encapsulates the data and indicates what type of data you have, as well as its relationship to other data. Those tags are not there for your eyes only, though.

Because the purpose of a piece of data is so clearly labeled, it's relatively simple for a programmer to write software that can read an XML document to use that data. This is one of the key features that makes XML such an open, platform-independent standard. If XML needs to be translated into another form (either another type of XML document or a document in a completely different file format, such as HTML or PDF), it's relatively easy to write an application to accomplish this task.

Business-to-Business (B2B) computing relies heavily on this capability. One business might have a specific XML format for a product order form, for example, while another business with which it operates could have a different, and incompatible, XML format for its product order forms. Because XML is easily machine-readable, it can be translated into other XML formats with little effort, so interoperability between businesses is greatly improved.

Nested Data

A lot of people will be happy with using Flash's `loadVariables()` method for the rest of their development and might never use or have need for XML. This method (and other non-XML methods for loading data into Flash) is perfectly fine for certain applications—and until Flash 5, was the only method in use. In fact, there are reasons that could make `loadVariables()` your method of choice for a particular project, but they are discussed later in Chapter 8, "Performance and Optimization."

XML does, however, make it easier to represent complex nested data. By "nested," we mean information contained within other information in a hierarchical fashion. The following example is *not* a particularly good example of nested data:

```
<street_address>189 King St E.<street_address>
<city>Toronto</city>
<country>Canada</country>
```

This data can be represented in name-value pairs and loaded into Flash via `loadVariables()`. This example might indeed be better served by `loadVariables()` because it can be easily converted to name-value pairs that are `loadVariables()`-friendly:

```
StreetAddress='189%20King%20St%20E.&city=Toronto&country=Canada
```

Another example is not as easily converted to name-value pairs: A Diablo is a model made by a company called Lamborghini, which is in turn a manufacturer of sports cars.

```
<sports_cars>
<make company_name='Lamborghini'>
  <model>Diablo</model>
  <model>Countach</model>
</make>
<make company_name='Audi'>
  <model>TT</model>
</make>
</sports_cars >
```

Clearly, converting this kind of nested data into name-value pairs would be a fairly difficult task. We're not saying it's impossible, but we are saying it's probably not worth it.

XML is clearly the more flexible representation of this type of complex data, and so should probably be the developer's choice in these situations. Quite often Web development (be it HTML or Flash development) requires some integration with a database on the server. Modern relational database designs typically structure data in a form that is more nested and less conducive to representation via simple name-value pairs. For this reason, XML is a capable tool for handling all your data-representation needs.

What Can Flash and XML Accomplish Together?

The possibilities are overwhelming. The main thing to be learned is that Flash is capable of being an application development environment. If you're a developer from the pre-Flash 4 days, you might remember when Flash was simply for Web-based multimedia. To be accurate, it is still focused in that direction, but its capabilities are far exceeding that now. XML fits in in a number of places. Many of today's applications are Web-based, both for ease of distribution and for interoperability on multiple platforms. XML can be the glue that binds your Flash applications to a database, or it can be the protocol used to keep your stock quotes updated so that you can be constantly reminded of just how much you're losing.

In this book alone, we will be covering Flash applications such as a multiuser message board, a file-system directory tree, a mock stock market ticker, and news log. A huge number of applications are equally possible in Flash because of XML, and it's important that you, as the reader, keep in mind that creativity is the main ingredient.

XML requires a little more creativity than HTML development. You write your own tags, so you have to be able to visualize how you want your data to be organized. It's not difficult, but it's also not a skill that is easily taught or memorized; it comes from practice and experience. We hope our examples will spur you on to bigger and better ideas and show you the beginning of what is possible.

Mix Flash, the most dynamic presentation method for the Web, with XML, the most easily manipulated data-structuring file format we have today, and you're bound to get bleeding-edge Web sites and Web-based applications.

Summary

In this chapter, we have highlighted the key aspects of XML and discussed how they can play well with Flash integration. You should now understand how powerful XML is for separating your content from your presentation as well as communicating with other systems or servers. You should also begin to see and understand the best type of content to use XML for: nested and hierarchical. XML works wonders with complex nested data structures, breaking them down into simple subsets of elements. There is no questioning the power and flexibility XML offers developers; it's only a matter of how you choose to apply this technology to your own projects.

So What's Next?

If we've sold you on XML and Flash integration so far, it's time to really get into the nuts and bolts of XML. It's certainly a lot like HTML, but there are a few key differences and a few other quirks to learn. If you know XML backward, upside down, and inside out, then feel free to skip the next chapter. We're mostly describing the syntax and rules of XML documents in general so that a newbie can start using XML in his or her Flash applications. On the other hand, if you *are* a newbie, don't fear: We supply a basic explanation of XML in general, and gloss over the details of the XML specification that aren't really necessary for Flash development. That will be the foundation for your work in later chapters, and will greatly facilitate your understanding of the examples.

{ Chapter 2 }

The Details of XML

This chapter lays down the foundation of XML knowledge that we build on throughout this book. If you can wrap your mind around the concepts, rules, and terminology of XML presented here, you are well on your way to applying it in your own unique Flash applications. If you already have some knowledge of HTML, you'll be surprised at how simple and familiar you will find XML to be.

Before we get up to our necks in XML syntax and structure, we'll start off easy by covering the basics of XML. We'll review XML's role and how it is used to communicate information. Then we will dig into the more intricate nooks and crannies that make XML the powerful markup language that it is.

Understanding XML terminology is important, but just as important is the proper structuring of the document. XML aggregates data and arranges it hierarchically, so it helps to begin thinking in this way. The animal kingdom, for example, is classified with a number of different categories, all arranged in a hierarchical fashion. XML's purpose is to similarly classify data in general.

This chapter covers the lingo and jargon of XML. What are elements and attributes? Is the DTD a new killer wrestling move? What the heck is whitespace? As daunting as XML might seem, it's basically about intelligent labeling of information. We'll discuss the terminology of these labels and a few basic building blocks you'll need to know by building a simple XML document based on music CDs we have lying around. After covering these examples, you'll be able to fully understand the possibilities and create an XML document of your very own.

Finally, in this chapter you'll take a look at XHTML, which is an implementation of HTML in XML. We'll explain how XHTML follows XML structure and syntax, making it compliant with the HTML 4.0 specification, and thus making HTML extensible. Because of XHTML's XML-based structure and syntax, it is slightly different from HTML, but you'll be surprised at how similar it is.

The Basics

So, how exactly does XML work? Start with a quick breakdown of what happens to the XML document before understanding what defines it. The XML document is meant as a carrier of information, as you now know. It can be a static file that you create and place on the server, or it can be generated dynamically server-side, based on a user's request.

Like HTML, XML uses tags. The key difference is that in HTML you must use a predefined set of tags, but in XML you are responsible for creating your own set of tags. This is what makes XML extensible and makes it not only a markup language, but also a *metalanguage*. You, the author, create the definitions for your content through your tag names. In HTML, for instance, you are familiar with tags such as

```
<BODY>
```

or

```
<TITLE>
```

In XML you can create tags with whatever name you like. The author creates the naming structure, and these names are used to classify and describe data. For instance, using an example of a music collection, you can create tags like these:

```
<name>Tosca</name>
```

or

```
<album>Suzuki Dub</album>
```

These custom tags are used to create your own content-specific data structure. Each set of tags is called an *element*, and it represents an independent piece of information. You can see from these examples how readable XML can be, which is what makes it such an incredible format for development. By having control over the nomenclature of your content, it becomes incredibly easy to communicate that content between different applications and even different people.

There's no better way to see how simple XML can be other than to start getting
your hands dirty with an example. We'll start by building an XML document
based on some CDs we have lying around while we're writing this. The first
three CDs we've grabbed are The Ramones, *All The Stuff & More*, Tosca, *Suzuki
Dub*, and Operation Ivy, *Hectic*.

XML Declaration

To organize this information as an XML document, you should first declare the
document as XML. When working with XML in Flash, this step isn't necessary;
however, when you're working with other applications, this declaration might be
required. It's a good habit to get into, and often necessary as well, so we'll go
with a standard XML declaration here:

```
<?xml version='1.0'?>
```

All this line is doing is defining the document as XML version 1.0 (based on the
W3C specifications); nothing more, nothing less.

Another commonly used part of the XML declaration is the `encoding` attribute.
An XML document is most often encoded with one of two Unicode standards:
UTF-8 or UTF-16. These encodings are denoted respectively as follows:

```
<?xml version='1.0' encoding='UTF-8'>
```

or

```
<?xml version='1.0' encoding='UTF-16'?>
```

UTF stands for Unicode Transformation Format. UTF-8 is compatible with the
ubiquitous ASCII, and UTF-16 allows for many more possible characters. For
this reason, UTF-16 is often used when dealing with foreign languages. For most
English-language applications, UTF-8 is completely adequate.

Elements

Elements are the containers of data in an XML document and thus XML's basic
building blocks. Tags are just the textual representation of elements in XML.
Typically, elements are denoted by an open tag and a closing tag. For instance, to
create an element for the title of one of our CDs, we would use the following:

```
<albumTitle>Suzuki Dub</albumTitle>
```

In HTML you might use this format:

```
<b>Suzuki Dub</b>
```

Both examples use tags; however, they serve different purposes. The element `<albumTitle>` defines the content, and the HTML tags merely define the visual format and presentation of this content (with "bold" tags).

In the XML element, we're defining both content and structure at the same time by saying that "Suzuki Dub" is the title of an album. In HTML we have no clue what "Suzuki Dub" is; we know only that it is to be bolded when formatted onscreen via HTML. This is the key difference between HTML tags and XML elements. Elements define content and HTML tags define their visual presentation.

All XML documents have at least one element, the *root element*, and any number of possible subelements. All content in an XML document is placed inside elements, which are really nothing more than tags. There are, however, several rules you must abide by when using elements in XML:

- All XML elements *must* contain closing tags. Unlike HTML, where you can get away with not using closing tags (`<BR>` and `<P>`, for example), doing this in XML results in a malformed document that's unusable by applications that adhere strictly to the W3C's XML specification. In many cases, it can also make the document unintelligible to humans.

- Another pitfall to avoid when naming your elements is using spaces or invalid characters in the element names. You cannot structure your element like this, for example:

  `<album title>Suzuki Dub</album title>`

  As with case-sensitivity, using spaces in element names produces errors when parsing the XML document because spaces are considered illegal characters when inside an element name. You must begin your element name with an alpha character, but after that first letter, you can use any combination of alphanumeric characters, hyphens, colons, or underscores in the element name.

- If you want to use element names made up of more than one word, you should replace those spaces with underscores or hyphens, like so:

  `<album-title>Suzuki Dub</album-title>`

  or

  `<album_title>Suzuki Dub</album_title>`

- XML is a case-sensitive format, so it is picky about the case of the characters in the element name. This example is invalid for that reason:

  `<Album-Title>Suzuki Dub</album-Title>`

The open tag capitalizes "Album-Title," but the closing tag lowercases it as "album-Title." The XML specification says that applications should recognize these tags as two different names and return an error that closing tags are missing. Therefore, it's essential that you adopt a standard for naming your XML elements. In general, it's good practice to keep these names all lowercase to avoid confusion and typos.

- When creating your element names, it is often useful to consider names for them as though you were considering names for the column of a spreadsheet or database table. By remaining consistent in your naming structure and in your actual names for content and objects, it becomes much easier to define your own standard and reduces opportunities for errors when working with the content.

- Although we did say that you can begin element names with letters, note that you cannot name your tags starting with the string xml in any combination of the lowercase *x*, *m*, or *l* because the W3C has reserved those characters for future extensions of the XML specification.

Now that you understand what an element is and its role in XML, let's build an XML document based on the three albums we originally grabbed.

The Root Element

The first thing you need to understand when creating this document is that all XML documents require a *root element*. This is a set of tags (making an element) that encapsulates the entire document, much like the way you use the <HTML> tag when creating HTML documents. This is your first glimpse at the extensibility of XML. You get to create your own root tag, and not be restricted to something as nondescriptive as <HTML>. Because we are creating an XML document of our CD collection, we will call our root element <cd-collection>:

```
<?xml version="1.0"?>
<cd-collection>
</cd-collection>
```

There's really not that much to it. Quite often the root element identifies the type of data structure being outlined. The "meta" nature of XML enables you to create simple and easy-to-remember elements to classify your data structures.

Notice how the first line (the XML declaration) has no closing tag. This is because it's not an element, and that is why we have included the closing tag </cd-collection> to complete the <cd-collection> element. We've also removed the encoding attributes in these examples for simplicity's sake. This attribute is by no means necessary to import XML information into Flash.

Subelements and the Element Family Tree

Now that the root element is set up, you can begin populating the document with elements. First, the CDs we have must be classified. To do this, we'll create an assortment of `<genre>` elements. By creating these elements now, we are creating a document that can be easily searched and referenced. This task is where any database experience will come in handy. You can structure your XML documents to mirror your database fields or vice versa. So based on the Ramones, Tosca, and Operation Ivy CDs, we have three genres: punk, electronic, and skacore. First we will enter these three `<genre>` elements:

```
<?XML version="1.0"?>
<cd-collection>
    <genre>punk</genre>
    <genre>electronic</genre>
    <genre>skacore</genre>
</cd-collection>
```

Now we have the CD collection consisting of three `<genre>` elements, and the text content for each genre matches the music we have gathered so far. These new `<genre>` elements are considered subelements of the root element `<cd-collection>`. As subelements, they are considered to be contained, or "nested," within the `<cd-collection>` element, thereby indicating a hierarchy.

Unlike HTML, which allows you to alter the order of tags such as `<i>` and `<b>`, XML is not as lenient. XML is strict in its handling of tags. Just as you need to properly nest table cells when building tables in HTML, you need to make sure that you properly nest your XML tags. Think of the XML document as a table of information. If the elements are not *properly nested*, the reference to the data becomes ambiguous.

For instance, in XML you can't place the closing tag for the punk `<genre>` element after the other genres:

```
<?XML version="1.0"?>
<cd-collection>
    <genre>punk
    <genre>electronic</genre>
    <genre>skacore</genre>
    </genre>
</cd-collection>
```

That just doesn't make sense. Under normal circumstances, people would logically avoid this kind of structure, but often in HTML you see examples like this one:

```
<b><i>tag cross</b></i>
```

If you try that in your favorite browser, it *will* work, and display bold, italicized text. XML, on the other hand, will not stand for those kinds of shenanigans.

Hierarchy

XML is structured in a hierarchical manner, similar to a family tree or the file system on your computer. A simple XML document such as the following example can be visually represented in a hierarchical fashion, as shown in Figure 2.1.

```
<?XML version="1.0"?>
<cd-collection>
    <genre>punk</genre>
    <genre>electronic</genre>
    <genre>skacore</genre>
</cd-collection>
```

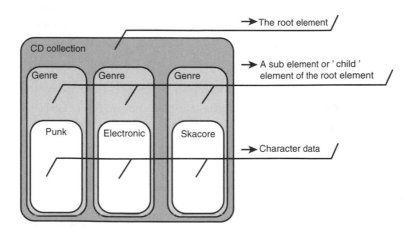

Figure 2.1   *A tree representation of the XML document.*

Basically, when referring to Figure 2.1, think of it as an upside-down tree with the root on top. All content information flows from this root element throughout the document.

The content is organized in the document in parent-child relationships. In other words, a subelement is a child of its parent element, as shown in this example:

```
<?XML version="1.0"?>
<cd-collection>
    <genre>punk</genre>
    <genre>electronic</genre>
    <genre>skacore</genre>
</cd-collection>
```

In the preceding code snippet, the parent element is `<cd-collection>` and the subelements, or children, are the `<genre>` elements. In a more complex XML document, each of the genres could contain subelements, making the `<genre>` elements parents of those subelements/children. This is the nature of XML structure: All content is placed in a hierarchical format.

Beyond the parent-child relationships that exist in XML structure, there are also sibling relationships. In the previous example, all the `<genre>` elements share a sibling relationship, with `<cd-collection>` as the parent. An element's siblings are the other elements that share the same parent. It's analogous to a family tree: There is a parent element that contains child elements, and all these child elements share a sibling relationship. The only major difference is that no subelements contain more than one parent, so maybe it's more like the family tree of an amoeba.

Ultimately, the family-tree analogy represents the concept of nested data. As you create more child elements, you further define the content. Parent elements are always much more general in nature than their children.

Empty Elements

Elements can also be empty. When or why would you have an empty element? Well, you would need one if your document requires the element, but currently there's no content (either a subelement or text). You can also include information using these empty elements, but we'll be covering that soon enough. Before we do, here is the syntax you can use for including empty elements:

```
<album-title></album-title>
```

This example is probably what you would expect—the traditional syntax with no content inside the tags. However, you can also use an abbreviated version:

```
<album-title/>
```

It looks a bit like the closing tag, but notice that the forward slash is at the end of the tag, not at the beginning as for the closing tag.

Now that we've discussed the different types of elements and how to use them, it's important to further investigate the concept of nesting. "Well-formed" is the term used to describe an XML document that is properly nested. It must follow these rules to be well-formed:

- All tags must be closed (for example, `<tagname>some text</tagname>` or `<tagname/>`).

- There must be a single root element encapsulating any other elements.

- Tags may not overlap (such as `<tagname><another>qwerty</tagname></another>`). In HTML, this improper nesting is often forgiven by the browser.

You can probably get away with breaking any or all of these rules in HTML, and the browser will still show your document. In XML, this is not the case. An XML document must, by definition, be well-formed. If it is not, it's not XML, and will be unreadable by XML-oriented applications.

Attributes

XML *attributes* are similar to attributes used in HTML. They are basically properties given to an element. In HTML you're familiar with the use of attributes in the `<anchor>` tag:

```
<a href="http://www.xmlinflash.com">link text</a>
```

In this line of HTML code, the attribute is the `href` value. This is exactly the same format you use when adding attributes in XML. For example, if you wanted to include further information in your `<genre>` element as an attribute, such as the genre name, you would do the following:

```
<genre name="punk"> </genre>
```

Note that any XML-specific characters should be escaped (such as `<` = `&lt`, `>` = `&gt`, `'` = `&apos`, `"` = `&quot`, and `&` = `&amp`), just as in HTML. You can encapsulate attribute data with single quotes (') or double quotes ("). If you want to include double quotes in your attribute content, you need to encapsulate them with single quotes or vice versa.

This is an example of improper encapsulation of the attribute `releaseDate`:

```
<album releaseDate="2000'>Suzuki Dub</album>
```

This is an example of proper encapsulation of the attribute `releaseDate`:

```
<album releaseDate="2000">Suzuki Dub</album>
```

Because you have the option of using either type of quote, remaining consistent is what's important. Use what you prefer and stick with it.

Like elements, attributes are also case sensitive, so `color="blue"` is not the same as `COLOR="blue"`. XML will treat them as separate attributes.

Now that you understand the role of attributes, let's populate the XML document with some more information. So far, you have the main root element `<cd-collection>` and three `<genre>` elements. Now we want to place the artist and album information inside these `<genre>` elements. Because this new information falls inside the `<genre>` element, `<genre>` becomes the parent to the information contained inside and, in essence, becomes the root element to the new album and artist content. Because `<genre>` will classify all information contained inside it, we'll need to use attributes to label the `<genre>` elements. Previously we had the following:

```
<?XML version="1.0"?>
<cd-collection>
    <genre>punk</genre>
    <genre>electronic</genre>
    <genre>skacore</genre>
</cd-collection>
```

Now we are going to use attributes to define the genres:

```
<?XML version="1.0"?>
<cd-collection>
    <genre name="punk"></genre>
    <genre name="electronic"></genre>
    <genre name="skacore"></genre>
</cd-collection>
```

After we have this laid out, we can begin populating the `<genre>` elements with the album information:

```
<?XML version="1.0"?>
<cd-collection>
<genre name="punk">
        <artist>
            <name>The Ramones</name>
            <album-list>
                <album>All The Stuff & More</album>
```

```
            </album-list>
        </artist>
    </genre>

  <genre name="electronic">
      <artist>
          <name>Tosca</name>
          <album-list>
              <album>Suzuki Dub</album>
          </album-list>
      </artist>
  </genre>

  <genre name="skacore">
      <artist>
          <name>Operation Ivy</name>
          <album-list>
              <album>Hectic</album>
          </album-list>
      </artist>
  </genre>
</cd-collection>
```

You can see how much more information this new document can store. We have now included a subelement called <artist> inside <genre>, and inside <artist>, we have created two further subelements: <name> and <album-list>. Last, we have <album> subelements inside <album-list>. Although it might seem like a lot of elements, you'll soon see how clean this organization is. As we add more artists to a <genre> element, we might want to incorporate attributes even further and structure the <artist> elements much as we did the <genre> element:

```
<?XML version=1.0?>
<cd-collection>
<genre name="punk">
      <artist name="The Ramones">
          <album-list>
              <album>All The Stuff & More</album>
          </album-list>
      </artist>
  </genre>

  <genre name="electronic">
      <artist name="Tosca">
          <album-list>
              <album>Suzuki Dub</album>
          </album-list>
      </artist>
  </genre>
```

```
            <genre name="skacore">
                <artist name="Operation Ivy">
                    <album-list>
                        <album>Hectic</album>
                    </album-list>
                </artist>
            </genre>
        </cd-collection>
```

It's certainly not necessary to transfer content from elements to attributes, but in some cases it's clearer. Actually, elements and text data are all you'll ever need, but sometimes you have a subelement that contains only simple text. It's often easier to read if you design your document to include that text as an attribute, rather than as text in an element. Attributes are obviously not useful for information that will contain more and more data in a nested, hierarchical fashion; for that, you'll need to rely on your elements and text data.

Although the example is coming together nicely and appears to follow proper XML formatting, there is a problem with the first <album> element for The Ramones. It's nothing serious, but in XML you cannot place characters that XML uses in the text data of elements, including characters such as <, >, &, ', and ".

If you take a look at the album *All The Stuff & More*, you'll notice that it contains an ampersand (&). In XML-speak, the ampersand is used to denote the start of an encoded character, but in this case we're not using it for that purpose; we simply want to show an ampersand. Because of this, an application built to read XML as outlined by the W3C's specs would choke on this XML if used as is. To avoid this outcome and extend functionality in other situations, you need to incorporate something called CDATA into your document.

CDATA

In general, *CDATA*, which stands for "character data," allows element text to contain reserved characters that XML uses (<, >, &, ', ") without having them interpreted as XML. CDATA includes letters, numbers, and other symbols that need to be used exactly as they appear. A CDATA section includes literal data that XML applications can use without modification.

A good example of using CDATA is if you want to include actual HTML code in your XML document. Without CDATA, the XML parser would see each set of HTML tags as elements—and you would not be able to access the content as it was intended.

To eliminate these problems so that the Flash parser can see the set of HTML tags and you can access this information, you need to create a CDATA section, but keep in mind that CDATA can be used only inside elements, not inside element attributes.

To remedy the problem with the ampersand in The Ramones `<album>` element, we will add some CDATA. All instances of CDATA must begin with the following:

```
<![CDATA[
```

You then drop in the information that you would like to have appear as is, and close it with two ending square brackets, as shown:

```
]]>
```

To fix the `<album>` element, you would need to do the following:

```
<album><![CDATA[All The Stuff & More]]></album>
```

Now when the XML is parsed, the album's proper title will be retained, including the ampersand, and not cause any parsing errors. Another popular use for CDATA sections is when you want to include HTML tags in your content. For instance, here is an example of integrating HTML tags inside an `<artist-link>` element of an XML document:

```
<artist-link>
<![CDATA[<a href="http://www.artistname.com>artistname</a>]]>
</artist-link>
```

This brings up the point of where to place data. Data that involves "reserved" characters can be placed as a CDATA section or can be escaped (entity-encoded). Basically, *escaping* means you are replacing special characters with their entity-encoded equivalents. Common encodings are as follows:

```
<       &lt;

>       &gt;

&       &amp;

'       &apos;

"       &quot;
```

If you don't mind escaping and unescaping this type of data, you can even use it in the values of attributes. CDATA is a simpler and more popular way of managing these issues, though.

Document Type Definition (DTD)

Okay, so a DTD isn't a new killer wrestling move, but it is important for what you're doing with XML. DTDs (Document Type Definitions) are used to define the legal elements of a particular type of XML document and are either contained inside the XML document or referenced as an external document with a specified location. Basically, the DTD declares the format of a specific kind of XML document so that an application knows what to expect as far as the elements, tags, attributes, and CDATA the document contains. The parser references the DTD to ensure that the XML is properly structured, a condition referred to as *valid*.

For example, if an HTML document was a type of XML document, the DTD would say that it must contain <html>, <head>, and <body> tags (among other things).

It's important to note here that Flash almost completely ignores the DTD and does no checking for validity. Other XML-centered applications certainly do use the DTD to allow the document to validate itself, but for the sake of simplicity, Flash does not. For this reason, we are discussing DTDs here, but we're not going into a lot of detail on how to create them. For Flash development, you simply don't need them. All you really need to know, as a Flash developer, is how to recognize DTDs if you are using documents that contain them.

Here's the CD example with the DTD declaration added in bold:

```
<?xml version="1.0"?>
<!DOCTYPE cd-collection [
  <!ELEMENT cd-collection (genre)>
  <!ELEMENT genre    (#PCDATA)>
]>
<cd-collection>
    <genre>punk</genre>
    <genre>electronic</genre>
    <genre>skacore</genre>
</cd-collection>
```

Essentially, this code says that <cd-collection> is the root element, and all subelements are called <genre>. All <genre> elements contain regular text, otherwise known as *parsable character data* (*PCDATA*). Obviously, these DTDs can get quite a bit more complicated for more complex XML.

In general, the use of a DTD is recommended, and most XML documents contain them. However, the fact remains that DTDs are optional, and Flash ignores them, so for the most part, we will, too. For completeness, though, here is an example of an *external* DTD that might be used for the <cd-collection> example:

```
<?xml version="1.0" encoding="UTF-8"?>
  <!ELEMENT cd-collection (genre)>
  <!ELEMENT genre    (#PCDATA)>
```

It's exactly the same as the internal DTD just shown, but this time it's in its own file. If you save that external DTD as cd-collection.dtd, you can reference it, if needed, by that name. It's nice to use external DTDs because they don't clutter up your content, and they allow multiple XML files to use the same DTD without having to paste it into each XML document. Here is the code you would need to include in the XML document to point externally to that DTD:

```
<?xml version="1.0"?>
<!DOCTYPE cd-collection SYSTEM "cd-collection.dtd">
<cd-collection>
    <genre>punk</genre>
    <genre>electronic</genre>
    <genre>skacore</genre>
</cd-collection>
```

A well-formed XML document can be valid only if it contains a proper Document Type Declaration (the section that contains the DTD) and follows the guidelines established in that DTD. If the document is valid, it will conform to the structure described in the DTD, meaning that whatever the DTD declares as necessary (elements, attributes, text, and so forth) must exist in the document, with no superfluous pieces of information.

Chemical Markup Language (CML; http://www.xml-cml.org/) and Mathematical Markup Language (MathML; http://www.w3.org/Math/) are just a couple of examples of XML document types defined by specific DTDs. By conforming to the CML DTD, a chemist can represent complex chemicals in a way that can easily be understood by other chemists, or even by applications built to read CML. A mathematician can use MathML similarly. Throughout this book, we will be informally creating our own document types to use with specific examples. We won't be using DTDs, but a set format will certainly be implied.

Comments

As in most languages, comments are invaluable for assisting team members (and even ourselves at times) in understanding and manipulating code. You are most likely familiar with the use of comments in HTML or ActionScript. Placing comments in XML is done exactly as it is in HTML:

```
<!-- comment here -->
```

You must simply begin your comment with `<!--` and end with `-->`. There's really not much else to it! Use comments as often as necessary to illuminate tricky parts in complex documents.

Processing Instructions

Processing instructions (PIs) are similar to comments, but they are not necessarily ignored by the application, whereas comments are. Flash ignores PIs, so understanding this difference is not all that essential unless you are using your XML with a non-Flash application and require that functionality.

Actually, you've already seen a few PIs in action. One example is the XML-specific PI `<?XML version="1.0"?>` used to describe the XML document. Although Flash doesn't really change its handling of the XML based on information in that PI, another XML application certainly could. For example, in the future, if version 2 of the XML specification is completely different from version 1, the application reading the XML might find version information extremely useful in dealing with the document.

Whitespace

Whitespace is a term used to define spaces, carriage returns, tabs, and line feeds in an XML document. When creating or editing XML documents, whitespace makes the document much more readable and convenient to use. In all the examples thus far, we have been formatting the XML structures with whitespace. Let's quickly illustrate the visual difference between using whitespace and not using whitespace.

Using whitespace:

```
<cd-collection>
    <genre>punk</genre>
    <genre>electronic</genre>
    <genre>skacore</genre>
</cd-collection>
```

Void of whitespace:

```
<cd-collection><genre>punk</genre><genre>electronic</genre><genre>skacore
⮥</genre></cd-collection>
```

Although it's simpler for applications to deal with documents that don't contain whitespace, you can imagine how difficult it would be for us humans to make any sense of the document when it's just one long string. By using tabs and line breaks, you can make the document display more of its inherent "nestedness," which better reflects the data structure. Whitespace also aids in debugging, as proper use reveals any missing closing tags.

When using whitespace in the Flash environment, you need to keep a number of issues in mind. We'll cover the pitfalls of whitespace in Chapter 3, "Getting Your Feet Wet."

A Familiar XML Document Type: XHTML

eXtensible HTML (XHTML) follows the rules of XML (therefore, it is extensible), but conforms to DTDs that specify many of the HTML 4.0 tags so that it can be used as an extensible HTML for the Web.

The XHTML structure adheres more closely to the XML specification than to the HTML specification, so you need to keep these guidelines in mind:

- The document must be well-formed (no overlapping tags, and all tags must be closed, including the infamous <br>, which should now be written as <br />).

- Write all element and attribute names in lowercase because XML is case sensitive.

- Make sure either single or double quotes enclose all attribute values.

After all that, use an XHTML validator, such as HTML Tidy (http://www.w3.org/People/Raggett/tidy/) or the W3C's HTML Validating Service (http://validator.w3.org/), or view it as XML in your favorite XML browser.

One of the most ubiquitous XML browsers is part of Microsoft Internet Explorer. Internet Explorer (for Windows or Macintosh) has a built-in XML parser that informs you of errors, if any exist. If you simply rename your .xhtml file to an

.xml file and open it in IE, IE should be able to detect any problems. (*Note:* We did find the MacIntosh implementation to be a bit buggy at times, reporting errors on documents that were correct, whereas the MS Windows version did not.)

Summary

We've laid the foundation of your XML knowledge in this chapter by discussing both the syntax and structure of an XML document. In some ways, these concepts are the difficult part, but it's over now. If you've followed along so far, you're going to have an easy time in the next chapters where this knowledge is applied.

If you're looking for even more detail about XML, check out these other resources:

- The XML FAQ: `http://www.ucc.ie/xml/`
- The W3C XML page: `http://www.w3.org/XML/`
- The basics: `http://www.xml101.com/`
- Usenet newsgroup: `comp.text.xml`

So What's Next?

In the next chapter you'll finally get a chance to actually create a Flash-XML example. Chapter 3 will explain the fundamentals of Flash's handling of XML, and you'll get a chance to import an XML document into Flash and access and use information from it.

{ Chapter 3 }

Getting Your Feet Wet

This chapter provides your first steps into Flash-XML integration. There's no better way to learn than by doing, so we're going to get into an example right away. The example will cover loading a simple XML document in Flash and teach the basics of Flash's handling of XML, with its built-in XML object. At the end of this chapter, you will essentially be able to load information from the Web server into your Flash movie at runtime (that is, while it is running in the user's browser). This is exactly the kind of capability you want to be able to create a Flash movie for a Web site, one that requires a content change from time to time. Just changing the contents of the loaded XML file will change how that Flash movie appears, making it easily updatable (and even automatically updatable, as you'll see in Part II, "Flash and Dynamic XML").

First, you'll be importing an XML document in Flash and accessing that data. The example will be as simple as possible, but it should give you a good idea of how this stuff works.

Next, you'll learn about the basics of Flash's XML object. Flash automatically puts imported XML into its own ActionScript object with the novel name of "XML object." You'll learn a bit about this object as you try to access the information in it. Later chapters will certainly explore the object, its methods, and its properties in greater detail, but this chapter will be essential to understanding the fundamentals.

Importing XML into Flash

Now is the time to fire up Flash, and put down your honey-glazed cruller. Create a new Flash file (an FLA), and save it as simpleXMLexample.fla in a convenient directory of your choosing. In the same directory, create a text file using your favorite plain text editor. Microsoft Word is not particularly good at plain text editing because it tends to format everything in its own rich text format. Notepad, on the other hand, is completely acceptable, as is SimpleText if you're on a Mac. Enter the following XML into the text document:

```
<?xml version="1.0" encoding="UTF-8"?>
<recipe>
    <name>peanut butter and jelly sandwich</name>
    <ingredient_list>
        <ingredient quantity='2 tbsp'>
            peanut butter
        </ingredient>
        <ingredient quantity='2 tbsp'>
            jelly
        </ingredient>
        <ingredient quantity='2 slices'>
            bread
        </ingredient>
    </ingredient_list>
</recipe>
```

Save the file as "pbj.xml" and give it a quick check in Internet Explorer to reveal whether any typos or other problems exist. When you've checked the XML document and fixed any errors, you're ready to load it into Flash.

Return to your empty simpleXMLexample.fla. Open your ActionScript editor for the first frame by double-clicking that frame in the timeline. Enter the following ActionScript:

```
recipeXML = new XML();
recipeXML.onLoad = function (success) { trace("Loaded!");}
recipeXML.load ("pbj.xml");
```

A quick test of this FLA in your Flash editing environment (choose Control | Test from the menu) should bring up the trace window with a message of "Loaded!". If this does not occur as described here, go back and ensure that your XML file has the correct name and is saved in the same directory as your FLA. You'll also want to make sure you've written the ActionScript exactly as it's shown in the preceding code lines. Keep in mind that the trace() function works only in the Flash editing environment, so there's no point in trying this in your browser. If everything went well and you have seen the "Loaded!" message, then you have successfully loaded your first XML document. It should look similar to Figure 3.1.

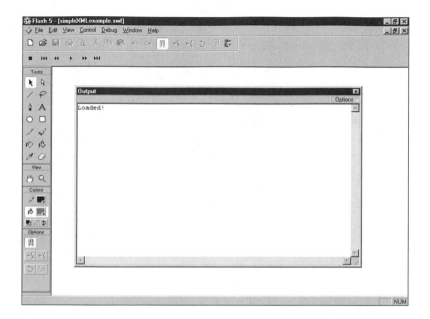

Figure 3.1 *This figure shows that the XML was loaded successfully.*

It doesn't look like much right now, but it's really the beginning of many things to come. Before you do something more useful, like extracting the data, take a look at what that ActionScript was actually doing.

Step 1: Create an XML Object

In the first line, the ActionScript says the following:

```
recipeXML = new XML();
```

XML() is the method that creates the XML object. You can tell what the method's purpose is because it has the same name as the XML object. For that reason, the XML() method (and methods like it for other objects) is called a *constructor method*. By using the new keyword, this method knows that it needs to return a reference to an object. That reference is then stored in the name you've created called recipeXML. After this, recipeXML will be an XML object.

Step 2: Override the onLoad() Handler Method

The onLoad() method in the second line of code is another special kind of method of the XML object:

```
recipeXML.onLoad = function (success) { trace("Loaded!");}
```

Now that you have an XML object called recipeXML, you need to tell it what to do after XML has been loaded into it. When Flash finishes reading XML (such as "pbj.xml") into your XML object (recipeXML), it automatically calls the onLoad() method . Methods that work this way are often referred to as *event handlers* because of the way they are called to handle events (the loading of XML, in this case). By default, the XML.onLoad() method does nothing, but you would like it to tell you when the XML is loaded. The only way to achieve that kind of functionality is to *override* the default onLoad() method of the XML object for your object, recipeXML.

The way that we've overridden that method in the preceding line of code is a little tricky and probably warrants some explanation. The following several lines of code work exactly the same as the previous one line of code, but it might make more sense spread out:

```
function aBetterOnLoad (success) {
  trace("Loaded!");
}
recipeXML.onLoad = aBetterOnLoad;
```

The code starts with a function definition that takes an argument named success, and then calls a trace() function with the string "Loaded!". That's simple enough. You don't know what success is (yet), but whatever it is, the string "Loaded!" will show up in Flash's Output window.

After defining that function, you set your object's onLoad() method to be equal to that new function. In that way, you override the default onLoad() method with your own aBetterOnLoad() function. From now on, when Flash calls onLoad() automatically, it will call your aBetterOnLoad() function. Now you have precise control over what Flash does when it loads XML into your recipeXML object.

Instead of messing around with creating and naming an otherwise unrelated function, you simply compress those lines into a more concise version:

```
recipeXML.onLoad = function (success) { trace("Loaded!");}
```

So what about success? It's an argument that indicates whether the XML was loaded successfully. It contains a true or false value, and you can do whatever you want with that information. In this example, we've done absolutely nothing with it, although we could have just as easily written something like this:

```
recipeXML.onLoad = function (success) {
trace("Loaded!");
trace(success);
}
```

Chances are that if you try this code, you're going to see something similar to Figure 3.2.

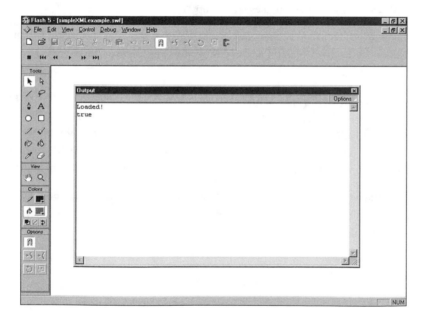

Figure 3.2   *The result when* success *is* true.

The only time success would be false is if the file didn't exist as you've called it, or if you're requesting the file from a network resource (such as a Web server) and a network error occurs (like the Web server has crashed). Errors in your actual XML document will not affect the value of success in any way (but you'll be detecting those errors later, in Chapter 4, "Using XML Data in Flash").

As a side note, you really didn't need to call this parameter success. You could've called it anything because it's your function. Flash simply passes a true or false value to the function, and whatever variable you enter as the argument will contain that value.

Step 3: Load the XML

The third step is pretty straightforward, if you have followed along through the two previous steps:

```
recipeXML.load ("pbj.xml");
```

The load() method is a simple method of the XML object that takes a filename or URL as a parameter and makes an attempt to load that document.

The onLoad() method is called automatically after the XML is loaded, so you don't need to worry about doing anything after the load(). The onLoad() method handles the rest.

So Where's the XML?

Well, XML uses a complicated structure because it is often used to represent complex data. Because of this, you should be aware that accessing XML from the XML object can also be somewhat complicated. We'll start gently, though.

The onLoad() method is where everything happens, so that's what you'll be modifying right now. Use the same code as before, but replace the original onLoad() definition with this one:

```
recipeXML.onLoad = function (success) {
if (success) {
    trace("This is the XML document:");
    trace(this.toString());
        } else {
            trace("Loading Error!")
        }
}
```

Running that code should give you output that looks like Figure 3.3.

There's not a lot of complicated code here, but what is here performs quite a bit. First, you are actually checking the value of success, and doing something based on that value. If success is false, the document was not loaded successfully and Flash displays the message "Loading Error!". Assuming you have the correct document name, and you're loading from your hard drive (as opposed to a Web server), you shouldn't see this error message at all.

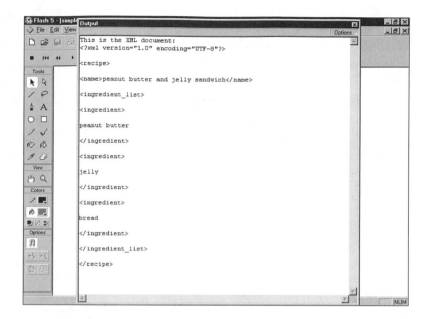

Figure 3.3   *The Output window with the new* onLoad() *method invoking* this.toString().

The really interesting bit of code is this line:

```
trace(this.toString());
```

The trace() function is the easy part; it's just putting the value of this.toString() in Flash's Output window, as it would with any other value passed to it. The method call this.toString() is the bit of code returning your XML document, though. Here's how it works. onLoad() is a method of recipeXML, so when you use the this keyword, you are referring to recipeXML. In fact, you could've just as easily said recipeXML.toString() instead of this.toString(). In general, XML.toString() (the toString() method for any XML object) returns your XML document in string form. Usually this format isn't useful for anything more than a quick check of your document because the data is not separated in any way. Fortunately, that's all you need right now to make sure your XML is all there.

Moving the Party to the Web

To get this code working on the Web, you're going to need get rid of the calls to the trace() function. In the first frame of your FLA, place a text box, and make it dynamic by selecting Dynamic Text from the Text Options panel. Next, select

Multiline from the drop-down list, name it "output," and select the BorderBG check box to make the border and background of the text box show up. You're going to put a good-sized chunk of XML into that box, so resize (both length and width) to match the size of the stage. You'll also overwrite the onLoad() method with a function that sends your XML to the output text box, instead of the trace() function:

```
recipeXML.onLoad = function (success) {
if (success) {
    output += "This is the XML document:\n";
     output += this.toString();
         } else {
             output += "Loading Error!";
         }
}
```

You should expect this new version to look something like Figure 3.4.

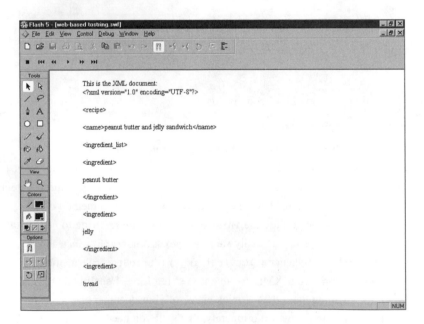

Figure 3.4 *A Web-based example.*

You're now safe to publish your FLA to an HTML file and an SWF file. Uploading the HTML, SWF, and XML files to your Web server will allow you to run the example over the Web.

The Basics of Flash's XML Object

Now that you've successfully imported XML into Flash, it's time to learn a bit more about Flash's handling of XML and, more specifically, the XML object.

All XML-based applications share the need to read in XML from a file and extract the meaningful data and data structures from that file. The portion of the application that does this is called the XML *parser.* Flash is no exception, and considering the size of the Flash plug-in, its built-in XML parser is quite sophisticated. XML.load() automatically starts the parser, and the parser reads through the XML, dividing up the individual elements, attributes, and other components, and puts them in the XML object (recipeXML, in our case).

After that XML object is created and fully populated with the XML data, Flash automatically calls the onLoad() method, and continues through any remaining ActionScript before moving on to the next frame in the timeline. It's good to understand this, because Flash's XML parser can be slow as documents get larger. We will discuss remedies for this problem later in Chapter 8, "Performance and Optimization," but for now, it's enough to realize that your Flash movie will freeze while Flash parses your XML for you. It will probably be unnoticeable on reasonably modern computers when the XML document is relatively small, but it can become noticeable under less-than-optimal conditions (like huge XML documents on slow computers).

Also, the XML parser in Flash is a *non-validating* parser. What this means is that although Flash can read a DTD, it does not do anything whatsoever with that information. It does not check your XML to ensure that it's valid, and it makes no attempt to determine whether your XML conforms to the document type. On the plus side, it can determine whether your document is well formed. The XML object has a simple property called status that returns the value 0 if there are no errors, and returns another number matching a corresponding error code if an error did occur. In the "XML.status" section of Appendix A, "The XML Object," we'll go into more detail on the subject of error codes. For now, however, it's enough to know that you want a value of 0 for your status, otherwise something has gone wrong. To see the status property for the loaded document, add the following line before the call to toString():

```
output += "The status is "+this.status+"\n";
```

Running this code now should produce results similar to Figure 3.5.

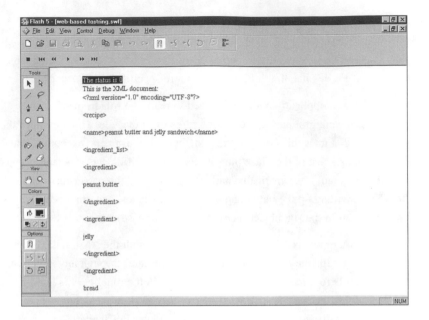

Figure 3.5 `this.status` *(notice the status line at the top).*

Whitespace Stripping

As we explained in Chapter 2, "The Details of XML," whitespace is irrelevant to most XML applications, and Flash-XML applications are no exception. Whitespace certainly makes things easier on human eyes, but to Flash it is a nuisance that just sucks up processing power. To make matters worse, there are different versions of the Flash 5 plug-in floating around that have different features for handling whitespace in XML.

If your user has revision 5.0.41 or later of the Flash 5 plug-in, you can just set a global property called `XML.ignoreWhite` to `true` with this simple code:

```
XML.ignoreWhite = true;
```

Unfortunately, to make this work for all plug-in versions, you still have to detect users' revision number and proceed appropriately. If they have an earlier player version, you will still need an alternative method of whitespace stripping.

For that reason, it usually makes more sense to write some ActionScript to remove the whitespace. You can do this a number of ways, as you'll see in Chapter 4 (the easiest method is to keep the whitespace out of the XML document altogether, but that would make it difficult for humans to read and edit).

It is important to do it, though, or Flash will store the spaces, tabs, carriage returns, and line feeds in your XML as character data, which can cause all sorts of problems when you are trying to get information from a specific element.

The Flash parser treats whitespace as character data, as it would if you had normal text between two tags. That's not necessarily the wrong approach, but it certainly isn't useful for normal use, when you don't care about the superfluous space. It's also essential that you make the first character in your XML document a non-whitespace character. If you don't, the parser will think you want your root node to be that whitespace text data. Of course, this is illegal XML, so it will generate errors.

Keep these things in mind during the following examples. You're going to have to remove the whitespace from your recipe example so that it doesn't interfere. Here's what it should look like:

```
<?xml version="1.0" encoding="UTF-8"?><recipe><name>peanut butter and
➥jelly sandwich</name><ingredient_list><ingredient quantity='2 tbsp'>
➥peanut butter</ingredient><ingredient quantity='2 tbsp'>jelly
➥</ingredient><ingredient quantity='2 slices'>bread</ingredient>
➥</ingredient_list></recipe>
```

It's not very readable from our point of view, but to Flash, it's perfect.

Knowing Nodes

XML elements are represented as *nodes* in a Flash object. For the most part, anytime we talk about XML nodes, we're talking about the representation of XML elements in Flash's XML object. In fact, there's an undocumented object in Flash called XMLnode that is much like the XML object, although it is made to represent a subelement rather than an entire XML document (which, as you've seen, is represented by the XML object). The XML object contains a single XMLnode object, just as an XML document contains a single root element. In Flash ActionScript, the root element of an XML document is represented as the firstChild of the object. In our example, recipeXML.firstChild is the XMLnode that contains the root element <recipe>. To verify this, change your onLoad() method to the following:

```
recipeXML.onLoad = function (success) {
if (success) {
    output += "Root Element: "+this.firstChild.nodeName;
    output += "\n";
```

```
output += "This is the XML document:\n";
output += this.toString();
    } else {
        output += "Loading Error!";
    }
}
```

The addition of the `nodeName` property lets you know the name of the node. You should get something that looks similar to Figure 3.6.

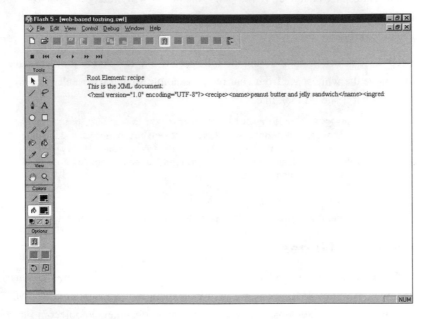

Figure 3.6 *Sample output with the addition of* `this.firstChild.nodeName` *(notice the* `nodeName` *at the top).*

Taking this one step further, you can get the name of the root element's first subelement simply by saying

```
output += "First SubElement: "+this.firstChild.firstChild.nodeName;
```

The output from this line is, of course, `name`, which is the element that names your recipe and contains the text `peanut butter and jelly sandwich`.

To start browsing other subelements, or *children* of the root element, you need to use the `nextSibling` property of the `XMLnode` object, which is actually a reference to another `XMLnode`. The reference points to the `XMLnode` that is the next child of the two nodes' common parent. For example, try this:

```
output += "fC-fC-nextSibling: ";
output += this.firstChild.firstChild.nextSibling.nodeName;
```

Now the output should include fC-fC-nextSibling: ingredient_list because the firstChild is <recipe>, <recipe>'s firstChild is <name>, and <name>'s nextSibling is <ingredient_list>. Keep in mind that although <ingredient list> is a child of <recipe>, it isn't the firstChild; <recipe> is. You can have only one firstChild, of course (because other ones wouldn't be first—they'd be second or third, and so on). This is one of the more complicated aspects of the XML object in Flash; Figure 3.7 shows a diagram that will help you understand how the XML elements are accessed by using Flash's XMLnode objects.

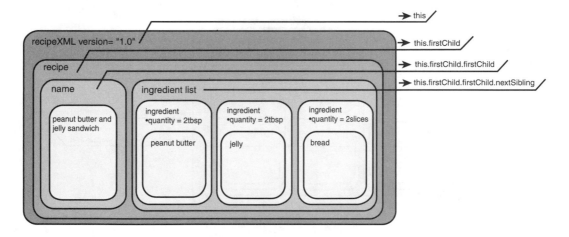

Figure 3.7   *This is a tree diagram of the* XML *and* XMLnode *objects.*

You can access *any* node in an XML object using these firstChild and nextSibling properties, so feel free to experiment, and make sure you understand how this naming works. For the most part, nodes are Flash's representation of the elements of an XML doc. One exception is for character data such as the text you find between tags in an XML document. Flash treats that text as nodes, too. It's a little confusing at first, but in the long run, it's nice to have all the XML data accessible through the single XMLnode object.

XMLnodes that contain text data instead of elements (we'll call them "text nodes" to make the distinction) are accessible by firstChild and nextSibling, too, because they are XMLnodes in their own right. It's pretty simple once you get used to it, but there is one little snag that often confuses people new to the technology:

If you want to get the text from a text node in Flash, use nodeValue instead of nodeName. You might be used to using nodeName to get the information from XMLNodes, but if it is an XMLnode containing text data, not element data, you need to use nodeValue to retrieve that data. To see it in action, try this quick example in your onLoad() function:

```
output += "fC-fC-fC: "+this.firstChild.firstChild.firstChild.nodeValue;
```

That line should add the string peanut butter and jelly to your output listing. Figure 3.8 shows a diagram similar to Figure 3.7, but with text elements mapped out, too. Notice the way nodeValue is used for text nodes and nodeName is used for elements.

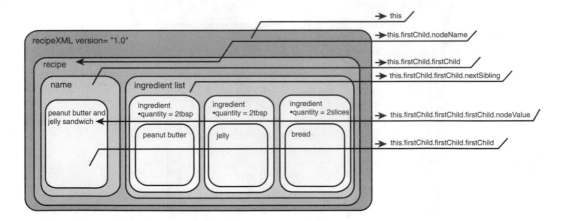

Figure 3.8 *This is a tree diagram showing the use of* XMLnode.nodeName *(for* recipe*) and* XMLnode.nodeValue *(for* peanut butter and jelly sandwich*).*

Aside from nodeName and nodeValue, another important property of XMLnode objects to learn is nodeType. Checking the nodeType of an XMLnode in Flash returns the value 1, denoting an XML element, or the value 3, denoting character data. Using our beloved PB&J recipe, you can see in Figure 3.9 exactly what the nodeTypes are for each of the nodes. This is pretty straightforward, but it's a useful property, as you'll see later.

The primary goal of using XML in Flash is to extract the information from the XMLNode objects; to determine whether you should be using nodeName or nodeValue, you need to know the nodeType. Later chapters go into more depth on extracting information from nodes when you don't necessarily know the type, so this property will be very handy then.

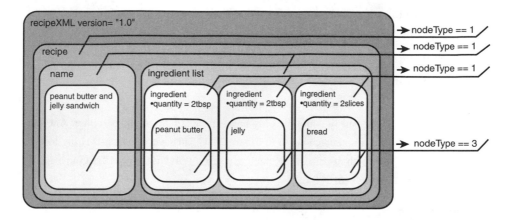

Figure 3.9   *This is a tree diagram showing the use of* `XMLNode.nodeType`.

The last important source of information is in the *attributes* of your elements. The `XMLNode` object also contains an `attributes` property, which is implemented as an associative array. If you've dealt with arrays before, associative arrays are even easier. Instead of referencing each object in the array by numeric keys, you can use literal keys. If you want to find how much peanut butter to use in the PB&J example, you need to target the first ingredient (peanut butter) at `recipeXML.firstChild.firstChild.nextSibling.firstChild`. Next, you access the `quantity` attribute in the `attributes` array with `attributes` `["quantity"]` (see Figure 3.10).

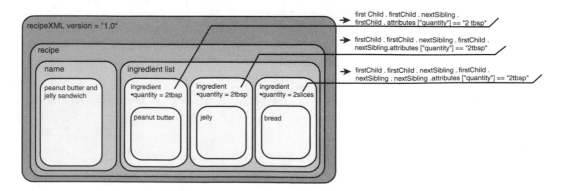

Figure 3.10   *This is a tree diagram showing the use of* `XMLNode.attributes[]`.

Putting this altogether, you can show the value 2 tbsp with the following amendment to your onLoad() function:

```
output += "pb quantity: ;
output += this.firstChild.firstChild.nextSibling.firstChild.attributes
➥["quantity"];
```

The attributes array is not the only array in the XMLNode object, either. Another array called childNodes, shown in Figure 3.11, can save you from writing long object strings with nextSibling, such as this.firstChild.nextSibling. nextSibling.nextSibling.

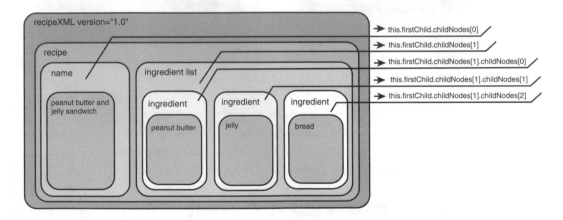

Figure 3.11   *This is a tree diagram showing the use of* XMLnode.childNodes[].

Quite often, you need to get an arbitrary child of an XMLnode, and using the childNodes array can get that information for you more directly. Here's a quick example:

```
output += "third ingredient:";
output += this.firstChild.firstChild.nextSibling.childNodes[2].firstChild.
➥nodeValue;
```

This code shows you the text in the third ingredient, bread. The first part, this.firstChild.firstChild.nextSibling, refers to the <ingredient_list> element, which you know has three elements: the three ingredients. The keys of the childNodes array start at 0 for the first child, and increase from there. So firstChild is at childNodes[0], firstChild.nextSibling is at childNodes[1], and firstChild.nextSibling.nextSibling is at childNodes[2]. Therefore, accessing `childNodes[2]` indicates that you want the third child node. You can continue further with `firstChild.nodeValue`, too, to make sure you get the value of the text in the element you've targeted with the `childNodes` array. The output, of course, is `bread`.

Summary

Those are the basics of the `XML` and `XMLNode` objects in Flash. There are a few more properties and methods to learn, but for now, the properties and methods discussed in this chapter should take you a long a way. If you want more detail about a particular object or property, check Appendix A. It might also be worth a browse to see what kinds of other methods and properties we'll be teaching later.

So What's Next?

In the next chapter, we're going to get heavier into this Flash-XML stuff by learning and using more methods and properties of the `XML` and `XMLnode` objects. Having read this chapter, you understand the fundamental properties and methods, but there are a few more to learn if you really want to harness the power of XML in Flash.

Having learned more about the `XML` and `XMLNode` objects, you'll be using ActionScript a bit more, too. ActionScript is a necessary tool for working with complex XML, so there will be three examples, each one using methods and properties you're familiar with, but the way we use them will be much more powerful. Of course, armed with this added power, you will be working through more complex XML documents, with the end goal of representing that data graphically. It's the next chapter that will bring you one step closer to more practical applications.

{ Chapter 4 }

Using XML Data in Flash

Now that you have a basic understanding of XML and the way XML and Flash communicate and pass information, it's time to start looking at some examples to solidify this knowledge with practical experience.

This chapter will offer a more in-depth understanding of working with the XML object and the XMLNode object when importing XML data into Flash. This chapter is particularly important as it covers some of the basic yet essential components to properly handling XML data.

We will cover methods of properly stripping whitespace in Flash so that you can create applications in Flash that use XML but operate on all versions of the Flash 5 player plug-in. As mentioned in Chapter 3, "Getting Your Feet Wet," whitespace is handled differently in several different versions of the Flash 5 player. This inconsistency means that creating a single Flash file that works on all player versions can be tricky when using XML. In this chapter, you'll learn about a whitespace stripper that will allow you to do just that.

This chapter is also the first one in which you see how to successfully extract XML data from the XML object. Through this process, you will gain an understanding of the relationship between XML objects and movieClip objects and can begin to visualize the transfer of XML object data into the visual and dynamic world of movieClips, which are used to visually display and represent the information in your XML documents.

After finishing this chapter, you will have a thorough understanding of how XML data can be successfully imported into Flash, manipulated and extracted from the XML object, and represented visually and graphically through the use of movieClip objects with full functionality and interactivity.

Whitespace, Thine Enemy

Whitespace in XML, as discussed earlier, is a nuisance to Flash. When Flash encounters whitespace between two tags, it automatically creates a text node to represent it. That's not very helpful if the whitespace is a simple carriage return, not real text data that you want to keep. Whitespace can be useful to humans to break up the XML and keep it organized visually, but the spaces, tabs, and carriage returns used to do that can confuse Flash and are just a nuisance in general. Since the release of its player version 5.041, Flash has included the ignoreWhite property, which allowed users to efficiently and easily drop or ignore whitespace in XML documents when parsing. However, this feature creates a new problem, as many users have different versions of the Flash player (build 30,41,42). Only releases after version r30 of the plug-in can handle this new property and remove the whitespace accordingly. Therefore, you need an efficient whitespace stripper to use in all your Flash 5 projects to handle the removal of whitespace when parsing in Flash so that you create reliable XML object structures. For further information on stripping whitespace in Flash, take a look at Chapter 8, "Performance and Optimization."

In-Flash Whitespace Stripping

As always, when working with XML in Flash, you must first create a new XML object to store your XML document. Select the first frame in your timeline of a new Flash file, go to the Actions panel, and enter the following code:

```
myXMLdoc = new XML();
```

Now that you have created the myXMLdoc reference for your newly created XML object, you must define where your XML will be loaded from. On the accompanying Web site (http://www.xmlinflash.com), in the Chapter 4 folder, is the stripWhite.xml file used in this example. You should copy this file to a directory on your local machine and make sure that the Flash file you're working on is saved in this same directory. To initiate loading the XML document, enter the following code:

```
myXMLdoc.load("stripWhite.xml");
```

As you learned in the previous chapter, this statement loads your XML document; however, you want to process this XML data as soon as it has been loaded into Flash so that you can properly handle any whitespace issues the document might have. This requires writing a custom function to act as an event handler to the onLoad event, which by default is automatically called after the XML document has been successfully loaded. To do this correctly, you must set the custom onLoad function before loading your XML document, so enter the following code snippet after initializing the myXMLdoc XML object:

```
myXMLdoc.onLoad = function(){
    this.firstChild.stripWhite();
}
```

All you've done here is overridden the default onLoad() method by setting it equal to a new function that performs the stripWhite() method on the firstChild or root element of the imported XML document. If you are already familiar with all the methods of the XML and XMLNode objects, you'll notice that stripWhite() is not a predefined method of either of these object prototypes. It's a custom-built method that you're going to create by modifying the XMLNode prototype. In Flash ActionScript, as well as other object-oriented programming languages, *overriding* an object prototype is a powerful way to define methods that are accessible to all instances of that particular object prototype. For instance, you could create a custom method that flips the horizontal alignment of any movieClip object. To do this, you would write the following code:

```
movieClip.prototype.flipX() = function{this._xscale *= -1;)
```

This one line of code now makes the flipX() method available to all movieClip objects in the movie—whether they already exist or not. You can now simply access this method by using the following code:

```
myMovieClip.flipX();
```

This line will cause myMovieClip to be flipped horizontally whenever this code is called.

Your custom onLoad() method calls a new method named stripWhite(), but it has not been created yet. So do that in the same location where you inserted the previous code, in the Frame 1 Actions panel:

```
XMLNode.prototype.stripWhite = function() {
    if (this.nodetype ==1) {
        var chLength = this.childNodes.length;
```

```
        for (var i=0; i < chLength; i++) {
            this.childNodes[i].stripWhite();
        }
    } else {
        if (this.nodetype ==3) {
            if (whiteTest(this.nodeValue)) {
                this.nextSibling.stripWhite();
                this.removeNode();
            }
        }
    }
}
```

You have successfully created the `stripWhite()` method, which you can use on all instances of the `XMLNode` object class. This means you can process this method on all nodes in your `XML` object. Let's walk through this method and pick it apart to get a better understanding of what it is doing.

To strip the whitespace from an `XML` object, you simply go though all the nodes in the object and remove any that contain only whitespace. The characters that are considered whitespace are carriage returns, line feeds, spaces, null characters, and horizontal and vertical tabs. It just so happens that these characters, along with a number of other unimportant characters, exist below 33 on the ASCII character chart. If any character in a `textNode`'s value is *not* below 33, that value contains a non-whitespace character. In that case, you do nothing, and keep looking at other nodes. If all characters are below 33, you remove that node completely because you know it is just whitespace and other useless characters.

Recursion and Recursive Algorithms

If it sounds complicated now, don't worry—it's not. For now, just concentrate on how to go through each node of the tree. To do that, you use a recursive algorithm, which most non-programmers are unfamiliar with. It's actually a simple way of navigating the complicated XML tree. In general, a *recursive function* is one that calls itself until a specific condition exists (this condition is called the *terminating condition*). This is just a lot of computer science mumbo-jumbo right now, so let's look at a simple example.

In mathematics, there is a function called a *factorial* that looks like *n*!. If you don't have a mathematics or an engineering background, you might at least have seen it on a scientific calculator. It looks impressive, but there's really nothing to it. If you are trying to compute 4!, for instance, you multiply

$$4 \times 3 \times 2 \times 1$$

If you want to compute 8!, it's

$$8 \times 7 \times 6 \times 5 \times 4 \times 3 \times 2 \times 1$$

If you wanted to write a function for this equation in English, you would say "Multiply the number by itself minus 1, and then multiple that by itself minus 2, carrying on in this way until you multiply by 1." It's easy to see how this function works, but it's another task entirely to convey that information in a program.

In ActionScript, you would do something like this:

```
function factorial(n) {
  if (n == 1) {
return(n);
  } else {
return(n * factorial(n-1));
  }
}
```

The function takes a value of n and checks to see whether it equals 1. If it does, you already have the answer: 1. That's the easy part. It's the terminating condition. If it doesn't equal 1, you return the value of n, multiplied by the value of `factorial(n-1)`. That's the tricky part: The function is calling itself. Let's see how it would work with an input of 4:

Call the factorial function on 4.

It's not equal to 1, so the answer is 4 multiplied by the factorial of 4-1, which is the factorial of 3.

Call the factorial function on 3.

It's not equal to 1, so the answer is 3 multiplied by the factorial of 3-1, which is the factorial of 2.

Call the factorial function on 2.

It's not equal to 1, so the answer is 2 multiplied by the factorial of 2-1, which is the factorial of 1.

Call the factorial function on 1.

It's 1, so the answer is 1.

Return the value 1 to the factorial function on 2.

Return the value 1×2 to the factorial function on 3.

Return the value $1 \times 2 \times 3$ to the factorial function on 4.

Return the value $1 \times 2 \times 3 \times 4$, which is 4!, what you wanted originally.

That's recursion in a nutshell. The function calls itself, and continues to do so until it reaches some terminating condition (in this case, it terminates when n equals 1). The stripWhite() method is a recursive function, too, so it's necessary to understand how recursion works before we explain the stripWhite() method. In fact, a lot of the work in this chapter and the following ones uses recursion in one way or another because it's useful for traversing the XML tree. If you're unclear about it at this point, read on. A few more examples should make it clearer.

The stripWhite() method is broken down into two separate if statements that are used in a similar recursive algorithm. The first step that this function performs is determining whether the referenced XMLNode is of nodeType 1 (an element) or nodeType 3 (a text node).

The method is separated into two separate if statements to make the first if block responsible for identifying all other elements in the XML document and applying the same method to them to identify all text nodes. The second if block handles the text nodes, so we need to ensure that you cycle through all the element nodes that might contain a text node to make sure we haven't missed any occurrences of whitespace. Here's a simplified version:

```
XMLNode.prototype.stripWhite = function() {
if (this.nodetype == 1) {
// element node handling here
    } else {
if (this.nodetype == 3){
   // text node handling here
}
     }
}
```

If the XMLNode object is of nodeType 1, you know that it's an element. In the following code, you then set the variable chLength equal to the childNodes.length of this particular node and perform a for loop that goes through these childNodes and subsequently calls the stripWhite() method on each element. This procedure shows the recursive nature of stripWhite(). That is, the same function that is initially called subsequently calls itself. In that way, calling stripWhite() on one node also calls the method on all its children.

```
    if (this.nodetype ==1){
        var chLength = this.childNodes.length;
        for (var i=0; i < chLength; i++){
            this.childNodes[i].stripWhite();
        }
    }
```

Eventually, as the first `for` loop drills down through the document, it will probably run into an occurrence of a text node, which you'll have to test for whitespace. When this happens, that text node gets handled by the second `if` block, which handles all nodes with a `nodeType` equal to 3 (text). All nodes are of type 1 or 3, so the `if (this.nodeType ==3)...` check is unnecessary; if it were a type 1 node, it would've already been handled. We've included it here, though, for the sake of clarity. Essentially, this `if` block is the one responsible for instantiating the removal of whitespace. Let's take another look at this portion of the code:

```
if (this.nodetype ==3) {
    if (whiteTest(this.nodeValue)) {
        this.nextSibling.stripWhite();
        this.removeNode();
    }
}
```

If the node has been identified as a text node, another `if` statement performs a secondary function called `whiteTest()` on the `nodeValue`. This `whiteTest()` function is responsible for determining whether the text node contains data or whitespace only. However, you have not created this `whiteTest()` function yet, so let's get that code into the movie to better understand the flow:

```
function whiteTest(str) {
    var allWhite = true;
    var strLength = str.length;
    for (var i=0; i<strLength; i++) {
        if (str.charCodeAt(i) > 32) {
            allWhite = false;
            break;
        }
    }
    return allWhite;
}
```

Basically, `whiteTest()` takes a string as input and returns a Boolean value (true or false) to indicate whether the string contains all whitespace. If you take a look at the previous `if` statement that calls the `whiteTest()` function, you can see that it sends the string `this.nodeValue` to the function, so the `str` parameter is filled with `this.nodeValue`, which is equal to the character data of the text node. That's what you need to process to determine whether the text node's text data contains only whitespace.

When this function is called, you instantly initialize two variables: allWhite and strLength. The first variable, allWhite, represents whether the string you're processing contains all whitespace and is given a default value of true. In other words, you assume that the string is all whitespace, so false is returned only if that's not the case. The variable strLength contains the numerical value of the string's length for use in the subsequent for loop. You are basically testing to see whether there are any *non*-whitespace characters. Every time you use a space in your XML data, you are technically using whitespace, so you don't want to test whether there is *any* whitespace, but whether there is *only* whitespace.

This for loop is the meat of the function and serves to determine whether the string contains all whitespace. Inside this loop you perform an if statement that checks the character code value at the current position in the string.

Take a look at Figure 4.1, which tables the character code values from 0 to 32. The character codes that represent whitespace (what you need to check for) are null (0), horizontal tabulation (9), line feed (10), vertical tabulation (11), form feed (12), carriage feed (13), and space (32).

If your code detects a character code value greater than 32 (meaning it's *not* a whitespace element), you know that the nodeValue you are checking is not all whitespace; therefore, you set allWhite equal to false and break from the loop. When you break from this loop, you are returning the Boolean value of false, which was set in the variable allWhite, to the if statement that called the whiteTest() function:

```
If (whiteTest(this.nodeValue)) ...
```

By doing this, the subsequent commands in the if statement are not performed on the node object. So what happens if the whiteTest() function loops through the string and finds only character code values that represent whitespace? Then the value of the allWhite variable is not altered and remains true. This boolean value true is then sent back to the if statement located in the stripWhite() method that called the whiteTest() function:

```
if (this.nodetype ==3){
     if (whiteTest(this.nodeValue)){
         this.nextSibling.stripWhite();
         this.removeNode();
         }
     }
   }
```

CHARACTER AND UNICODE MAPPINGS		
dec	**unicode**	**description**
0	\u0000	[null]
1	\u0001	[start of heading]
2	\u0002	[start of text]
3	\u0003	[end of text]
4	\u0004	[end of transmission]
5	\u0005	[enquiry]
6	\u0006	[acknowledge]
7	\u0007	[bell]
8	\u0008	[backspace]
9	\u0009	[horizontal tabulation]
10	\u000a	[line feed]
11	\u000b	[vertical tabulation]
12	\u000c	[form feed]
13	\u000d	[carriage feed]
14	\u000e	[shift out]
15	\u000f	[shift in]
16	\u0010	[data link escape]
17	\u0011	[device control one]
18	\u0012	[device control two]
19	\u0013	[device control three]
20	\u0014	[device control four]
21	\u0015	[negative acknowledge]
22	\u0016	[synchronous idle]
23	\u0017	[end of transmission block]
24	\u0018	[cancel]
25	\u0019	[end of medium]
26	\u001a	[substitute]
27	\u001b	[escape]
28	\u001c	[file separator]
29	\u001d	[group separator]
30	\u001e	[record separator]
31	\u001f	[unit separator]
32	\u0020	[space]

Figure 4.1 *Whitespace character codes.*

With the if statement returning true, the subsequent two lines are executed. The first statement performs the stripWhite() method on the nextSibling to the node you just processed and then removes the node that just returned allWhite == true from the myXMLdoc XML object.

The stripWhite() method will continue to go through all child nodes of the root element and any child nodes they may have, removing all nodes that contain only whitespace until the method has traversed the entire XML object. When it has, you are left with a completely whitespace-free XML object that is ready to be accessed and manipulated cleanly inside the Flash environment.

Before you move on to translating the XML document with a custom-written toString() method, take one final look at the complete code and an example of its use:

```
XMLNode.prototype.stripWhite = function(){
    function whiteTest(str){
        var allWhite = true;
        var strLength = str.length;
        for (var i=0; i<strLength; i++){
            if(str.charCodeAt(i) > 32){
                allWhite = false;
                break;
            }
        }
        return (allWhite);
    }

    if (this.nodetype ==1){
        var chLength = this.childNodes.length;
        for (var i=0; i < chLength; i++){
            this.childNodes[i].stripWhite();
        }
    } else {
        if (this.nodetype ==3){
            if (whiteTest(this.nodeValue)){
                this.nextSibling.stripWhite();
                this.removeNode();
            }
        }
    }
}


myXMLdoc.onLoad = function(){
    this.firstChild.stripWhite();
}
myXMLdoc.load("example.xml");
```

You'll notice that the whiteTest() function is placed inside the stripWhite() method you created. This is done to keep the code together. This function is used solely by the stripWhite() method, so placing it inside the prototype keeps your code clean, compact, and portable.

Also, keep in mind that you call `stripWhite()` on the `firstChild` of the XML object, not the object itself. That's because you've extended the `XMLNode` prototype, not the XML object prototype. The `firstChild` is the first occurrence of an `XMLNode` in this representation of the XML document.

You now have a streamlined piece of portable code that can be used to strip whitespace from any XML document. Feel free to use it when you need to deliver XML content across all versions of the Flash 5 player.

CDATA Handling in Flash's Parser

The only remaining caveat is that CDATA is also stored in Flash's `XMLNodes` as a text node. This is a bit of a sloppy implementation because Flash gives no indication in the `XMLNode` object as to whether you're dealing with CDATA. If you wanted to purposely add whitespace to your document, you might consider using CDATA to make sure it doesn't get stripped out. Unfortunately, with this stripping method, even that whitespace will be eliminated. For that reason, and for more efficiency, we suggest you use other methods for stripping whitespace *before* you even load it into Flash. We will cover some of those methods in Chapter 8, but for now this method should be adequate for most applications of XML in Flash. In fact, this is the method that most Flash developers use because all-white CDATA is usually unnecessary.

Rewriting the `toString()` Method

Why on earth would you want to rewrite the `toString()` method? Good question! For starters, you need a better demonstration of how to traverse the XML tree. Like the previous example of stripping whitespace from an XML document, in this example you will also travel through an entire XML document, but this time with the intent of rewriting the `toString()` method and actually adding whitespace.

Whitespace is a beautiful thing to us humans. It's a visual way to help make XML readable and understandable. When you are working with XML in Flash, even if it's just for debugging, reading lines and lines of unformatted XML source code doesn't help you visually interpret your data's hierarchical nature at all. For the sole purpose of debugging, rewriting `toString()` is an invaluable tool for quickly determining how your XML is formed or forming.

To Start toString()

Rewriting toString() also acts as an excellent lead-in to the example in "Creating a Custom toHTML() Method," later in this chapter, that will incorporate HTML formatting. But before we get ahead of ourselves, for the toString() example, you'll need the toString.fla file, which is in the toString folder of the Chapter 4 directory on the accompanying Web site. If you are still rolling from the previous example, you can keep that file handy and build on it along with our explanation.

After you have the file open, you'll see the same code from the previous example, except that the XML and XMLNode prototypes have been extended to include a new custom toString() method. At the bottom of the code in Frame 1, you will see that the onLoad() handler has been modified slightly:

```
myXMLdoc = new XML();

myXMLdoc.onLoad = function () {
  this.firstChild.stripWhite();
  trace(this.toString());
}

myXMLdoc.load("toString.xml");
```

The only thing added is a trace() statement that takes the XML document myXMLdoc and displays the results of the toString() method in the Flash Output window. The code is still performing the stripWhite() method and stripping the document of whitespace. The catch is that the default toString() method was rewritten to alter how your XML source code is represented as a string. In other words, after you have removed the whitespace from your XML document, you are rewriting the toString() method to then visually display this stripped XML with whitespace! Crazy, we know, but bear with us. Let's take a look at how you go about accomplishing this.

It's important to understand that when dealing with an XML object, you need to work with the XML object class as well as the XMLNode object class. The XMLNode object covers all nodes in an XML document, from the firstChild down. The XML object includes the XML declaration as well as the DocType declaration, which are not considered nodes in the object hierarchy. For this reason, you need to extend the toString() prototype for both the XML object and XMLNode object classes.

This code is called in the onLoad() handler:

```
trace(this.toString());
```

In this line, this refers to myXMLdoc, which is the newly created XML object. After whitespace has been stripped with the stripWhite() method, the toString() method is then performed on this stripped XML object. Here's the code associated with the XML object:

```
1  XML.prototype.toString = function () {
2    var xStr = "    ";
3    if (this.xmlDecl != null) {
4      xStr += this.xmlDecl+"\n";
5    }
6    if (this.docTypeDecl != null) {
7      xStr += "    " + this.docTypeDecl+"\n";
8    }
9    xStr += this.firstChild.toString();
10   return(xStr);
11 }
```

The main objective of the toString() method is to handle the string representation of the XML document's XML declaration (xmlDecl; line 3) and DocType declaration (docTypeDecl; line 6). First you create a variable called xStr in line 2 that stores and represents the string of XML data. Remember, the purpose of rewriting the toString() method is to give you a formatted string representation of your XML document—using whitespace. You first instantiate the xStr variable with four spaces (line 7), which are used to represent a horizontal tab.

Next, the code checks to see whether the XML object contains an xmlDecl value. If there is an XML declaration property (returning not null), you add the XML declaration to the xStr variable followed by a newline character (carriage return). The code does the same check on the docTypeDecl property, and if there is one, you add another four spaces and the DocType declaration to your string.

After adding these elements to xStr, you then add the value of the toString() method applied to the firstChild or root element of your document. This firstChild is represented by the XMLNode object, so you need to extend the toString() method for this object class, too. Let's take a peek at that code:

```
XMLNode.prototype.toString = function () {

  function spaceOut() {
    var sStr = "";
    for(var i=0;i<XMLNode.spaces;i++){
      sStr += "  ";
```

```
    }
    return(sStr);
}

var xStr = "";
XMLNode.spaces += 4;
if (this.nodetype == 1) {
    //it's an element; check its kids
        xStr += spaceOut()+"<"+this.nodeName;

        var attr = this.attributes;
        for (var eachAttr in attr){
          xStr += " " + eachAttr+"='"+this.attributes[eachAttr]+"'";
        }
        xStr +=">";

        if (this.firstChild.nodeType == 1){xStr += "\n";}
        var chlength = this.childNodes.length;
        for (var i=0;i < chlength; i++) {
          xStr += this.childnodes[i].toString();
        }
        if (this.lastChild.nodeType==1){xStr += spaceOut();}
        xStr += "</"+this.nodeName+">\n";
        XMLNode.spaces -= 4;

    } else {
      //it's text
      xStr += this.nodeValue;
      XMLNode.spaces -= 4;
if (this.nextSibling.nodeType == 1) {xStr += "\n";}
//useful if children are mixed content.  puts elements on a new line.

    }
  return(xStr);
}
```

For the moment, we'll skip over the spaceOut() function. As in the rewritten
toString() method, you create a variable (called xStr) to hold the string representation of your XML data. You also create a variable called XMLNode.spaces
that's used throughout your method to add space representing horizontal tabs
between child and sibling elements/nodes. This variable is set to 4, which is the
number of spaces used to display your initial XML object declarations.
Throughout this function, the value of this variable will change to represent the
depth level of your parent/child nodes.

Next, the toString() method checks to see whether the first node is of type 1
(an element). If it is, you call the spaceOut() function, which is used to determine how many spaces to add. It simply determines the value of XMLNode.spaces

and adds a space character (" ") equal to its value. Because that value has not changed, the root element is indented four spaces, lining it up with the string output from your XML object's `toString()` method. Next, you output a "`<`" followed by the `nodeName` of this node.

Of course, nodes can contain any number of attributes, so you use the following piece of code to handle processing attributes:

```
var attr = this.attributes;
for (var eachAttr in attr){
  xStr += " " + eachAttr+"='"+this.attributes[eachAttr]+"'";
}
xStr +=">";
```

This code first sets the `attr` variable equal to the current node's attributes. Then you run a `for` loop through each attribute in the node's associative array of attributes. As it cycles through each attribute, the loop adds a character space between each attribute and places the attribute value within quotes. When you finish processing the attributes of the node in the `for` loop, you close the tag in the string representation with "`>`".

This next piece of code is what makes this function so powerful. You'll notice here that this function is recursive, meaning it calls on itself for all its children:

```
if (this.firstChild.nodeType == 1){xStr += "\n";}
var chlength = this.childNodes.length;
for (var i=0;i < chlength; i++) {
  xStr += this.childnodes[i].toString();
}
```

This code detects whether the root element has a child node that is an element (a type 1 node). If it does, you insert a carriage return ("`/n`") in the current string, and then use `childNodes.length` to determine how many `childNodes` there are. With this value, you then loop through all `childNodes` and subsequently apply the `toString()` method to them. That means as each `childNode` is processed, it in turn runs through this very same `for` loop if it contains `childNodes`. This function will keep running recursively, traveling deeper through the XML hierarchy, until all nodes have been added to `xStr`.

When this `for` loop is finished, you run into this next piece of code:

```
if (this.lastChild.nodeType==1){xStr += spaceOut();}
xStr += "</"+this.nodeName+">\n";
XMLNode.spaces -= 4;
```

This code determines whether the `lastChild` is an element node. If so, you perform the `spaceOut()` function to add the appropriate number of spaces, representing horizontal tabs. You then close off the element you just looped through and reduce the `XMLNode.spaces` variable by four characters, returning you to the appropriate horizontal spacing of the parent node.

After traversing the entire `XMLNode` hierarchy and placing the data—with whitespace—into the `xStr` variable, you then return `xStr`'s value to the `XML.toString()` method, which returns that value to the original `trace()` statement. You have successfully transformed the representation of your XML object in Figure 4.2.

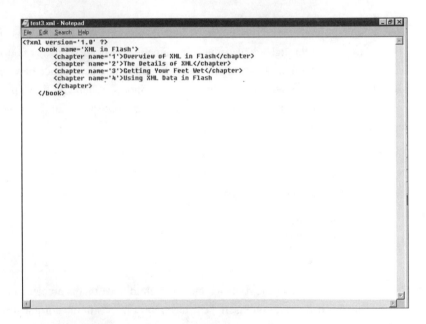

Figure 4.2 *Sample XML in MS Notepad.*

Although it was a little work, this custom `toString()` method is handy. Whenever you want to check or confirm how your XML is being formed inside Flash, you can simply call this method on your `XML` object and use `trace()` to send it to the Output window. This method can instantly give you a visual indication of where you might be having problems with your XML structure.

Figure 4.3 shows the Output window with the correct output you should get when this code runs.

Figure 4.3   `XML.toString()` *in the Output window.*

Creating a Custom `toHTML()` Method

Now that you have taken a look at tree traversal in an XML hierarchy and understand the concept of a recursive algorithm—in which the same function calls itself as it drills down through child nodes—you will take the custom `toString()` method a little further and incorporate HTML functionality. You'll rework the method to incorporate syntax highlighting of elements, text nodes, attributes, and declarations in your XML structure to improve the display of the data you have.

Along with the addition of XML in Flash 5, some rudimentary HTML display was provided. Although Flash 5's handling of HTML is very basic and adheres only to the HTML 1.0 standard, it is incredibly handy and efficient for formatting text or creating syntax highlights.

To follow along, open the toHTML.fla file in the Chapter4 source code from the companion Web site. The script in Frame 1 is set up almost exactly the same as the previous `toString()` method, except that you're extending the XML object to include the `toHTML()` method. As before, you will need to enhance the prototype for both the XML object and the XMLNode object to correctly display your entire XML document.

The handling of the output is also a little different, as shown in this code:

```
myXMLdoc = new XML();
myXMLdoc.onLoad = function () {
  this.firstChild.stripWhite();
  output = this.toHTML();
}
```

Instead of using the `trace()` function to display the string representation in the Output window, you are using a text field on the stage to display the information. You are setting the `output` variable equal to the XML `toHTML()` method so that it will be displayed in the dynamic text field on the stage and labeled `output` with the HTML option selected in the Text Options panel.

As before, in the `toString()` method, you are processing the XML object with the `stripWhite()` method before performing the `toHTML()` function. This ensures that you're using a clean XML structure.

First, you need to extend the XML object's prototype by adding the custom `toHTML()` method to the XML object. This is done much like the `toString()` method, with a few minor differences, as shown in the following lines:

```
XML.prototype.toHTML = function () {

  function tagKiller(str) {
     str = substring(str,2,(str.length-2));
     return(str);
  }

  var xStr = "     ";

  if (this.xmlDecl != null) {
    xStr += "<font color='#00ee00'>&lt;"+
    xStr += tagKiller(this.xmlDecl)+"&gt;</font><br />";
  }

  if (this.docTypeDecl != null) {
      xStr += "<font color='#00ee00'>
➥&lt;"+tagKiller(this.docTypeDecl)+"&gt;</font>+<br />";     }
  xStr += this.firstChild.toHTML();
  return(xStr);
}
```

The first thing you'll notice is that the code immediately sets a function called `tagKiller`. This function's main purpose is to strip out the brackets (< and >) of an `xmlDecl` or `docTypeDecl` so that they can be added as `&lt;` and `&gt;` later to correctly display your strings.

Following this function, you set the xStr variable equal to four blank spaces to represent a horizontal tab indentation in the document's visual display.

The first of the two if statements handles the xmlDecl of the XML document, if there is indeed one:

```
if (this.xmlDecl != null) {
    xStr += "<font color='#00ee00'>&lt;";
    xStr += tagKiller(this.xmlDecl)+"&gt;</font><br />";
  }
```

If an xmlDecl is present, you populate it and add it to the xStr variable. You'll notice that in the middle of the if statement, you're accessing the tagKiller function just mentioned. You send the xmlDecl to the tagKiller function to rip out the less-than (<) and greater-than (>) characters so that you can manipulate the string data independently of the brackets.

In setting xStr, notice that you begin with the font property, where you set the color to #00ee00, which happens to represent green. This is the type of basic HTML support you can access in the Flash 5 environment, which is perfect for performing this type of syntax highlighting. Inside the <font> tags, you also reinsert the tag brackets by using the < and > encoded entities. Also, instead of using "/n" to insert a line break as you did in the previous example, you can use the well-known HTML tag <br> to perform this same function.

The second if statement is almost identical, but you're syntax-highlighting the XML document's docTypeDecl the same green as the xmlDecl and inserting a line break.

The next line is responsible for returning the HTML for the firstChild of your XML object. Note that this is *not* a recursive call because the firstChild's toHTML() method is the toHTML() method of the XMLNode object, not the XML object written here. Therefore, you'll need to define the XMLNode.toHTML() method for that purpose. Take a look at the entire code before you begin to dissect it:

```
XMLNode.prototype.toHTML = function () {

  function spaceOut() {

    var sStr = "<pre>";
    for(var i=0;i<XMLNode.spaces;i++){
     sStr += " ";
    }
```

```
        sStr += "</pre>"
        return(sStr);
    }

    var xStr = "";
    XMLNode.spaces += 4;

    if (this.nodetype == 1) {
            xStr += spaceOut();
            xStr +="<font color='#0000ee'>&lt;</font><font color='#996600'>";
            xStr +=this.nodeName+"</font>";
            var attr = this.attributes;
            for (var eachAttr in attr){
              xStr += " <font color='#ff0000'>" + eachAttr;
              xStr += "</font><font color='#0000ee'>='</font>";
              xStr += this.attributes[eachAttr]+"<font color='#0000ee'>'
➥</font>";
            }
            xStr +="<font color='#0000ee'>&gt;</font>";

            if (this.firstChild.nodeType == 1){xStr += "<br />";}


            var chlength = this.childNodes.length;
            for (var i=0;i < chlength; i++) {
              xStr += this.childnodes[i].toHTML();
            }

            if (this.lastChild.nodeType==1){xStr += spaceOut();}
            xStr += "<font color='#0000ee'>&lt;/</font>
➥<font color='#996600'>";
            xStr += this.nodeName;
            xStr +="</font><font color='#0000ee'>&gt;</font><br />";
            XMLNode.spaces -= 4;
    } else {
        //it's text
        xStr += this.nodeValue;
        XMLNode.spaces -= 4
        if (this.nextSibling.nodeType == 1) {xStr += "<br />";}
    }
    return(xStr);
}
```

The initial spaceOut() function is used to output a certain number of spaces, as specified by XMLNode.spaces. The XMLNode.spaces variable creates the indentations in your document's display; it's included in the prototype to make its value a global one that's available to other nodes. Note that sStr += "<pre>"; is included to represent spaces as . Plain spaces do not work in version r30 of the Flash player, so they are preformated in this code.

The following code handles the main syntax highlighting of the element nodes:

```
if (this.nodetype == 1) {
      xStr += spaceOut();
      xStr +="<font color='#0000ee'>&lt;</font><font color='#996600'>";
      xStr +=this.nodeName+"</font>";
      var attr = this.attributes;
      for (var eachAttr in attr){
        xStr += " <font color='#ff0000'>" + eachAttr;
        xStr += "</font><font color='#0000ee'>='</font>";
        xStr += this.attributes[eachAttr]+"<font color='#0000ee'>'
➡</font>";
      }
      xStr +="<font color='#0000ee'>&gt;</font>";

      if (this.firstChild.nodeType == 1){xStr += "<br />";}
}
```

After the initial `if` statement determines that the node is indeed an element node
(type 1), you call the `spaceOut()` function to insert the proper number of spaces,
depending on how many child levels down you are in the XML document, and
then insert the `nodeName`. However, you are also adding an open tag bracket (<)
first and coloring it blue (#0000ee) before you highlight the `nodeName` as
brown(#996600) with the preceding HTML <font> tag.

After we have placed the open tag bracket (in blue) and `nodeName` (in brown) in
the `xStr` variable, you need to process any and all attributes of the current node.
To do this, you set the variable `attr` to the node's attributes. The `.attributes`
property returns an associative array containing all the node's attributes, which
allows you to then loop through each attribute, adding it to `xStr` with a simple
`for-in` loop, as shown here:

```
for (var eachAttr in attr){
      xStr += " <font color='#ff0000'>" + eachAttr;
      xStr += "</font><font color='#0000ee'>='</font>";
      xStr += this.attributes[eachAttr]+"<font color='#0000ee'>'
➡</font>";
        }
```

This code uses color to highlight the attribute name, the attribute value, the
quotes, and the equal sign. First add the attribute name, referenced as `eachAttr`
in the loop, using the color red (#ff0000). You follow this by adding a blue
(#0000ee) ='. No <font> properties are included for the attribute's value; instead,
it's displayed with the default color black. Last, you add another blue (#0000ee)
quotation to close off the attribute value.

After looping through all the attributes and adding them to xStr, you close off the closing tag bracket in blue (#0000ee). If you're closing off an element node, you add a <br> tag to create a carriage return before processing any further children of this node:

```
xStr +="<font color='#0000ee'>&gt;</font>";

if (this.firstChild.nodeType == 1){xStr += "<br />";}
}
```

Now that you have processed a node, you make the recursive call. Again, this is where you call the same function that you're currently in to filter through children of the current node:

```
var chlength = this.childNodes.length;
for (var i=0;i < chlength; i++) {
  xStr += this.childnodes[i].toHTML();
```

This code determines the number of children in this node and runs the toHTML() method on all of them, placing the end results back into xStr.

You should have a pretty good understanding of the rest of the code, so we'll just show the rest of it with comments:

```
//if the last child is not text, indent
if (this.lastChild.nodeType==1){xStr += spaceOut();}
// </nodename>, where '</' is blue, nodename is brown, and > is blue
xStr += "<font color='#0000ee'>&lt;/</font><font color='#996600'>";
xStr += this.nodeName;
xStr +="</font><font color='#0000ee'>&gt;</font><br />";

// reduce the indentation level, we're leaving the children
XMLNode.spaces -= 4;
//it's text
    } else {
// output the text
      xStr += this.nodeValue;

//reduce the indentation level, we're leaving the text node
      XMLNode.spaces -= 4;

    //useful if children are mixed content.  puts elements on a new line.
  if (this.nextSibling.nodeType == 1) {xStr += "<br />";}
    }
  return(xStr);
}
```

Although this book is printed in black and white, trust us that the screenshot in Figure 4.4 does include the color syntax as described here. Try running it on your own with your own XML to see how the color-coding turns out.

```
<?xml version='1.0' ?>
<book name='XML in Flash'>
  <chapter name='1'>Overview of XML in Flash</chapter>
  <chapter name='2'>The Details of XML</chapter>
  <chapter name='3'>Getting Your Feet Wet</chapter>
  <chapter name='4'>Using XML Data in Flash
     <example>Interactive Representation</example>
  </chapter>
</book>
```

Figure 4.4   *The color-coded results of the new* `XML.toHTML()`.

A Graphical Representation of XML in Flash

By the end of this section, you will have successfully created a Flash application that loads XML content and displays it through the use of `movieClip` objects. This graphical representation of the XML document gives you more information about the XML structure and how each piece of information in that document relates to the others. The final result will be a split-paned display that allows you to navigate an XML structure displayed with `movieClips` so that you can roll over individual elements and nodes in the XML document to display more details about that element in the opposite panel.

So let's get moving! To follow along, open the graphical.fla file in the graphical folder of the Chapter 4 directory of the accompanying Web site.

Before you start examining the code, it's a good idea to open the file and test it to see what you're creating and what the end goals of this particular example will be. Figure 4.5 shows how it should look eventually.

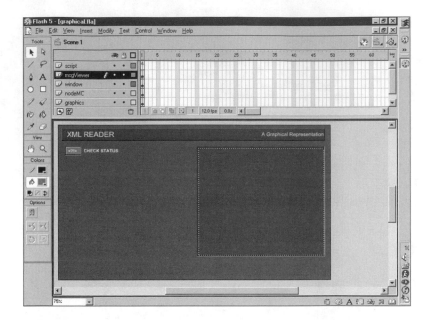

Figure 4.5   *The XML Reader: A graphical representation of XML in Flash.*

After you have the Flash file open, notice that the main timeline consists of four separate layers: script, msgViewer, window, and nodeMC. All these layers contain just a single frame. Let's quickly go over the purpose of these components so that you can familiarize yourself with the conceptual approach we are taking.

The script layer is where you place the majority of your code. All code directly related to handling the transfer of your XML document is handled in the first frame of this layer. This layer has no graphical elements or movieClip objects; it is meant to contain only your scripts.

The msgViewer movieClip, shown in Figure 4.6, is the clip containing the information about the nodes in your XML tree. As in the previous toHTML() method example, you have a text field called output inside this clip, where the information generated from the XML content is displayed.

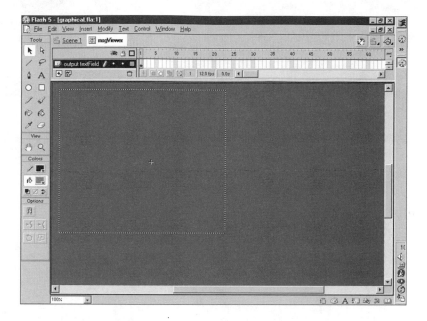

Figure 4.6   *The msgViewer* movieClip.

The window movieClip, shown in Figure 4.7, serves two main purposes. First, it's used as a design element to lay out the header title and some simple design elements. Second, it holds information about the XML document declarations. Inside this clip is a small question mark (?) button. When you roll over it with your mouse, the document's XML declaration and DocType declaration are displayed.

The nodeMC movieClip, shown in Figure 4.8, is the main clip you'll be using to display nodes in your XML tree. This clip is positioned offstage, as all instances of it are generated dynamically based on your XML document. This clip is duplicated as the code goes through each node when you traverse the XML data. Inside this movieClip are several other elements of significance, used to display node information and generate interactivity with the mouse.

You'll notice in Figure 4.9 that there are four layers inside the nodeMC movieClip: viewBtn, icon, fields, and msgBox. Each of these layers contains a single element.

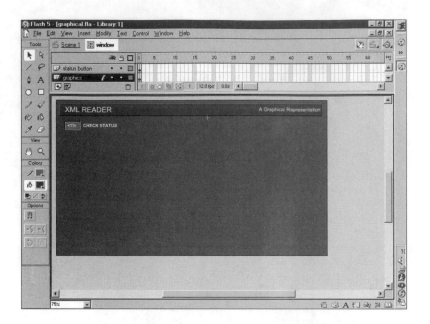

Figure 4.7 *The window* movieClip.

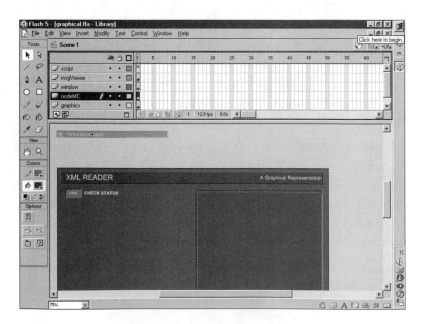

Figure 4.8 *The* nodeMC *movieClip.*

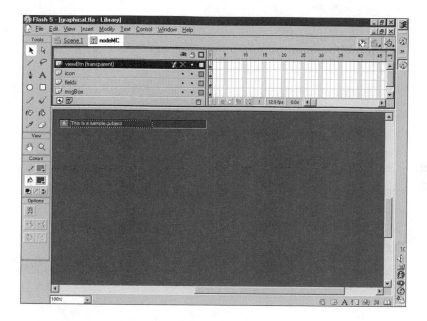

Figure 4.9   *The layers of nodeMC.*

The viewBtn layer holds a transparent button that sits on the top layer and contains rollover code that sends the information for the particular node instance to the output in the msgViewer `movieClip`.

The icon layer is a two-framed `movieClip` that contains an icon in each frame. One icon is displayed if the node is of type 1 (element), and the other icon is displayed for a node of type 3 (text).

The fields layer simply contains a text field called titlefield, which is used to display the node name if it's an element node or the node value if it's a text node.

Last, the msgBox layer holds a simple blue graphical element used as the background for the `movieClip`. All of the previously mentioned `movieClips` are situated next to or directly above this graphic on stage. This layer is responsible for the actual look of your `movieClip`.

Now that you have an overall idea of how this movie is put together, let's start digging through the code and see how it interacts with the elements we have discussed.

Scripting for Graphical XML Output

If you take a look at the code in graphical.as, you can see that a lot is going on. It might seem daunting at first, but once we dissect it, you'll see how it makes sense.

When coding in Flash, you need to make sure that functions are made available for use immediately when they're called. For this reason, the meat of the code—all the juicy stuff that makes it all happen—is at the top. For explanation purposes, however, we will be covering the code from the bottom up. Let's start with what you should be familiar with now: loading your XML and customizing the onLoad() handler:

```
_root.nodeNum = 0;
linkdata = new XML();            // creates a new XML object
linkdata.onLoad = linkdata_onLoad;
linkdata.load("test.xml");  // loads the local file test.xml into the
➡ object and parses it
stop ();
```

This code creates the new XML object called linkdata and modifies the onLoad() handler to perform the linkData_onLoad after the test3.xml document has been loaded into Flash. Also, the nodeNum variable is initialized and set equal to 0. This variable's purpose is to tally the number of nodeMCs that you currently have—that is, the number of movieClips you have duplicated that represent nodes in your XML document.

Let's move on and take a look at the custom onLoad() handler:

```
function linkdata_onLoad(success) {
    this.firstChild.stripWhite();
    _root.depth = 0;
    _root.msgViewer.output = "Status: "+this.status+"\n";
    this.firstChild.displayNodes();
}
```

This custom function, which overrides the default onLoad() handler, is used to set some global variables as well as display the status of your XML load to the main Output window.

The nodeNum value is for determining the number of nodes you have, and depth is used to track the highest depth level of your movieClips.

After you have set these variables and displayed their status, you then perform the custom method displayNodes() on the firstChild. This method, as in the previous examples, was created when you extended the prototype for the XMLNode object, as shown here:

```
XMLNode.prototype.depth = XMLNode_depth;
XMLNode.prototype.node2Viewer = XMLNode_node2Viewer;
XMLNode.prototype.nodeDetail = XMLNode_nodeDetail;
XMLNode.prototype.displayNodes = XMLNode_displayNodes;
```

A bunch of functions have been added to the XMLNode prototype to make them methods of the XMLNode object. The actual functions are described and defined in the preceding code. Note the use of the underscore (_). It's used to represent the division between object and method, with XMLNode being the object and displayNodes() being the new prototyped method. Take a closer look at this method, which is responsible for representing the XML visually with movieClips each time it is called:

```
function XMLNode_displayNodes(){
  var nodeNum = _root.nodeNum++;
  _root.nodeMC.duplicateMovieClip("nodeMC"+nodeNum, nodeNum);
  _root["nodeMC"+nodeNum]._x = 85 + this.getDepth() * 18;
  _root["nodeMC"+nodeNum]._y = 90 + _root.nodeNum * 20;
  _root["nodeMC"+nodeNum].nodePtr = this;

  if (this.nodeType == 1) {
    _root["nodeMC"+nodeNum].titlefield = this.nodeName;
    _root["nodeMC"+nodeNum].nodeIcon.gotoAndStop(2);
  } else {
    _root["nodeMC"+nodeNum].titlefield = this.nodeValue;
    _root["nodeMC"+nodeNum].nodeIcon.gotoAndStop(1);
  }

  if (this.childNodes.length > 0) {
    for (var i = 0; i < this.childnodes.length; i++) {
      this.childnodes[i].displayNodes();
    }
  }
}
```

This function in essence becomes the visual engine in displaying your XML onscreen. It dictates what the user will see—in other words, how the XML is presented and how the nodes are displayed. Because this function is responsible for generating the movieClips, you begin by grabbing the global nodeNum value from the _root and making it local with var nodeNum. This is the variable used to label and place movieClips in a tracked depth order. With this value, you can create instances of your XML through movieClips by using the duplicateMovieClip() method. Let's quickly dissect the duplication of these movieClips:

```
_root.nodeMC.duplicateMovieClip("nodeMC"+nodeNum, nodeNum);
```

You duplicate the movieClip nodeMC and give the duplicates the names nodeMC1, nodeMC2, and so on, based on the numerical value obtained from nodeNum. You then assign the duplicate's depth to the same nodeNum value:

```
_root["nodeMC"+nodeNum]._x = 90 + this.getDepth() * 18;
```

This line of code is responsible for placing these clips horizontally across the stage, using their x position. You use getDepth, which represents how deep in the tree the clip is, to make sure all childNode graphics are indented from their parents:

```
  _root["nodeMC"+nodeNum]._y = 20 + _root.nodeNum * 20;
```

This code line sets the y-coordinate of the nodeMC at the proper position in the tree so that siblings will show up below their previous siblings and children will appear below their parents. Next, you create a new variable called nodePtr that acts as a pointer to the XMLNode you are representing visually:

```
_root["nodeMC"+nodeNum].nodePtr = this;
```

This method will come in handy later when you want to grab further data from this node for use in your movieClip representation.

After you have created and displayed this movieClip, you populate its text fields with data contained in the node. To do that, first you ascertain what type of node it is:

```
if (this.nodeType == 1) {
   _root["nodeMC"+nodeNum].titlefield = this.nodeName;
   _root["nodeMC"+nodeNum].nodeIcon.gotoAndStop(2);
 } else {
   _root["nodeMC"+nodeNum].titlefield = this.nodeValue;
   _root["nodeMC"+nodeNum].nodeIcon.gotoAndStop(1);
 }
```

If the node is determined to be an element node (type 1), you set titlefield, the name of the text field, to the nodeName of the node you are processing. This is the name of the element. You then assign the appropriate icon, in this case a <>

inside the nodeMC movieClip, as mentioned earlier. Frame 2 contains a graphic symbol of the element tags, so you advance the movieClip to that frame.

If the node is a text node (type 3), you set the text field of the duplicated movieClip to hold the nodeValue—or the character data—of that node.

As we've stressed several times in this chapter, recursion is your friend when working with XML, and it's no different now. After you've dealt with your node's visual display, the code then detects whether this node has any children:

```
if (this.childNodes.length > 0) {
    for (var i = 0; i < this.childnodes.length; i++) {
      this.childnodes[i].displayNodes();
    }
  }
```

If the current node does contain childNodes, you move through those nodes and recursively perform the same function on these children. This method, as you can see, will go through an entire XMLNode object and properly display both vertically and horizontally the tree structure of your XML data.

Graphical Display with Mouse Interaction

Now that you have all the XML elements displayed onscreen with movieClips, you can begin to display further information based on user interaction, particularly mouse interaction in this example. As we mentioned in the overview of the elements, the nodeMC movieClip contains a transparent button on the top layer. All duplicated movieClips will contain this button as well as the following code, which is attached to the on(rollover) handler:

```
    _root.msgViewer.output = this.nodePtr.nodeDetail();
```

You've already come across a use for the nodePtr variable that was created to reference the node the movieClip represents. You're now performing a new method, which was created in the XMLNode prototype extensions, called nodeDetail(). The rollOver of the button will display in the output text field the information gathered from the following code:

```
function XMLNode_nodeDetail () {
  var outString = "<u><pre>                                    </pre></u>";
  outString += "<br /><b>nodeName: </b>"+this.nodeName;
  outString += "<br /><b>nodeValue: </b>"+this.nodeValue;
  outString += "<br /><b>nodeType: </b>"+this.nodeType+" ";
  outString += (this.nodeType==1)?(" (element)"):(" (text)");
```

```
if (this.nodeType == 1) {
  outString += "<br /><b>string: </b>";
  outString += "<b>&lt;</b><font color='#ffff00'>";
  outString += this.nodeName+"</font>";
  for (var eachAttr in this.attributes){    //for each attribute...
    outString += " <font color='#66ccff'>"+ eachAttr;
    outString += "</font><font color='#d8d8d8'>='</font>";
    outString += this.attributes[eachAttr];
    outString += "<font color='#d8d8d8'>'</font>";
  }
  outString +="<b>&gt;<b>";  // put on the closing bracket, >, in bold
} else {
    outString += "<br /><b>string: </b>"+ this.nodeValue;
}
outString += "<br /><b>Number of childNodes: </b>";
outString += this.childnodes.length;
outString += "<br /><u><pre>                         </pre></u>";
return(outString);
}
```

Notice that you initiate the outString variable with the following:

```
var outString = "<u><pre>                  </pre></u>";
```

This creates the top border line that appears above the node information. You'll notice that this same string information is placed at the end of the function to create the bottom border line.

The next thing this function does is grab information on the nodeName, nodeValue, *and* nodeType of the current node and places it inside the outString variable. Notice that you're using HTML to format this data, with the <br>, <font>, and <b> tags to alter its final display.

After you have gathered and displayed this information, you perform an if statement to determine the rest of the output, based on the node being an element type or text type. If the node is of type 1 (an element), you need to display further information:

```
if (this.nodeType == 1) {
    outString += "<br /><b>string: </b>";
    outString += "<b>&lt;</b><font color='#ffff00'>";
    outString += this.nodeName+"</font>";
    for (var eachAttr in this.attributes){    //for each attribute...
      outString += " <font color='#66ccff'>"+ eachAttr;
      outString += "</font><font color='#d8d8d8'>='</font>";
      outString += this.attributes[eachAttr];
      outString += "<font color='#d8d8d8'>'</font>";
    }
    outString +="<b>&gt;<b>";  // put on the closing bracket, >, in bold
  }
```

Just as in the toHTML() method, you use HTML to format the text, in this case attributes, to not only be rendered to screen but also colored differently. First the element nodeName is colored yellow, and then the attributes are colored light blue.

The final piece of this function displays the nodeValue of the node if it is not the element node detected in the if statement, and then displays the number of childNodes before adding the formatted bottom line divider:

```
else {
     outString += "<br /><b>string: </b>"+ this.nodeValue;
  }
  outString += "<br /><b>Number of childNodes: </b>";
  outString += this.childnodes.length;
  outString += "<br /><u><pre>                        </pre></u>";
  return(outString);
```

The last line is where this information is returned for display. Once it's complete, this entire string representation, formatted in HTML and contained in outString, is placed into the output text field in the msgViewer movieClip.

There is one other interactive way to present information in this example. If you roll over the question mark button at the window's top left, you trigger an action on another transparent button that calls the function show_doc_details:

```
function show_doc_details() {
  function tagKiller(str) {
    /* This function rips the brackets off an xmlDecl or a
       docTypeDecl, so they can be added as &lt; and &gt;
       later, for proper output. */
    str = substring(str,2,(str.length-2));
                 // take the first and last characters off the string
    return(str);
  }
  _root.msgViewer.output = "Status: "+_root.linkdata.status+"\n";
  _root.msgViewer.output += _root.linkdata.xmlDecl + "\n";
  _root.msgViewer.output += _root.linkdata.docTypeDecl;
  if (_root.linkdata.xmlDecl != null) {  //if there is an xmlDecl...
    _root.msgViewer.output += "<font color='#00ee00'>&lt;";
    _root.msgViewer.output += tagKiller(_root.linkdata.xmlDecl);
    _root.msgViewer.output += "&gt;</font><br />";
  }
  if (_root.linkdata.docTypeDecl != null) {  //if there is an xmlDecl...
  _root.msgViewer.output += "<font color='#00ee00'>&lt;";
  _root.msgViewer.output += tagKiller(_root.linkdata.docTypeDecl)
  _root.msgViewer.output += "&gt;</font>+<br />";
  }
}
```

This function is written to display the details of the XML document to the dynamic text field called output in the _root.msgViewer movieClip. Specifically, this function displays the XML document's XML declaration and DocType declaration, if they exist.

The tagKiller subfunction is responsible for removing the brackets from the declaration tags so that they will be interpreted as HTML, not formatted correctly. To avoid this error, later you add the tags back in by using the encoding entities < (<) and > (>).

You now have access to all of your XML data via movieClips. Figure 4.10 shows a final display.

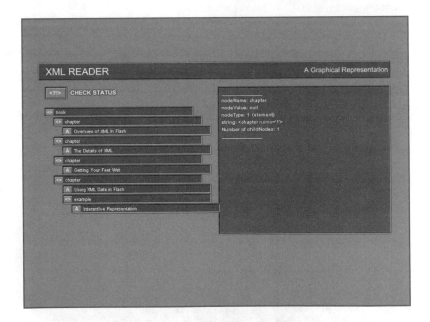

Figure 4.10 *A graphical representation of an XML document.*

You can see by this third graphical example how you are merely adding on or modifying code that was created earlier in this chapter. After you have moved to transferring the information to movieClips, you can shift display and interactive elements to the movieClip itself, as you will see in the last example incorporating interactivity.

Interactive Display of XML In Flash

Now that we've covered everything from translating your XML to both string and HTML format and then displaying that data with `movieClips`, you can explore further by extending control with `movieClip` interactivity.

You are going to turn everything you have learned in this chapter into a basic interactive XML editor that looks similar to Figure 4.11.

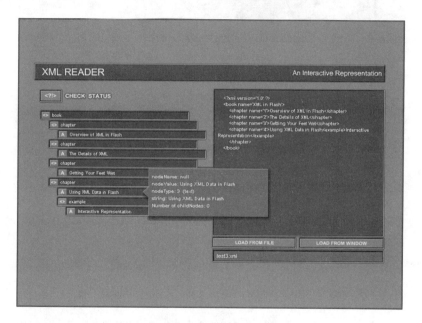

Figure 4.11 *The goal: An interactive representation of an XML document.*

In this editor, you will have a split-pane interface with the `toString()` method displayed on the right and the interactive `movieClip` displayed on the left. You can manually enter or copy and paste XML into the editor, or you can load a file locally or remotely. You'll also transfer the `nodeDetail` information into a ToolTip that is triggered by the user's mouse position.

Open the interactive.fla file in the folder with the same name (in the Chapter 4 directory) to follow along.

If you take a look at the main timeline and layers, you'll notice that it is set up almost identically to the previous graphical version, as shown in Figure 4.12.

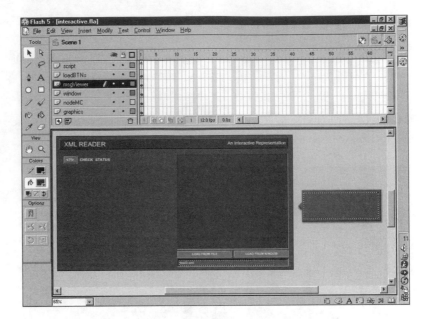

Figure 4.12   *Interface for interactive.fla.*

The only differences are found in the addition of a new layer called loadBTNs and the modification of the msgViewer layer.

Because you're creating an editing environment to modify the XML source code, you need to create an interface for loading XML source or for updating XML that is being modified in the editor. This new loadBTNs layer contains the buttons that trigger the new functions located in your script layer, which control loading and updating XML content.

The modification to the msgViewer layer is placing the same content into a movieClip that will be influenced by the user's mouse position. The display and structure are identical; the content is just placed into a movieClip object that can be controlled and affected by a range of interactive factors.

Before we cover these new areas, let's take a look at the onLoad() handler, which we've customized a little differently:

```
linkdata = new XML();
linkdata.onLoad = linkdata_onLoad;
```

The onLoad() handler is now defined like this:

```
function linkdata_onLoad(success) {
    for (var i = 0;i < _root.nodeNum+1;i++) {
      _root["nodeMC"+i].removeMovieClip();
    }
    _root.nodeNum = 0;
    _root.depth = 0;
    _root.msgViewer.output = "Status: "+this.status+"\n";
    this.firstChild.stripWhite();
    this.firstChild.displayNodes();
    _root.window.xString = this.toString();
}
```

Because you can now dynamically load XML documents as opposed to hard-coding them into your scripts, you need to remove all movieClip instances from the old file. This is accomplished with the for loop at the top of the function.

After you have removed the clips, run the XML through the stripWhite() method to remove all whitespace. When that's done, and you have clean crisp XML, render this structure again to screen with the displayNodes() method covered in the previous example.

You also use the toString() method, performing it on your XML and placing it into the xString text field in the window layer for display and editing purposes. You handle this process rather similarly with the new load buttons. The action on the Load From File button is as follows:

```
on (release) {
  if ((this.filename != "")  && (this.filename != null)) {
    _root.linkdata.load(this.filename);
  }
}
```

Here you load the new XML file into the linkdata XML object, thus calling the custom onLoad() handler to properly format the display. However, if you alter the information at all in the editing window and want to update it, you need to use the Load From Window button. Clicking this button will call the loadFromWindow() function.

This function is called from the Load From Window button on the stage. Essentially, it takes the data from the window layer and puts it into an XML object by using parseXML(). It then strips the whitespace (as usual), displays all the nodes by calling displayNodes(), and sends the XML back to the editing window by using toString().

There is one small catch, though: The toString() method actually displays a couple of spaces before any XML data to create the proper indenting. That's all well and good for updating the window, but if you try to load an updated window, that extra space causes load errors. For that reason, you need to manually strip that leading whitespace from the string before you let Flash parse it. The subfunction killLeadingSpaces does that for you. It takes a string as input (an XML string, you hope!) and returns that same string with the whitespace removed from these areas:

- Before the XML declaration
- Between the XML declaration and the DocType declaration
- Between the DocType declaration and the root element

You can go through the code to figure out how it works if you're really keen, but for now it's more important that you know it works and why you're using it.

It's more important to jump to the core of the loadFromWindow() code:

```
var holder = new XML
holder.parseXML(inXStr);
```

Here you're creating a new temporary XML object called holder to test your new string. Next, parse this string into the new XML object. After you have this new temporary object, you remove all previous nodeMC clips:

```
for (var i = 0;i < _root.nodeNum+1;i++) {
    _root[nodeMC+i].removeMovieClip();
}
```

Now that you have a blank screen, you can regenerate the visual XML representation. Reset the nodeMC counter back to 0 and parse the new XML string into the linkdata XML object. After the string has been transferred to the XML object, you perform the stripWhite() method to remove whitespace and then use the displayNodes() method to place the new XML structure on stage.

```
_root.nodeNum = 0;
_root.linkdata.parseXML(inXStr);
_root.linkdata.stripWhite();
_root.linkdata.firstChild.displayNodes();
```

You then issue an if statement to test whether the temporary XML object holder was loaded successfully. If so, put the final toString() into the editing field:

```
if (holder.status == 0) {
  _root.window.xString = _root.linkdata.toString();
}
```

Now that you understand how to display your XML both graphically and with the toString() method, take a look at how the data is being manipulated by user interactivity.

When you test the movie after you have entered or pasted text into the editor or loaded it from a file, you'll notice that you can interact with this content. By rolling over the movieClips generated with displayNodes(), the msgViewer movieClip containing the node details follows the mouse in a ToolTip. This ToolTip is controlled by the nodeMC_rollover() function, which is called by each of the loaded nodeMCs anytime the movieClip is rolled over. You call the nodeMC_rollOver() function like this:

```
onClipEvent(enterFrame){
  _root.nodeMC_rollOver(this);
}
```

The this that is passed is the calling movieClip, known inside this function as nodeMC. If there is a positive hitTest with this movieClip and the mouse, you set the claim variable to true, meaning that this movieClip claims the msgViewer to display its information. It also makes the msgViewer visible and makes it follow the mouse coordinates, as shown in the following code:

```
1   function nodeMC_rollOver(nodeMC) {
2       if (nodeMC.hitTest(_root._xmouse, _root._ymouse, false)) {
3           nodeMC.claim = true;
4           if (!_root.msgViewer._visible) {
5               _root.msgViewer._visible = true;
6           }
7           _root.msgViewer._x = _root._xmouse+280;
8           _root.msgViewer._y = _root._ymouse+150;
9       } else {
10          if (_root.msgViewer._visible) {
11              nodeMC.claim = false;
12          }
13      }
14  }
```

Lines 7 and 8 of the preceding code, which set the x and y properties of the msgViewer movieClip, illustrate how easily you can affect the interactivity of the movieClip. You could set any number of values to not only the x and y positions, but also of alpha and of scale. You could even add inertia and friction to the movement. It's really up to you how far you want to go. We encourage you to explore this function to create interesting navigational concepts.

You might have noticed that there's nothing here to make msgViewer invisible when it's done, though. Well, don't worry; you've got another loop calling a prolog_rollOver() function that will make msgViewer invisible after checking that no movieClip still has a claim on it. It's a little bit better for performance if you have only one loop checking for that condition, rather than *all* your movieClips. This call to prolog_rollOver() is found on a button in the window layer, represented by <?!>.

Another modification to this version is found in the show_doc_details() function, where you have a statusMsg(code) function for displaying the status of your XML. Consider it a primitive debugger that merely reports whether there's an error parsing the XML. As you can see, it simply returns a string based on the status value:

```
function statusMsg(code) {
    if (code==0)
        {var returnVal = "No error; parse completed successfully.";}
    if (code==-2)
        {returnVal = "A CDATA section was not properly terminated.";}
    if (code==-3)
        {returnVal = "The XML declaration was not properly terminated. ";}
    if (code==-4)
        {returnVal = "The DOCTYPE declaration was not properly ";
         returnVal += "terminated. ";
        }
    if (code==-5)
        {returnVal = "A comment was not properly terminated. ";}
    if (code==-6)
        {returnVal = "An XML element was malformed." ;}
    if (code==-7)
        {returnVal = "Out of memory. ";}
    if (code==-8)
        {returnVal = "An attribute value was not properly terminated. ";}
    if (code==-9)
        {returnVal = "A start-tag was not matched with an end-tag. ";}
    if (code==-10)
        {returnVal = "An end-tag was encountered without a ";
         returnVal += "matching start-tag. ";
        }
    return(returnVal);
}
```

This is just a slight modification that was added in this example. At this point, you should be able to see the interactive potential you have when you incorporate movieClips with your XML content.

Summary

We've covered a tremendous amount of ground in this chapter. By now, you should be thinking about how content can be integrated into Flash by using XML. Whether the information is coming dynamically from a server or from static XML files, the same rules apply. As we moved from text representation to graphical and finally interactive, we wanted to illustrate the flexibility in displaying this content. Any sort of interactive behaviors you use in your work you can use here by simply attaching the code to the appropriate movieClips or functions.

For instance, to add sound only requires adding the sound on the appropriate button states. The nodeMC clips could easily be programmed to bounce or interact with the cursor on rollover and on click. Even simple scaling could be added. So play with these files—create a new XML file from the default file and populate it with data, for example. Check the status to see whether it's well formed and parses correctly. Experiment with altering the graphics for the icons and the node representations. The more you look under the hood, the more ideas and possibilities will arise. We all know Flash is fun, and now you know that XML in Flash can be easy.

So What's Next?

Now that you're well versed in the XML in Flash thang, you're ready to jump into Part II, "Flash and Dynamic XML," where we go into depth on dealing with server-side integration using ASP and PHP. After understanding how to work with these middleware languages, you will walk through an example of dynamically reading a directory on the server and representing that information in Flash. In this next chapter, you'll wade into application development waters, priming you for the following chapters.

{ Part II }

Flash and Dynamic XML

{ Chapter 5 }

Importing Dynamically Created XML Documents

So far we have covered the ins and outs of XML and how to incorporate it into your Flash files. By now you should be familiar with the concept of importing data as XML into your Flash environment, manipulating that data, and representing it graphically through movieClips. Handling XML input is important in the development of any Web application; however, until this point you have been using only static XML documents. In true application development, you will be working with database servers and middleware to dynamically generate and transfer your data via XML. This is called *dynamic XML*.

Dynamic XML is the generation of XML documents on-the-fly. This means that the actual XML document does not exist, but is created by the server when the user requests it. This is one of the features that makes XML integration so powerful when working with Flash. Unlike the HTML counterpart, using Flash means you never need to load additional HTML pages to receive data sent from the server. This, in turn, offers the user a much more seamless experience and blurs the line between what is dynamic and what is not. Flash can dynamically handle its input without tipping the user off that it is communicating with the server.

The ability to update content quickly is invaluable for many Web initiatives. More often than not, content is king, and having current and relevant information is integral to the success of many Web sites. As in previous chapter examples, you are free to update XML files by hand. It's actually quite a nice way to manage Flash sites with content that isn't changed often and is much easier to administer than going through master FLA files. However, for sites that are updated more often, you need the type of dynamic content that's explored in this chapter.

Server-Side Integration

Server-side integration is the same as loading static text files, except you use your server-side script to create and transfer the data on-the-fly. The data is handled the same after it is inside Flash; it's just how the data gets to Flash that is different. Anyone who's familiar with creating HTML on-the-fly can use the same methods to return plain text or XML to the Flash environment—again illustrating why XML is so powerful with Flash.

By using server-side integration, you can create dynamic and personalized content for your sites or applications. Information can be continuously updated on the back end via the database and pulled in dynamically to the client's machine. For applications, this process works beautifully because you can store user information and have it available for future visits. Especially with the amazing interactive possibilities of Flash, it becomes easy to create dynamic personalized sites, in terms of both content and presentation.

With server-side scripts, you can separate your content from its display. All the content can be stored in your database and updated separately while you alter the look, feel, and layout of your Flash file. You can have a live version of your site and simultaneously build a different display with another version. After redesigning the display, you can simply switch Flash files on the server and instantly have a "new" version of the site.

This separation of content from display makes the workflow process much more streamlined and parallel. It becomes an easy task to create multiple views of the same data. Using the same XML information, for instance, you could create different graphs, such as line, bar, or pie, to represent the data. All these display differences would be completely controlled and created in Flash, so there's no need to alter your XML. It can also work the other way—after you have a view established, you can incorporate multiple data feeds.

Server-Side Scripting and Scripting Languages

In general, server-side scripts are used to dynamically retrieve data and relay it back to the client side. Often these scripts target a database with a query and then return these results to the browser or Flash movie. Many different languages and technologies can be used to transfer this data, including ASP, PHP, JSP, Perl, or ColdFusion, to name a few of the prominent platforms.

PHP, Perl, and ColdFusion are what we would call languages, but ASP and JSP are technologies that incorporate different languages, usually VBScript and JScript for ASP; JSP uses only Java, however.

The examples in this chapter will focus on the two most common middleware languages used today: PHP and ASP. ASP (Active Server Pages) is popular because of its integration with Microsoft Windows NT and Internet Information Server (IIS). Many corporations use Microsoft solutions, so they rely on ASP to generate dynamic Web pages and applications. PHP (PHP Hypertext Pre-Processor—yes, that acronym is recursive), on the other hand, is the fastest grow-ing Web-oriented scripting language for two reasons: It's free, and it runs on many highly coveted server operating systems, namely the many different flavors of Unix, including Linux. Together, these two languages account for a substantial part of the booming Web application frontier.

If you are new to server-side integration using PHP or ASP, that's okay. What you really need to understand is that Flash doesn't care where the XML content comes from, whether it's receiving text from a file in its directory or from a PHP or an ASP script running on the server. All XML is handled the same way inside Flash. PHP or ASP scripts merely create the XML dynamically for import to and use in Flash. You could do this by creating an XML document based on informa-tion sent to the PHP/ASP script or by generating XML based on information the script gathers and extracts from a database. The main concept to grasp is that server-side integration generally means you are dynamically creating or extract-ing content from some other source, such as a database.

Web Server Integration Methods

In Flash 4 there are two ways to communicate variables to Flash from the Web server: the query string method, and the `loadVariables()` method, both of which are discussed here. Flash 5 enables a developer to use both methods in addition to the new ability to import XML. First, you'll focus on learning those Flash 4 methods; they are still useful and probably used more frequently than XML in Flash development. Their level of simplicity can be irresistible, but keep in mind that complex data is difficult to represent with these simple methods. To do many amazing things with your Flash applications, you need the sophistication of XML. If you're aware of the query string and `loadVariables()` methods, feel free to skip this next section, or skim it as a refresher. If you've never dealt with them before, you'll be glad you have them in your bag of tricks.

Old School Integration: `loadVariables()` and the Query String Method

This explanation of `loadVariables()` with ASP or PHP requires a basic under-standing of ASP or PHP. For the sake of clarity, the examples are very simple: They don't show what you can do with the variable in Flash, but a simple knowledge of ActionScript should be all you need to apply this example to prac-tical solutions. Also, these examples don't show how to get the value from a database or form, but a basic knowledge of ASP or PHP will be enough for you to do that on your own. What they do show is how to make ASP or PHP *talk* to Flash by using these non-XML methods.

Of course, ASP and PHP aren't the only server-side technology capable of this type of communication. JSP, CGI, and ColdFusion are other possibilities well suited for the task. The two methods discussed in this chapter are equally appli-cable to those other technologies.

The Query String Method

The query string method (at least that's what we call it!) is a little complicated at first, but it requires no ActionScript at all in the Flash movie, so it's much faster to implement. If you take a look at the `<object>` and `<embed>` tags in the HTML that Flash produces when you publish a Flash movie, you can see two spots where the SWF is mentioned:

```
<OBJECT classid="clsid:D27CDB6E-AE6D-11cf-96B8-444553540000"
➥codebase=
➥"http://active.macromedia.com/flash2/cabs/swflash.cab#version=4,0,0,0"
➥ID=amovie WIDTH=750 HEIGHT=400>
<PARAM NAME=movie VALUE="amovie.swf">
<PARAM NAME=quality VALUE=high>
```

```
<PARAM NAME=bgcolor VALUE=#FFFFFF>
<EMBED src="amovie.swf"
➥ quality=high
➥ bgcolor=#FFFFFF
➥ WIDTH=750
➥ HEIGHT=400
➥ TYPE="application/x-shockwave-flash"
➥ PLUGINSPAGE=
➥"http://www.macromedia.com/shockwave/download/index.cgi?P1_Prod_Version=
➥ShockwaveFlash">
</EMBED>
</OBJECT>
```

You need to focus on only those two spots where the SWF is mentioned (formatted in bold) to be able to use the query string method. The query string method works much like a query string in a browser URL, if you're familiar with those. Instead of just saying amovie.swf, as we have in the preceding HTML code, you can say something like amovie.swf?id=3. That will pass the id variable to Flash with the value 3. Here's an example:

```
<OBJECT classid="clsid:D27CDB6E-AE6D-11cf-96B8-444553540000"
➥codebase=
➥"http://active.macromedia.com/flash2/cabs/swflash.cab#version=4,0,0,0"
➥ID=amovie WIDTH=750 HEIGHT=400>
<PARAM NAME=movie VALUE="amovie.swf?id=3">
<PARAM NAME=quality VALUE=high>
<PARAM NAME=bgcolor VALUE=#FFFFFF>
<EMBED src="amovie.swf?id=3"
➥ quality=high
➥ bgcolor=#FFFFFF
➥ WIDTH=750
➥ HEIGHT=400
➥ TYPE="application/x-shockwave-flash"
➥ PLUGINSPAGE=
➥"http://www.macromedia.com/shockwave/download/index.cgi?P1_Prod_Version=
➥ShockwaveFlash">
</EMBED>
</OBJECT>
```

When loaded, your movie will have an id variable with the value 3. There's nothing more to be done in Flash, except to use that variable as you would in any other ActionScript. If you need to load multiple variables, use & to append them:

```
amovie.swf?id=3&firstName=Jane&lastName=Smith
```

These strings that come after the ? all need to be URL-encoded, meaning that special characters (such as spaces) need to replaced with special codes (%20, for example). If you want to pass a name variable with a space in it (like name=Jane Smith), you would do so like this:

```
amovie.swf?id=3&name=Jane%20Smith
```

You can use a chart like the one in Figure 5.1 as a reference for encoding the string:

	0	1	2	3	4	5	6	7	8	9	A	B	C	D	E	F
2	SPACE	!	"	#	$	%	&	'	(	)	*	+	'	-	"	/
3	0	1	2	3	4	5	6	7	8	9	:	;	<	=	>	?
4	@	A	B	C	D	E	F	G	H	I	J	K	L	M	N	O
5	P	Q	R	S	T	U	V	W	X	Y	Z	[	|	]	^	
6	'	a	b	c	d	e	f	g	h	i	j	k	l	m	n	o
7	p	q	r	s	t	u	v	w	x	y	z	{	\	}	~	

Figure 5.1 *A URL-encoding chart.*

To be able to use the URL-encoding chart, notice that the space character is in row 2 and column 0. That means it's represented as %20 after being encoded. Similarly, the letter A is represented as %41 because it's in row 4 and column 1. You simply find the character you want to encode and put its row and column values together with a percent sign in front.

Only the following characters really need to be encoded, however:

spaces

quotation marks (single and double)

brackets: ( ), { }, [ ]

the pound character (#)

the percent character (%)

other miscellaneous characters: ~ ^ ` \ |

You can actually use Flash to test these characters, and even find out the proper values without the URL-encoding chart. ActionScript's built-in escape() and unescape() functions can encode and decode these characters (respectively). For a quick test, open up a fresh FLA and try this ActionScript:

```
trace(unescape("%41"));
trace(escape("A B"));
```

The output will be

```
A
A%20B
```

The decoded value of %41 (as you can see from row 4 and column 1 of the chart) is A. The encoded value of the space between the A and B is %20. Notice that the function doesn't bother to encode the A or B characters because it's not really necessary. You can sometimes get away with not encoding spaces and other characters we're warning about here. Despite that, you should try to always encode these problem characters, because they don't always work as you would expect, and then you're left trying to figure out what went wrong.

If you're using ASP there is an even easier way to do this encoding, so now we'll discuss the ASP integration. So far everything you've seen has been in plain HTML, but it's also possible to generate these query strings dynamically using ASP or PHP. If you have an ASP page that you add these same `<object>` and `<embed>` tags to, you would have something like this:

```
<%
'this is where you set a variable called name
name = "Jane Smith"
%>
<html>
<body>
<OBJECT classid="clsid:D27CDB6E-AE6D-11cf-96B8-444553540000"
➥codebase=
➥"http://active.macromedia.com/flash2/cabs/swflash.cab#version=4,0,0,0"
➥ID=amovie WIDTH=750 HEIGHT=400>
<PARAM NAME=movie VALUE="amovie.swf?id=3">
<PARAM NAME=quality VALUE=high>
<PARAM NAME=bgcolor VALUE=#FFFFFF>
<EMBED src="amovie.swf?id=3"
➥ quality=high
➥ bgcolor=#FFFFFF
➥ WIDTH=750
➥ HEIGHT=400
➥ TYPE="application/x-shockwave-flash"
➥ PLUGINSPAGE=
➥"http://www.macromedia.com/shockwave/download/index.cgi?P1_Prod_Version=
➥ShockwaveFlash">
</EMBED>
</OBJECT>
</body>
</html>
```

The PHP equivalent would look like this:

```
<?
//this is where you set a variable called name
$name = "Jane Smith";
?>
<html>
<body>
<OBJECT classid="clsid:D27CDB6E-AE6D-11cf-96B8-444553540000"➥
➥codebase=
➥"http://active.macromedia.com/flash2/cabs/swflash.cab#version=4,0,0,0"
➥ID=amovie WIDTH=750 HEIGHT=400>
<PARAM NAME=movie VALUE="amovie.swf?id=3">
<PARAM NAME=quality VALUE=high>
<PARAM NAME=bgcolor VALUE=#FFFFFF>
<EMBED src="amovie.swf?id=3"
➥quality=high
➥ bgcolor=#FFFFFF
➥ WIDTH=750
➥ HEIGHT=400
➥ TYPE="application/x-shockwave-flash"
➥ PLUGINSPAGE=
➥"http://www.macromedia.com/shockwave/download/index.cgi?P1_Prod_Version=
➥ShockwaveFlash">
</EMBED>
</OBJECT>
</body>
</html>
```

You can have the variable name generated in any way you want (from a database, from a form, from variables appended to a URL, and so forth), but for clarity's sake, we've simply declared it in the code to be equal to "Jane Smith". The name needs to be URL encoded first, so you need to alter that line slightly. In ASP, you would change

```
name = "Jane Smith"
```

to

```
name = Server.URLEncode("Jane Smith")
```

With VBScript, it's that simple; the URL encoding is all done automatically with the Server.URLEncode() function. PHP has a similar function called urlencode(). The same PHP line would be changed to

```
$name = urlencode("Jane Smith");
```

The only thing left is to dynamically generate the query string for the SWF. The final result will look like this in ASP:

```
<%
'this is where you set a variable called name
name = Server.URLEncode("Jane Smith")
%>
<html>
<body>
<OBJECT classid="clsid:D27CDB6E-AE6D-11cf-96B8-444553540000"
➡codebase=
➡"http://active.macromedia.com/flash2/cabs/swflash.cab#version=4,0,0,0"
➡ID=amovie WIDTH=750 HEIGHT=400>
<PARAM NAME=movie VALUE="amovie.swf?id=3&name=<%=name %>">
<PARAM NAME=quality VALUE-high>
<PARAM NAME=bgcolor VALUE=#FFFFFF>
<EMBED src="amovie.swf?id=3&name=<%=name %>"
➡ quality=high
➡ bgcolor=#FFFFFF
➡ WIDTH=750
➡ HEIGHT=400
➡ TYPE="application/x-shockwave-flash"
➡ PLUGINSPAGE=
➡"http://www.macromedia.com/shockwave/download/index.cgi?P1_Prod_Version=
➡ShockwaveFlash">
</EMBED>
</OBJECT>
</body>
</html>
```

Similarly, in PHP you use the following:

```
<?
//this is where you set a variable called name
$name = urlencode("Jane Smith");
?>
<html>
<body>
<OBJECT classid="clsid:D27CDB6E-AE6D-11cf-96B8-444553540000"
➡codebase=
➡"http://active.macromedia.com/flash2/cabs/swflash.cab#version=4,0,0,0"
➡ID=amovie WIDTH=750 HEIGHT=400>
<PARAM NAME=movie VALUE="amovie.swf?id=3&name=<?=$name ?>">
<PARAM NAME=quality VALUE=high>
<PARAM NAME=bgcolor VALUE=#FFFFFF>
<EMBED src="amovie.swf?id=3&name=<?=$name ?>"
➡ quality=high
➡ bgcolor=#FFFFFF
➡ WIDTH=750
➡ HEIGHT=400
➡ TYPE="application/x-shockwave-flash"
➡ PLUGINSPAGE=
➡"http://www.macromedia.com/shockwave/download/index.cgi?P1_Prod_Version=
➡ShockwaveFlash">
</EMBED>
```

```
</OBJECT>
</body>
</html>
```

When loaded in the user's browser, your SWF will automatically have variables called id and name with the values 3 and Jane Smith respectively, as though you had set those variables yourself by using Set Variable (in Flash 4) or an "=" assignment, such as name='Jane Smith'; (in Flash 5). There's nothing more to it. Flash even automatically decodes the URL encoding you performed so that you don't have to use the unescape() function.

If you can't get it to work, the key to troubleshooting this method is to view the PHP or ASP file in your browser (by its correct URL) to ensure that it was rendered into the proper form, as shown in this example. You'll want to make sure you didn't include extra carriage returns or characters that aren't URL encoded.

This method is great for small amounts of data that is loaded only at the start of the movie, but for data that is loaded and reloaded multiple times, or for larger amounts of data, the loadVariables() method, which we discuss next, is best.

The loadVariables() Method

The loadVariables() method is the one that people use when they load a simple static text file from the Web server into Flash. Basically, the text file is just like the previous query string. It's a bunch of name-value pairs separated by ampersands (&) and URL encoded. You can imagine that the same query string might appear in the file like this:

```
id=3&name=Jane%20Smith
```

If you call loadVariables() with that text file as a parameter, the id and name variables are automatically set up in Flash as ActionScript variables.

Of course, this method can also be used with ASP or PHP. If you change your text file's name to textfile.asp or textfile.php, and change your loadVariables() statement to load that file by name, instead of textfile.txt, you will see that the variables are still loaded as though this was a normal text file. (So far, so good!) The only thing left to do is add the VBScript or PHP to write the text file dynamically.

The ASP version would then look like this:

```
<%
id = 3
name = Server.URLEncode("Jane Smith")
%>id=<%=id%>&name=<%=name%>
```

And here's the PHP version:

```
<?
$id = 3;
$name = urlencode("Jane Smith");
?>id=<?= $id ?>&name=<?= $name ?>
```

That's really are there is to it. What most people learning this method fail to recognize is that ASP and PHP are not restricted to generating dynamic HTML pages. They can be used (as they are in this case) to generate a plain-text page or even an XML page (we'll get to that soon enough!).

The key to troubleshooting these dynamic text files is to look at the text files themselves by their own URL to ensure they are in the correct format for a Flash-readable text file. They will load up in your browser on their own (if you have the correct URL), and you can make sure you didn't accidentally include additional carriage returns or characters that need to be URL encoded. It's also important to note that you shouldn't test these files in the Flash editing environment. The Flash player in the editing environment *is not* the same as the Flash player you have installed in your browser. They do behave differently, so test in your browser, preferably from your Web server, not from a local directory. (PHP and ASP files simply do not work from a local directory, so you might as well move the whole party to the Web server.)

The following are some simple examples of how you might use `loadVariables()` to access data in a file:

```
loadVariables("myData.txt") ;
```

```
myMovieClip.loadVariables("myData.txt");
```

```
loadVariables("myData.php", _root.someMC, "GET");
```

The first example is a simple one in which you're just loading the information directly into Flash. The second example simply demonstrates that you can load variables directly into a `movieClip` instead of the third example, which sets that location as a parameter (_root.someMC). The third example is also more complex, as you are receiving information dynamically from a server-side script and determining where this information is to be returned in your Flash file.

In the third example, myData.php is set as the source for the variables you are loading, but you then determine the location of the returned values, which in this example are set in the movieClip pointed to by _root.someMC. Last, you set the request method to GET.

When transferring information via the browser (HTTP), you can use one of two methods: GET or POST. The HTTP specifications technically define the difference between these two methods so that GET means form data is to be URL encoded, and POST means the form data is to appear within the HTTP header.

GET is basically used for retrieving data, but POST could include storing or updating data, sending an e-mail, and so on. There are several key differences between these two methods.

As mentioned, GET puts variables on the actual URL when submitting, for instance, ourPage.html?userID=23. By using GET, you are limited to a maximum of 255 characters. You also have this string of variables displayed in the browser, visible to the user.

When using the POST method, you include your data in the HTTP header and in essence make this data invisible to the user. Because you are not placing this data in the URL, you are not limited to the number of characters you can send. This makes the POST method necessary when you need to transfer long pieces of data information.

You can also send variables with loadVariables(), as deceiving as that might seem. This same example can be extended so that you are submitting information by using loadVariables() to your PHP script to define specific results, as shown here:

```
loadVariables("myData.php", _root.myData, "GET");
```

This method still hits your myData.php file and returns it to _root.myData, but when you hit the PHP file, you also send along additional information. Variables in the current timeline get sent as well; for instance, if you had the variable userID=23, you would really be sending myData.php?userID=23. The PHP script then uses that extra piece of information to return a specific set of data correlating with the userID number sent to the script.

The version of `loadVariables()` that is tied to a specific `movieClip`, `movieClip.loadVariables()`, actually allows a little extra functionality over the old `loadVariables()`, too. In the days of Flash 4, when there was no `movieClip.loadVariables()`, the common practice was to have the loaded variables contain an extra variable on the end, something like `received=1`. This variable could denote whether all the variables were received, so a Flash programmer could create a frame loop to keep checking whether `received` equals 1. When `received` was found to be equal to 1, the frame loop could be broken because the data was surely all loaded. With the advent of Flash 5, there is actually a new, more efficient method of detecting whether all the variables are loaded. If you use a `movieClip` that does the loading for you with `movieClip.loadVariables()`, you can also assign a `clipEvent` to that `movieClip`. The important `clipEvent` to handle is called `data`, which means that data has been completely loaded. Here's how it might look:

```
onClipEvent(data){
  trace ("All the variables were loaded!");
}
```

This is actually quite a nice advance for `loadVariables()` because it makes it faster and easier to detect whether the variables were loaded. It's very similar to the `onLoad()` handler that the XML object uses, although it needs to be tied to a `movieClip`, of course.

Remember that loading variables from a script and loading variables from a static text file are essentially the same, as far as Flash is concerned. The code inside the myData.php file determines what values are returned to Flash, but the first static example has predetermined values that are hard-coded in the actual text file.

XML.load() **Integration**

Like the `loadVariables()` and query string methods, the new XML object in Flash 5 also uses HTTP and HTTPS to transfer information to and from the server. Generally, you can use the XML object in three distinct ways to communicate with the server: `XML.send()`, `XML.load()`, and `XML.sendAndLoad()`. Note that this information must be sent in XML format, meaning all data must exist as XML source code and be contained as elements or attributes of elements. You can still use name/value pairs with XML; however, they need to be included as attributes of an element, shown here:

```
<book name="XMLinFlash" />
```

This example places a name/value pair as an attribute of the <book> element.

When trying to understand the three distinct methods of interacting with the server, it's easier if you think of it this way: XML.send() sends data to the server for processing, XML.load() loads data from the server, and XML.sendAndLoad() sends information to the server and then loads the server's response into another XML document of your choosing.

For those who are familiar with HTTP, it's useful to know that XML.send() sends XML via POST. This information is essential for allowing your server-side scripts to access the XML document that's being sent.

The loadVariables() and movieClip.loadVariables() methods are a lot like XML.sendAndLoad() in that they do double duty. They all send *and* receive data, although the sending in loadVariables() happens implicitly. All the variables with the correct scope are sent (if it's movieClip.loadVariables, that scope is the referenced movieClip; if it's loadVariables(), the variables in _root are sent). XML.sendAndLoad() sends the actual referenced XML object (in string format). It is, as we said earlier, sent via POST (in all cases), but loadVariables() allows you to specify GET or POST methods. POST is usually the better method because it doesn't have the 255-character limit for the URL, as GET does.

It should be noted that even in complex Flash applications, loadVariables() can come in handy. It's simple and easy to use for small, simple sets of data. If you want to send only a name and password, you can see that it's easier to use the following code than to use ActionScript to somehow build an XML object containing the name and pass information:

```
name = "Mojo";
pass = "Nixon";
loadVariables("login.php", 0, "POST");
```

It's certainly possible to use XML for this example, but XML's sophistication is surely wasted on such a tiny set of information. At the same time, before your server-side script can handle the XML, it needs to retrieve and parse it. Using loadVariables(), you can simply access the Request.Form() and Request.QueryString() methods in ASP or the $HTTP_POST_VARS[] and $HTTP_GET_VARS[] arrays in PHP. Here's a simple example of retrieving those variables (assuming that you're using POST):

In ASP with VBScript:

```
name = Request.Form("name")

pass = Request.Form("pass")
```

In PHP:

```
$name = $HTTP_POST_VARS["name"];

$pass = $HTTP_POST_VARS["pass"];
```

In fact, we think you'll find that most data you send *from* Flash *to* the server is simple in nature. It's not often that a large amount of data is created in Flash or entered from the user. For this reason, we recommend that you use loadVariables() for sending data in most cases. XML is more useful and offers better performance for larger, more complex data or for receiving data *from* the server.

Of course, sometimes your server deals with a lot of XML anyway, so XML as a transport method from Flash makes more sense. For that reason, and for the sake of completeness, you'll be looking at XML.send() and XML.sendAndLoad(), too. Basically, you just need to understand the methods you have at your disposal for transferring information between Flash and the server by using XML. To get a better understanding of the actual process, take a look at a simple example of receiving information from several different types of middleware languages.

A Simple Flash/XML "Hello World" Example

Roll up your sleeves because it's time to start talking with the server! You're going to connect via XML with several middleware languages and retrieve data dynamically from server-side scripts. This is your first step before you begin to use the same methods to pull information from a PHP file that dynamically retrieves its data.

This first example is used to transfer information from a PHP script to Flash. Flash requests the data from the PHP script, and the results are sent back to Flash via XML. Following this, you'll take the same approach, but create and obtain values dynamically. It's a piece of cake. There's no difference at all on the Flash side, only in creating the middleware scripts. This part of the process is usually where the true programmers take over to interface these scripts with databases and other sources of content.

If you are a designer, you should be familiar with at least the structure of these documents. This is about everyone being on the same page and understanding how to communicate content. Now that you have an understanding of what XML is and how to use it, you'll have a better understanding of how it is handled dynamically when you start to examine the code.

The following code is in the Chapter 5 directory in the helloWorld folder on the accompanying Web site; however, we're not using that file now because it needs to reside on a properly configured server. We are using the code in the file only as a reference, so you can simply follow along in the book until we get to the directory tree example later in the chapter. First, just take a look at a simple PHP file that you will use to send XML information to Flash.

PHP

When you want to use or access server-side scripts, you call the file just as you have called static XML documents in previous chapters, by using `XML.load()`. For example, in the Flash file you call a PHP script by using the following:

```
myXML.load("myVariables.php");
```

In this example, you're loading the file myVariables.php, which contains the following code:

```
<?
$output = "<message msgContent='Hello World!' />";
echo $output;
?>
```

The first line of code creates the string variable `output` containing the XML source code `<message msgcontent='Hello World!'>`. This is the XML you'll be sending back to Flash. In PHP, you do that with `echo`, which "echoes" the variable you just created containing your XML back to where the script was originally called from.

Generally, you create custom `onLoad()` event handlers to process your XML. For now, though, the following code (inserted before the call to the `XML.load()` method) creates a handler used to detect whether this XML content has been successfully imported from your PHP file:

```
myXML.onLoad = function(success) {
    trace (myXML.firstChild.attributes.msgContent);
}
```

You can trust us when we tell you that your Output window will display `Hello World!`. Remember that there's no magical difference between using static XML and dynamic XML. The only difference lies in programming the middleware, which acts as the conduit between your content and Flash.

Many programmers are familiar with handling XML with ASP or PHP pages, so we are focusing on handling that XML information successfully inside Flash. The main goal when working with dynamic XML is simply to successfully import it. PHP and ASP programming are beyond the scope of this book; it's the thoughtful integration of the two technologies that we're covering.

We'll quickly cover some other languages to give you an idea of how similar the structure is. It's merely a matter of writing code to handle structuring and building XML before sending it to Flash.

VBScript/ASP

Again, with ASP, you use the same structure except that the methods are different. You use `response.write(output)` to transfer the XML content to the `XML` object in Flash:

```
<%
output = "<message msgcontent='Hello World!' />"
response.write(output)
%>
```

Perl/CGI

Other than the initial Perl declaration, you can see that this code is identical to the PHP example, with the exception of using Perl's `print` instead of `echo` to relay the content back in Flash:

```
#!/usr/bin/perl
$output = "<message msgcontent='Hello World!'>";
print $output;
```

You still call this file in exactly the same manner as the previous example; just change the file you are accessing to `myVariables.cgi`.

ColdFusion

Finally, here's an example of this data exchange using ColdFusion:

```
<cfset output = "<message msgcontent='Hello World!'>">
<cfoutput>#output#</cfoutput>
```

You can instantly notice the familiar structure of ColdFusion's tag-based format, but it still performs the same task as all the previous examples.

Inherent XML Support in PHP and ASP

Despite the Microsoft marketing machine putting millions behind XML and related technologies, such as Simple Object Access Protocol (SOAP) and the .NET framework, we've had some problems with its current XML parser. Recent versions are certainly better than previous ones, but we find that the parser can behave inconsistently depending on a number of factors, especially in Macintosh IE.

Unfortunately, XML in PHP is not much better, for the most part. It's officially supported only "experimentally," and finding a good Apache/PHP host that offers it is difficult at best. Obviously, ASP and PHP developers are working quickly to support XML, but it's not quite there yet.

For ASP, you need to install the latest version of MS XML (3.0 at the time of this writing, although 4.0 is available for "preview"). It must be installed on the machine that is the platform for your Microsoft Web server of choice (either Personal Web Server on Windows9x/ME or Internet Information Services on Windows NT/2000), which is available at `http://msdn.microsoft.com/down-loads/default.asp?URL=/downloads/sample.asp?url=/msdn-files/027/001/596/msdncompositedoc.xml`.

Microsoft also has a few examples of using ASP with XML at `http://msdn.microsoft.com/downloads/samples/internet/default.asp?url=/Downloads/samples/Internet/xml/asp_samples/Default.asp`.

ASP actually has excellent DOM support, similar to that of ActionScript, but far superior. A quick look at `http://www.devguru.com/Technologies/xmldom/quickref/xmldom_intro.html` will show you the available properties and methods of the `MS-XML` object. You'll be relieved to see properties such as `nodeValue`, `firstChild`, and `nextSibling`, along with the `hasChildNodes`, `createTextNode`, and `Load` methods.

{ Note }

If you plan on learning more about XML in ASP, it's a good idea to learn about the eXtensible Stylesheet Transformation Language (XSLT) standard. XSLT is actually a programming language on its own, used to define how an XML document can be translated into another format. The other format can be XML or not, and can even be binary (JPEGs, PDFs, or MS Word documents, for example). Using the MS XML parser, ASP has excellent support for XSLT (server side *or* client side, but IE 6.0 is the only browser that supports it out of the box), and it enables you to do some interesting things with XML documents.

PHP does have comparable XML support, but it's not currently included as a standard extension and is difficult to find on a Web host unless you're serving in-house. Server administrators would need to download and install James Clark's Expat from `http://www.jclark.com/xml/` as part of their PHP installations. For more information, check out `http://www.php.net/manual/en/ref.xml.php`. If you want DOM functionality similar to the MS XML component, or Flash ActionScript, there is slightly less support. Using libxml (the Gnome XML library), most of the same DOM features can be used. The biggest problem is that these DOM features are not part of the standard PHP configuration, so it can be difficult to find a Web host that supports them. PHP.net itself labels XML-DOM use in PHP as experimental.

Because of the less-than-perfect support for XML in both platforms, our examples parse the XML directly as a string. These examples don't need anything more sophisticated, and this parsing method makes the sample code more portable and usable on a wider array of servers. Just keep in mind that more inherent XML support *is* on its way for both platforms. For now, you can use more basic configurations of ASP and PHP to achieve the results you want.

Creating a Directory Tree

Now you get to the nuts and bolts of this example, which creates two scripts—one in ASP and one in PHP—that dynamically create an XML document representing the server's root directory. Once inside Flash, this XML will be displayed dynamically, as in the previous chapter; however, we add some further interaction by making the folders collapsible, as they are in most operating system GUIs, such as Macintosh or Windows. Although this is your first dynamic XML example, don't be fooled! This stuff is easy, and not much different from previous examples. The differences are in the dynamic creation of XML on the server side. Integrating XML content into Flash will never change, so now that you have a good understanding of working with XML in Flash, you should be able to follow along easily.

The Flash Side of the Directory Tree

First, open the dirTree.fla file, which you can find at www.xmlinflash.com in the dirTree folder under the Chapter 5 directory. When you open this file in Flash (see Figure 5.2), you'll notice that two key elements are missing. You no longer have the loadBTNs layer or the xString text field used in the previous chapter to edit and view your XML source code. However, you don't need these elements because this example deals strictly with the display of dynamic XML generated via PHP and ASP.

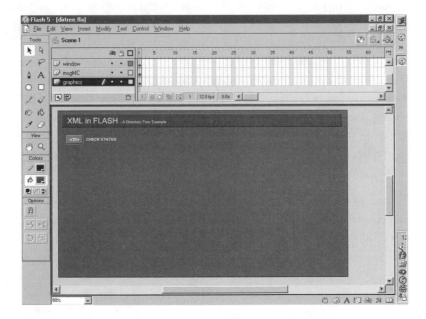

Figure 5.2 *The work area and layers of dirtree.fla in Flash.*

The only other visual difference you'll notice in this file is the graphical representation of your elements, using the nodeIcon movieClip instance in the nodeMC movieClip (see Figure 5.3). Previously, you've used icons that represent elements and text nodes. Because this example displays a directory structure, however, it seems appropriate to modify the icons to represent files and file folders of your directory structure.

There's one more major difference: the added interactivity you are placing on the buttons, which represent elements of the XML tree structure. Before, you had no control over these elements, but in this example you'll add the capability to open and close the "folders" so that you can reveal and hide the files and folders that are children of the selected button. You'll find it surprising how little code is needed. All the same code from previous examples is being used, which is why handling XML is such a quick and easy way to get information into Flash to be manipulated.

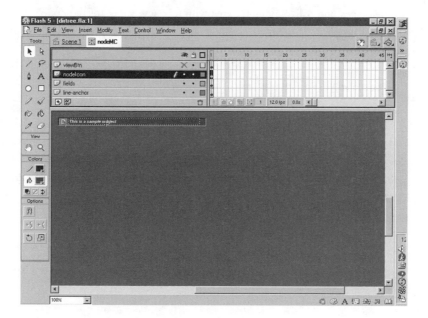

Figure 5.3   *The nodeMC* movieClip *with a file icon.*

If you take a look at the code in the script layer you'll notice one new function called nodeMC_expand. This function is responsible for setting the expanded property of the XML node to the opposite of its current state, simulating closing and opening a folder. First, you have to extend the XMLNode prototype to include this new expanded property:

```
XMLNode.prototype.expanded = false;
```

You can see how this property is handled in the nodeMC_expand function:

```
function nodeMC_expand(nodeMC){
nodeMC.nodePtr.expanded = !nodeMC.nodePtr.expanded;
    for (var i = 0;i < _root.nodeNum+1;i++) {
// erase all nodeMCs from the last XML representation
      _root["nodeMC"+i].removeMovieClip();
    }
    _root.nodeNum = 0;
```

```
// note that there are now 0 nodeMCs
   _root.linkdata.firstChild.displayNodes();
// display all the nodes (as usual)
  }
```

You are basically modifying the state of the selected node, removing all previous clip instances and redisplaying the tree with this new value for the node's expanded property. This action is called by the on(release) handler of a duplicated nodeMC movieClip instance:

```
on (release) {
   _root.nodeMC_expand(this);
}
```

You are still using the same displayNodes() function from the Chapter 4 examples; however, you are also including information about the open/close state of a parent element. This information is added to the displayNodes function as follows:

```
if ((this.childNodes.length > 0) && (this.expanded)) {
    for (var i = 0; i < this.childnodes.length; i++) {
     // graphically display each of the childnodes!
     this.childnodes[i].displayNodes();
      }
}
```

Here you are determining whether the current node has any childNodes thereby indicating it is a folder. If it does—and is a folder—you check to see the current value of expanded for that node. If the node's expand property is true, the next step is to go through the node's children and recursively call displayNodes() on all children until there are no further children. The final step is to return to the nextSibling of the parent node.

Now that we have covered the differences in the display and interaction of the XML tree, you can look at how this XML is generated dynamically by using a general algorithm before illustrating the particulars in PHP and ASP. But before you do, quickly take a look at a sample XML file so you can understand why we chose the structure we did and what impact it will have when handled by Flash:

```
<folder name="ourFiles">
   <folder name="sub1">
     <file name="file1.txt" />
     <file name="file2.txt" />
     <file name="file3.txt" />
```

```
      </folder>
      <folder name="sub2">
        <folder name="subsub">
          <file name="file1.txt" />
        </folder>
        <file name="file1.txt" />
        <file name="file2.txt" />
        <file name="file3.txt" />
        <file name="file4.txt" />
      </folder>
      <folder name="sub3">
        <file name="file1.txt" />
      </folder>
      <file name="file1.txt" />
</folder>
```

You can see that we are using two elements here: `<folder>` and `<file>`. We're clever like that. The `<folder>` elements actually encompass the `<file>` elements in the XML document, just as folders contain files on the server. We've modeled the data's structure on the real-world structure of a Web server's file system. Also notice that we are embedding the file and folder names as attributes, not as elements. This makes the XML traversing a bit simpler because we don't have to deal with text nodes. We've streamlined this XML document to be easily readable by humans *and* Flash.

The Server Side of the Directory Tree

As far as the server-side scripts go, you'll be doing quite a bit of recursion, too. Basically, you write out the XML declaration and the opening tag of the root node. Next, you call a function that shows the directory structure as XML, and follow that with the root element's closing tag.

The tricky part, of course, is the function that shows the directory structure as XML. Essentially, it goes through the "things" in the directory. If it's a file, the function displays it like this:

```
<file name="filename.txt" />
```

That's the easy part. If it's a folder, the function opens the `<folder>` tag like this:

```
<folder name="foldername">
```

Then it calls the same `folder2XML` function, using that folder, before it finally closes the `<folder>` tag. In this way, the XML is written out as you navigate through the server's directories recursively. Listings 5.1 and 5.2 are the PHP and ASP versions of the script, heavily commented for you to peruse.

Listing 5.1   PHP Version

```php
<?
//==================== Folder2XML function DEF'N =====================
function folder2XML(){
/* This function takes a folder as input and outputs that folder in XML
format.  The folder is represented in XML as
      <folder name='foldername'></folder>
and it contains all its subfolders and files as childNodes.  This
is written from scratch, so there is no whitespace added to it at
all.  That way, you don't need to strip any whitespace later!        */
    $fp = opendir('.');
                                        // make $fp hold the current directory
    while (false !== ($file = readdir($fp))) {
                            // for each file or folder in the directory...
        if ($file != "." && $file != "..") {
                // if it's not the current folder or the parent folder...
            if (is_dir($file)) {                  // if it's a folder...
                echo "<folder name='$file'>";
                    // open the folder tag and put the folder name in it
                chdir($file);
                                           // change to that directory
                folder2XML();
              // make your recursive call to display this directory too.
                chdir("../");
                                    // change back to previous directory
                echo "</folder>";           // close the folder tag
            } else {                              // if it's a file...
                echo "<file name='$file' />";
                // create the self-closing file tag, and add the filename
            }
        }
    }
    closedir($fp);                              // close the open directory
}
//======================= Main Code ============================
echo("<?xml version='1.0' ?>");
            /* echo out the XML declaration.  You can simply output it
               outside the PHP code because the <? and ?> tags of
               the XML declaration will conflict with PHP's short tags
               and really confuse the PHP processor. */
?><folder name='/'><?
         // Open the root element's tag (it's the root folder, of course)
folder2XML();         // Display the folder as XML (and all subfolders!)
?></folder><?                                 // close the root element
?>
```

Listing 5.2   ASP Version

```
<%

'================= Folder2XML function DEF'N =======================
Function folder2XML(Folder)
'This function takes a folder as input and outputs that folder in XML
'format.  The folder is represented in XML as
'       <folder name='foldername'></folder>
'and it contains all its subfolders and files as childNodes.  This
'is written from scratch, so there is no whitespace added to it at
'all.  That way, you don't need to strip any whitespace later!

    Dim S                        'output variable (holds the XML string)
    Dim SubFolder
    Dim File

    For Each SubFolder In Folder.SubFolders       'for each subfolder...

       S = S & "<folder name='" & SubFolder.Name & "'>"
                       'put them all in <folder name='foldername'></folder>
                       'format and make the XML node contain any further
                       'subfolders or files.

       S = S & folder2XML(SubFolder)
                       'Here is the recursive call to output any subfolders
                       'or files of this folder.

       S = S & "</folder>"                          'close the XML tag!
    Next

    For Each File In Folder.Files
                'wrap each file in XML tags too: <file>filename</file>
       S = S & "<file name='" & File.Name &"' />"
    Next

    folder2XML = S                               'return the XML string
End Function

'=========================== Main Code ============================

pathStr = request.servervariables("PATH_TRANSLATED")
scriptStr = Replace(request.servervariables("SCRIPT_NAME"), "/", "\")
Dim nameArr
nameArr = Array()
nameArr = split(scriptStr, "\")
scriptStr = nameArr(UBound(nameArr))
currentDir = Replace(pathStr, scriptStr, "")
                               ' the code above gets the current directory


%><?xml version='1.0' ?><folder name='/'><%
                               ' output the top of the XML file (the XML
```

Listing 5.2　continued

```
                               ' declaration, and the root element, dirread)

Set fso = CreateObject("Scripting.FileSystemObject")
                               ' create a filesystem object to read the
                               ' contents of your file system

Set Folder = FSO.GetFolder(currentDir)
                     ' start in the folder that this script resides in

response.write(folder2XML(Folder))
                     ' output an XML representation of that folder
%>
</folder>           <%  ' close the root element %>
```

Putting the Pieces Together

If you publish the SWF and HTML from Flash and upload them along with the
script that your Web server supports, you'll be ready to test it out. There won't be
much to see if you don't have many files or folders in the folder that you upload
this to, so feel free to upload a few files and create a few folders to get an interesting data source. Figure 5.4 shows what it should look like, although you
should get different results for your own server's folders.

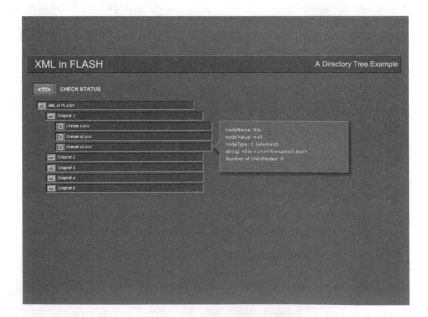

Figure 5.4　*The Flash-based directory tree in action.*

Summary

In this chapter, you have begun to examine the relationship Flash has with XML and server-side languages. Most of today's Web applications use dynamic content and these middleware languages, so understanding their connection is important.

You've learned that most of the work is spent on the server-side writing scripts to handle the XML build dynamically. In Flash, the goal is to successfully import this XML and master the ability to handle and manipulate this data. You can practice with static XML files preparing your Flash files, as long as you know how your XML is going to be structured.

This is why XML is such a powerful tool for developers. You can create and program your Flash separately from the back-end developers; all you need to do is come to a common understanding of how the XML will be formed. After you understand how the content is going to be structured, you can easily create a sample XML file to represent the XML to be generated dynamically on the server side. So even though it might take days for programmers to actually write the scripts that will properly generate this XML, designers and Flash coders can already be working on the display end of this content, based on the static XML representing the data.

So What's Next?

It's one thing to take XML, but Flash can also dish it out. In the next chapter, you'll begin to understand the process of creating XML documents in Flash. You'll move on from loading and manipulating XML data to creating it from scratch inside your Flash applications. By now, you can surely imagine how simple it will be to assign variables and values to XML nodes and elements.

You'll tackle this process by creating something we're all familiar with: the "news box" or "Web log." You will be creating a customizable, updatable Flash 5/XML-based Web log, starting with creating an interface for the user/administrator to generate new entries. You'll then transfer this information to a PHP script that writes this XML to a text file on the server. This file contains the news box items in XML format and is read back into Flash and displayed with a separate interface. After you have tackled the next chapter, you'll have a firm grasp on reading *and* writing XML from within Flash.

{ Chapter 6 }

Creating XML Documents in Flash to Send to the Server

You have finally reached the point where you can begin to communicate data back to the server, not just pull it into Flash. Until now, you have been using static XML files or merely pulling from XML on the server side with PHP/ASP files, but in this chapter you will start to send data back to the server. This is the next big step in server-side integration. After this chapter, you will understand the complete cycle of communicating with the server via XML. Sending data to the server is often a more important step then receiving data. If you never send information back to the server, you aren't creating real interaction with the user.

By sending information to the server, you can begin to think about applications that incorporate such features as personalization and content management, in which the user determines the content or data and uses Flash/server-side integration to transfer and store this new information. Sending XML to the server is integral in creating these types of Web applications.

If you've worked with server-side integration previously using the `loadVariables()` method, you'll quickly be up and running with XML in no time.

Transmitting Data from Flash to the Server

This chapter covers both aspects of XML data interaction with the server—reading and writing. You'll see how the Administration console is used to send content as XML source code to the server via PHP/ASP. This is a password-protected console used to update the news. The second aspect of this Web log example is the ability to then read these XML posts dynamically through Flash and display them onscreen.

With the knowledge you have gained so far, you'll find that this simple example clearly demonstrates sending XML to the server for processing. You have been continually building on previous examples and code, and this chapter is no different. First, take a step back and look at communicating with the server by using `loadVariables()`.

Using `loadVariables()` to Send Data to PHP/ASP

Here, you'll look at a login procedure because it's a nice simple example of the use of `loadVariables()`. Later you'll contrast it with using `XML.sendAndLoad()`.

Here's a quick snippet of ActionScript. For the sake of simplicity, assume that it is in a frame in the timeline of _root (_level0).

```
name = "Mojo";
pass = "Nixon";
loadVariables("login.php", _level0, "POST");
```

That's pretty much all there is to it. You set the `name` variable equal to the value `"Mojo"` and the `pass` variable equal to the value `"Nixon"`. With those variables declared and assigned values in the current timeline, which is _root, or _level0, you call `loadVariables()` and those values (along with any other variables in the timeline because the target _level0 has been specified) are sent off to the server via POST. It's as though a user had entered those variables into an HTML form and clicked Submit. The script won't know any difference.

In fact, the script accesses them exactly the same way. In ASP with VBScript, you would access them like this:

```
name = Request.Form("name")

pass = Request.Form("pass")
```

The PHP version isn't much different:

```
$name = $HTTP_POST_VARS["name"];

$pass = $HTTP_POST_VARS["pass"];
```

At this point, in either language, you're free to manipulate and test the values however you want. The logical next step might be to open a database connection and verify that the password is the correct one for the given username. You can then decide to return some information (in URL-encoded name/value pairs), depending on whether that user is authorized. We're not going to start on database integration yet, but it's coming in Chapter 7, "XML/Flash with Database Connectivity." For now, you just need to see the possibilities.

Clearly, `loadVariables()` is a nice simple method for getting nice simple variables from Flash to the server. When your data and its structure get a little hairier, though, you'll definitely want to turn to XML.

Using `XML.sendAndLoad()` to Send Data to PHP/ASP

There aren't many surprises as far as `XML.sendAndLoad()` goes. Clearly, it's a method for sending the referenced `XML` object to the server as a string and for loading XML from the server. We won't be doing any loading at the same time here, but it's certainly possible. The sending method is `POST`, so again, there's not much shocking there. Let's look at a couple of quick examples:

```
myXML = new XML("<message content='hello server!'/>");
var garbage = new XML();
myXML.sendAndLoad("receive.asp", garbage);
```

This ActionScript will simply create a new `XML` object with this single self-closing tag:

```
<message content='hello server!'/>
```

This code simply sends the XML document, as basic as it is, to a script called receive.asp (or receive.php!). The second parameter, `garbage` in this case, is an `XML` object that `sendAndLoad()` will attempt to populate with XML *from* the server, just as though you had called `garbage.load()`. In this case, we don't care about the response, but we've put an object there just for a placeholder. `XML.sendAndLoad()` handles server communication behind the scenes (just as with the `loadVariables()` method) so that your user is not bothered by windows popping up all over the place. Take a look at the ASP and PHP scripts:

```
<% 'XML to ASP to XML:
  If (Request.Form = "<message content=""hello server!"" />") then
    response.write("<message content='hello Flash!' />")
  end if
%>
```

The ASP is obviously quite simple. The XML document is stored in
`Request.Form` because it was sent via POST. You check whether it's the message
you expected, and then send your reply. If the ActionScript had actually made a
call to `XML.sendAndLoad()`, this response from ASP would be readable in the
`onLoad()` handler of the XML object in Flash. It's a clear example of round-trip
communication via XML. The PHP version is very similar. Here's a look at its
primary fragment:

```
<?
  if (getXML() == "<message content=\"hello server!\" />"){
    echo("<message content='hello Flash!' />");
  }
?>
```

It's all pretty straightforward except for the `getXML()` function, which you have
to define. The problem with PHP is that it actually trusts Flash to send it the correct content type for the document it is receiving. This would be perfectly okay if
Flash didn't erroneously send the wrong content type. Instead, by default Flash
sends `"application/x-www-form-urlencoded"` for the content type. Therefore,
PHP expects a regular HTTP form posting that's URL-encoded. What ends up
happening is that your XML document gets mangled into a name/value pair format because of the equals (=) signs you might have in your attributes. Because of
that, the `getXML()` function needs to repair the XML string by putting these
name/value pairs together (and adding the equals signs in the process). Because
much of your XML is crammed into variable names, PHP had to convert many
spaces to underscores (spaces aren't allowed in variable names, after all!) and
escape your quotes with slashes. The `getXML()` function needs to take all this into
consideration.

Let's take a look at the complete PHP version:

```
<?
// ==== getXML() function definition ================================
function getXML(){
  global $HTTP_POST_VARS;  // access $HTTP_POST_VARS as a global
  $xString = '';
```

```
    while(list($key, $value) = each($HTTP_POST_VARS)){
      $xString .= $key . '=' . $value;
    }
    /* In the preceding code you're reconstructing the broken XML.  You
    take the false name/value pairs from the $HTTP_POST_VARS array
    and put them together in a way that re-creates the XML string. */
    $xString = stripslashes($xString);
    // remove backslashes from any quotes that might have been escaped.
    $xString = str_replace('_', ' ', $xString);
    /* replace underscores with spaces because spaces in variable names
    were automatically translated to underscores */
    return($xString);
}
    if (getXML() == "<message content=\"hello server!\" />"){
      echo("<message content='hello Flash!' />");
    }
?>
```

Now, it's true that you could set the `contentType` property of the `XML` object to `"text/xml"` in Flash, which would certainly help. The problem is that only revisions 40 and 41 of the Flash player support that property. If your users are using revision 30 (and many are!), `contentType` is useless. If you could be assured that all your users were using a plug-in that supports the `contentType` property, you would be safe just accessing the XML in PHP as `$HTTP_RAW_POST_DATA`. Unfortunately, that's not usually the case, but this is just a small speed bump. If you copy and paste that `getXML()` function into your PHP scripts, you shouldn't have to worry about it again.

Creating a Dynamic News Box or Web Log

Now that we've demonstrated the methods necessary to transfer data via XML from Flash to the server, it's time to open the Web log example to see how an actual real-world application might be structured.

Web logs are everywhere. Every design portal, personal site, and news-related site seems to have one these days. With the addition of freely available Web-based software such as Blogger (`http://www.blogger.com/`), thousands of sites rely on these tools to update and keep content fresh. It's a useful application, obviously, but it is also an excellent illustration of the interaction between Flash and the server when sending XML content.

Before you look at the FLA aspect of this example, let's review the XML format you will be using so that you can get a sense of how these Flash elements integrate. Let's take a look at a small sample XML file, which is representative of what you would be generating. In this sample XML document, we are using just one single entry element in the Web log to simplify the discussion.

```
<weblog>
<entry name="lee7h4x0r" title="XML in FLASH rocks" date="Wed Sep 19
04:42:17
➥GMT-0400 2001">Since the introduction of Flash 5, we flashers have been
able
➥to play with many new features, but one of the most dynamic new addi-
tions
➥is the use of XML. And it rocks!</entry>
</weblog>
```

Notice that the root element `<weblog>` is created dynamically by the PHP/ASP scripts. What you want to focus on, however, is the `<entry>` element, which contains the data that the user submits in Flash and that is sent via XML to the server for processing. The XML is formatted in such a way that all the information about the entry, such as `name`, `title`, and `date`, is included as attributes to the `<entry>` element, which makes sense. The actual user entry is placed as a child `textNode` of the `<entry>` element node. This structure makes it easy to understand the information at a glance. You know that you have as many entries in your Web log as there are `<entry>` elements and that all information on the entry is embedded as attributes. It's an incredibly clean XML format that, as you'll see, makes the process of communicating between Flash and the server easy.

Deconstructing the Visual and Server-Side Interface

Now that you have an idea of what you will be ultimately generating, open the Flash file so that you see how this information is transferred. You can find the weblog.fla file in the Chapter6 directory of the source code on the Web site. Start by taking a look at the main timeline, layers, and components of the file in Figure 6.1.

This FLA has six layers used to control and display the different aspects of the Web log application. For the most part, the layer names are self-explanatory; however, we'll quickly outline the purpose of several of them.

As in previous examples, the script layer is used to hold all the scripts and functions that control both the XML and core functionality.

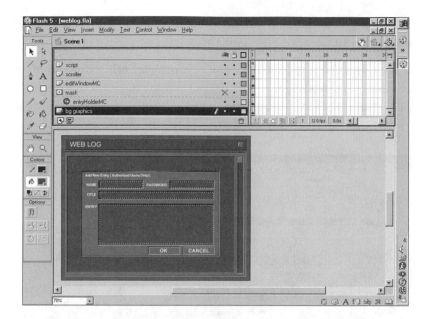

Figure 6.1   *The main timeline of the Web log.*

The two primary layers in the weblog.fla file, editWindowMC and entryHolderMC, are responsible for displaying and submitting the XML content. The editWindowMC layer contains the console box for entering content and submitting it to the PHP/ASP page. The entryHolderMC layer, on the other hand, is used to display the XML information read from the server.

Before we illustrate how to access and read the content, we'll start by demonstrating how to enter and submit information with the Administration console in the editWindowMC layer of the movie. This layer has one self-contained `movieClip` that contains all the elements needed to submit your entries to the server.

This editWindowMC `movieClip`, by default, is set to `_visible=false` and triggered by the editBTN button icon in the lower-left corner of this layer. This button contains the following code, which triggers the function in the script layer:

```
on (release) {
  showEditWindow();
}
```

The purpose of the showEditWindow() function is merely to make the editWindowMC clip visible by setting its _visible property to true.

If you take a look at the editWindowMC clip in Figure 6.2, you can see all the elements you're working with. Four text input fields are used to collect user-entered data: Name, Password, Title, and Entry. You'll use these text fields to transfer user input into XML and subsequently send it to the server.

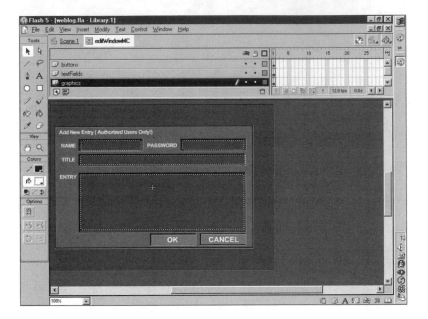

Figure 6.2 *The Add Entry button is used to edit the Web log.*

After users enter information in all the fields, they click on the OK button to submit their information. This button contains the following code:

```
on (release) {
 _root.submit(this);
}
```

All you're doing here is passing the information stored as variables to the submit() function in the script layer. You use this as the reference to the movieClip containing the button; subsequently, it contains the variables you want to translate to XML.

All the server interaction takes place in this script, so let's start dissecting the
submit() function to understand how to successfully move the user-entered data
from Flash to the server.

{ Note }

In this specific example, we will document the process using PHP. We
will outline and document the ASP script later in the chapter.

Because you want to transfer the information stored as variables in the
editWindowMC layer into XML, first you must create XMLNode objects in which
to store this data. You accomplish this in the first part of the submit() function:

```
function submit(window) {
  /*  This function is used to submit a new entry and
      refresh the display. */

  var newNode = linkdata.createElement("entry");
          //create a new entry element

          // Insert it into the firstChild spot.
  if (linkdata.firstChild.hasChildNodes()) {
   // if a firstChild exists, insert the newnode before it.
   linkdata.firstChild.insertBefore(newNode,
   linkdata.firstChild.firstChild);
  } else {
    /* if no firstChild exists, just append it so that it
       can be the firstChild.      */
    linkdata.firstChild.appendChild(newNode);
  }
```

First, a new element called "entry" is created and inserted into the linkdata XML
object. You create the name of this element by using createElement("entry").
That's all there is to creating elements in Flash; however, you need to make this
element part of your existing linkdata XML object. The goal here is to insert this
node as the first "entry" node in the root element because it's a little more user-
friendly to have the most recently added entries appear on top of previously
added entries. To achieve this, you need to use the insertBefore() method to
insert the node before the existing firstChild node, thus making it the new
firstChild node. If there is no existing firstChild (meaning the root element
has no child nodes), this node is appended to the root element directly by using
the appendChild() method. The appendChild() method is similar to
insertBefore(), except that it always inserts the node after the lastChild.

```
newNode = linkdata.firstChild.lastChild;
```

Next, you pass along some of the user-entered variables as attributes into the newly constructed <entry> element. In the following three lines of code, you are beginning to populate the XML with actual content:

```
newNode.attributes.date = (new Date()).toString();
newNode.attributes.title = window.title;
newNode.attributes.name = window.name;
```

The first attribute, date, is not received from user input, but is created dynamically. You simply use the Flash 5 Date() method and output this value to string format. You then set the next two attribute values of title and name equal to window.title and window.name. The parameter window in the submit() function equals the object reference this you sent previously, representing the editWindowMC layer it was sent from.

You still need to transfer the entryContent variable to XML; however, you will add this data as a text node to the newly created element node. Here you are using the createTextNode() method to add the users' entry comment:

```
var newTextNode = linkdata.createTextNode(window.entryContent);
newNode.appendChild(newTextNode);
```

You use this method to add text nodes to the XML object. This is used only for creating text nodes inside existing element nodes. To actually place this text node in the XML object, you need to use appendChild(). Because you are operating within the element node, appending a child automatically places the data inside the element tag/node. You must make sure to use creatTextNode() first and then append this newly created node to the appropriate element node.

You have successfully transferred the data the user has entered into text fields in the linkdata XML object. The only additional information you need to work with is the password field, which you need to verify before successfully submitting this information. This verification is done in the PHP script, so you need to forward this password value to the script. To do this, you set a variable called url equal to the path of the PHP script, but also append the name/value pair pass/window.password for the PHP script to process:

```
var url = "admin.php?pass="+window.password;
```

The preceding line loads the PHP script and passes the variable pass with the value equal to window.password to the script for verification. You'll look at this PHP script in detail shortly.

Now that you have transferred all the content to the XML object structure, you can clear all the window items so that they are empty the next time the submit() function is called:

```
window.name = "";
window.title = "";
window.password = "";
window.entryContent = "";
window._visible = false;
```

You also set the _visible property of the editWindowMC layer to false because as far as the user is concerned, the content has already been submitted. These same lines of code are used in the cancel() function, which is triggered by the Canel button in the editWindowMC layer:

```
function cancel() {
  // clear the window items
  editWindowMC.name = "";
  editWindowMC.title = "";
  editWindowMC.password = "";
  editWindowMC.entryContent = "";
  //close the window
  editWindowMC._visible = false;
}
```

However, it is in the following lines of the submit() function that you complete this process and the transfer of your XML. Here you send the XML to the value of url, which you set earlier:

```
var garbage = new XML();
linkdata.sendAndLoad(url, garbage);  // send the new log to the server

_root.nodeNum = 0;
linkdata.firstChild.displayNodes();
}
```

This is the location of your PHP script, which processes the XML and places it in an XML file on your server that you can read from. Last, you reset the nodeNum value to 0 before you call the displayNodes() function, which, as in previous examples, is responsible for visually displaying the XML content.

Before you take a look at the modifications you have made to importing and displaying your XML, look over the PHP and ASP Admin scripts in Listings 6.1 and 6.2 to understand what happens to your data after it leaves Flash and is headed for the server.

Listing 6.1   The PHP Admin Script

```php
<?
$password = "fishbone";
function getXML(){
  global $HTTP_POST_VARS;
  $xString = '';
  while(list($key, $value) = each($HTTP_POST_VARS)) {
    $xString .= $key . '=' . $value;
  }
  $xString = stripslashes($xString);
  $xString = str_replace('_', ' ', $xString);
  return($xString);
}
$pass = $HTTP_GET_VARS["pass"];
if ($pass == $password) {
  $XMLdoc = trim(getXML());

  if ($XMLdoc != "") {
    $fileName = "weblog.XML";
    // for this to work, you have to chmod weblog.XML to 777
    //weblog.XML must at a minimum contain the Web log root element: <weblog />
    $fp = fopen($fileName, "w");
    fputs($fp, $XMLdoc);
    fclose($fp);
  }

} else {
  echo "Access Denied";

}
?>
```

Listing 6.2   The ASP Admin Script

```asp
<%

password = "fishbone"


' ==== fileRead() function definition ==============================
function fileRead(filename)
  dim f, fs
  Set fs=Server.CreateObject("Scripting.FileSystemObject")
  Set f=fs.OpenTextFile(Server.MapPath(filename), 1)
  fileRead = f.ReadAll
  f.Close
  Set f=Nothing
  Set fs=Nothing
end function
```

Listing 6.2   continued

```
pass = request.querystring("pass")
filename = "weblog.xml"
if (pass = password) then

  xmldoc = trim(request.form())

  if (xmldoc <> "") then
    ' When using with IIS and not PWS, you have to make sure the
    ' permissions granted to IUSR_machine name are set correctly
    ' or you'll get "Permission Denied" errors.  You can probably
    ' get around this by checking the security settings of the
    ' specific folder containing the script (right-click on the
    ' folder, and go to Properties, and then the Security tab).

    ' weblog.xml must at a minimum contain the Web log root element: <weblog />

    dim fs,f
    set fs=Server.CreateObject("Scripting.FileSystemObject")
    set f=fs.OpenTextFile(Server.MapPath(filename), 2)
    f.Write(xmldoc)
    f.Close
    set f=nothing
    set fs=nothing
  end if

end if

response.write(xmldoc)

%>
```

Importing Dynamically Created XML from the Server

Now that you understand how to send the XML to the server for processing, let's go back and take a look at how this movie is initialized, and how the XML content is pulled into Flash.

Like all previous examples—and any time you want to import XML data—you need to use the handy XML.load() method. By now, you should be familiar with this method as well as the onLoad() handler, so just take a look at the initializing code, again in the script layer:

```
function linkdata_onLoad(success) {
        _root.nodeNum = 0;     // the number of nodes is now 0
        linkdata.firstChild.stripWhite();
        linkdata.firstChild.displayNodes();
}
```

First, the custom-defined onLoad() handler defines the actions to take after the XML has been successfully loaded. As in earlier examples, you then perform the stripWhite() function on the XML to ensure that you have removed all white-space. Next, you use the displayNodes() function, which is responsible for visually displaying the XML in Flash.

After you have set the onLoad() function, you can instantiate the XML document called linkdata in this example and use the load() method to import the XML:

```
linkdata = new XML();

linkdata.onLoad = linkdata_OnLoad;

linkdata.load("weblog.xml");
```

Notice that you are loading weblog.xml as the source for your XML. As mentioned earlier, the PHP script outputs the XML into a text-based XML file called weblog.xml. Now you're loading it into Flash to view. This procedure should be familiar to you by now, so let's revisit the displayNodes() function, which has been modified to specifically deal with this example.

Displaying the Imported XML

As mentioned in previous chapters, the displayNodes() function is written to extend the XMLNode object as a new method. This method uses the MovieClip.attachMovie() method on a movieClip, attached from the library, so that you can create graphics for each of the Web log entries. Using the attachMovie() method in this example becomes advantageous.

The main reason it becomes advantageous is that you cannot mask duplicated movieClips. Because you are creating a scrollable area that houses dynamic content, you need to use a mask, which makes the duplicateMovieClip() method useless. Although the duplicateMovieClip() method is useful in that it can contain an onClipEvent that can be transferred to all duplicates, you don't need this functionality here. What you need is the ability to mask your movieClips, so attachMovie() becomes your only real option.

Each time the attachMovie() method is performed, you create a new node graphic. You position the graphic correctly on the screen, populate the text fields with the correct node information, and then do the same for all the current node's child nodes by going through the children recursively, as shown here:

```
function XMLNode_displayNodes(){
    if (this != linkdata.firstChild) {
```

You don't want to perform this method on the firstChild, however, because it doesn't need to be displayed. The firstChild is your <weblog> element. All you really want to display in this application are the actual <entry> elements—the children to your firstChild—and their associated text elements that represent the entries' content.

To do that, check to see whether the node is of type 1, signifying that it is an element node. If so, increase the nodeNum value by one, simply because you have found a new element and need to keep track of it for display purposes:

```
if (this.nodeType == 1) {
    var nodeNum = _root.nodeNum++;
```

Now that you know you have a new element node to work with, use the attachMovie() method to visually represent the node onscreen:

```
entryHolderMC.attachMovie("nodeMC", "nodeMC"+nodeNum, nodeNum);
```

Next, attach the nodeMC movieClip from the library, which has been built to hold your Web log entries, as shown in Figure 6.3.

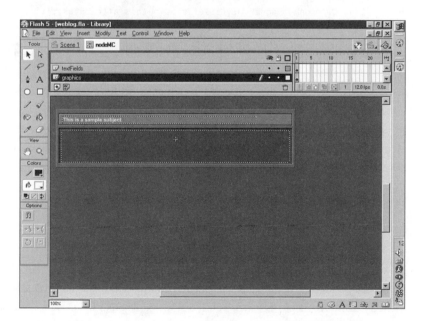

Figure 6.3 *The nodeMC* movieClip *used to display Web log entries.*

The following lines of code are the ones responsible for positioning the attached movie in the proper position. This is where you need to reference the nodeNum variable. By knowing how many entries or nodes you have, you can precisely place the clips dynamically on stage with this information.

```
entryHolderMC["nodeMC"+nodeNum]._x = 250;

entryHolderMC["nodeMC"+nodeNum]._y = 20 + nodeNum * 100;
```

This nodeNum value is also used, as you can see, to label the name of the attached movieClip, thus giving each movieClip a unique identifier in incremental format. To further identify the clips, you create the nodePtr variable to reference the node's position in the XML object, like so:

```
entryHolderMC["nodeMC"+nodeNum].nodePtr = this;
```

The last step in modifying each attached movie is to fill its dynamic text fields with the appropriate content:

```
entryHolderMC["nodeMC"+nodeNum].titlefield = this.attributes.name;
entryHolderMC["nodeMC"+nodeNum].titlefield += " | ";
entryHolderMC["nodeMC"+nodeNum].titlefield += this.attributes.date;
entryHolderMC["nodeMC"+nodeNum].titlefield += " | ";
entryHolderMC["nodeMC"+nodeNum].titlefield += this.attributes.title;
```

You can see from the preceding code that you are merely grabbing the current node's attribute values and plopping them into the titlefield text field. You are also adding " | " to visually separate the elements, yet have them appear on the same line. To actually include the entry's content, you need to target the firstChild of the node. You do this because you are currently working with the element node (type 1), but the data for the entries is placed in the element's text node. Therefore, you need to target the firstchild, like so:

```
entryHolderMC["nodeMC"+nodeNum].entryText.output =
this.firstChild.nodeValue;
    }
   }
```

Now that you have successfully transferred the content from the imported XML to the newly attached movieClip, you need to continue through the XML document by using recursion, as usual. You'll test to see whether the current node has childNodes and, if so, recursively call the displayNodes() method on them:

```
  if (this.childNodes.length > 0)  {
    for (var i = 0; i < this.childnodes.length; i++) {
```

```
       // graphically display each of the child nodes!
       this.childnodes[i].displayNodes();}
  }
}
```

This recursion continues until you have traversed the entire XML document and dynamically placed all <entry> elements on stage by using attachMovie().

You are using the same recursion that you have in previous examples. However, you aren't working with heavily nested data in this Web log example. You are essentially using the for loop to go through the element node children of your root element. The XML consists of only <entry> elements under the root element <weblog>, so in this instance you are going through only one level of nested elements.

Further Specifics

Now that you understand how the XML is displayed, we'll quickly go over some further specifics. Because you do not know how many entries there might be, you need to place these attached movies inside another movieClip that you can scroll, if necessary. You'll notice that there is an entryHolderMC layer, which of all things contains an entryHolderMC movieClip. This layer is masked by the mask layer located above it in the main timeline.

You control the entryHolderMC movieClip with the scroller movieClip in the scroller layer. This scroller is ultimately controlled by a function that is called on an enterFrame action:

```
onClipEvent(enterFrame) {
  _root.handleDragger(this);
}
```

We won't go into detail here about the mechanics of the scroller, because you are more than likely familiar with such interface components. If not, you can take a quick look here and decipher how it works:

```
function handleDragger(bar){
  if (bar.dragging) {
    var track = bar._parent;
    bar.ratio    = ((bar._y - 1)/(track._height - bar._height));
                    /*  figure out the fraction of the scroller track
                        that has been scrolled.  If it's been scrolled
                        halfway down, this value should be 0.5 */
```

```
var contentheight = _root.nodeNum * 120;
                /* figure out just how tall the entries are, when
                   stacked on top of one another. */
    var contentMaxScroll = contentheight - 344;
                /*  a simple calculation to determine what y value the
                    entryHolderMC should be at if it is scrolled to 100% */
    EntryHolderMC._y = 72 - (contentMaxScroll * bar.ratio); //scroll formula
                /*  set the y value of entryHolderMC so that it is
                    correct and in accordance with the scrollbar. */
    }
}
```

The button in the scroller clip also contains the following calls to functions that can be found in the script layer:

```
on (press) {
  _root.startscroll(this);
}


on (release, releaseOutside) {
  _root.stopscroll(this);
}
```

Keep in mind that this is a basic example that was created to demonstrate passing XML information to the server. We hope you can see a number of possibilities for improving on this particular file or augmenting it for use in your own applications.

Security

The password is sent by using plain text with no encryption whatsoever, so technically it's not very secure. For most purposes, however, this method is probably secure enough. In reality, you'll probably want to remove the Admin interface and maybe put it in an SWF in a completely separate password-protected directory. In any case, the Edit button just might be too much for potential crackers to resist. You could always try something sneaky, such as detecting specific keystrokes to make the window open, and you could remove the button altogether. We'll leave this up to you as an exercise, though. The point of what we've done here is to show how XML can be sent and stored on the server.

Summary

After reading through this chapter, you should have a solid understanding of how XML is sent from Flash to the server as well as how it is manipulated for display when imported. You have covered all the fundamentals necessary to start working with and creating your own XML-based applications.

So What's Next?

Now that you have successfully covered importing and exporting XML with server-side languages, it's time to take the next step. In the next chapter, you use XML and middleware to enable Flash to communicate with a server-side database. This is where true application building begins. Most of you programmers reading this book frequently work with database development. The following chapter will shed light on how you can incorporate this practice with Flash.

Quite often, companies export their content and data with XML, but use HTML as the display method. If you are comfortable doing this, you'll see how easy it is to make the transfer to Flash. You now know how to properly manipulate and display XML content in Flash, so now's the time to start incorporating your database content.

{ Chapter 7 }

XML/Flash with Database Connectivity

You've come a long way, baby. You've walked through the basics of XML and learned how it applies to the world of Flash. You've dynamically imported XML from the server and sent XML from Flash back to the server. Now you're ready to take the plunge into true dynamic application building.

Web applications are perhaps one of the fastest growing segments in Web development these days. Although the days of "brochureware" will perhaps never be behind us, average Web developers are quickly learning—out of necessity—how to build Web applications. From simple dynamic forms to large content management systems, applications are fast becoming integral in the suite of tools available to developers. With middleware languages, such as PHP, that are both free and open source appearing on the scene, it's incredibly easy and barrier-free to begin experimenting with and ultimately publishing dynamic Web applications.

It goes without saying that you cannot truly have a powerful Web application without interacting with some sort of database system. This is where you can truly publish dynamically with dynamic content. We are seeing a new generation of Web applications being built with Flash as the front end. With the capabilities in Flash 5—particularly XML—there is very little reason it would not be considered for Web application development these days. Flash allows you to visually and interactively display your content in ways that are not possible with the standard HTML interface and, on top of that, be totally cross-platform, cross-browser compatible. Why wouldn't you consider using Flash?

Throughout this chapter you are going to explore strictly the development of a Flash-based message board. This message board will communicate to a MySQL database by using two separate middleware options: PHP and ASP. One of this message board's advantages is that, unlike traditional HTML boards where you need to reload new HTML pages every time a new post is selected, you can dynamically import this content into Flash with no need for a page refresh or reload. This feature makes the application much more interactive and responsive to the user.

It is assumed that you have some experience working with databases, as we cannot cover a Database 101 course here. We will be going through the PHP and ASP code to identify how information is being sent and read from the database, and all code is well documented. However, this chapter is not for the faint of heart. If you are a designer with no knowledge of middleware or databases, this is no excuse to skip through this chapter, though! In today's development world, designers must work with programmers and vice versa.

Structuring Your Data

Before you start analyzing custom functions, prototypes and server-side code, take a peek at the actual XML content you will be working with. Although this message board is the most complex example in this book, it is still made up of many small and basic pieces that when linked create a sophisticated application.

By now, you've seen enough XML to easily understand its structure and begin thinking about how you might work with it inside Flash, so take a look at what a sample post might look when formatted as XML:

```
<msgBoard>
<entry name="Craig" title="I wish I had a cruller" date="2001-09-18
03:28:13">
I'm all out and need inspiration! Can someone hook a brother up?
</entry>
</msgBoard>
```

You should be able to look at this piece of XML code and instantly break it down and understand how it is structured. It's very simple. As we've stressed throughout this book, this is the beauty of XML: the ability to format content into logical, readable constructs—readable by machines *and* people.

The preceding example illustrates just one post in the board. You can see that the root element or firstChild of the XML document is—ta-da!—<msgBoard>.

We think we're pretty clever coming up with that one. Each post is then given the element name `<entry>`. For each post, we have separated the content between `textNodes` and attributes. You'll see later, as you dig into the Flash file, that this content is handled and displayed differently. We house name, title, and date of the post as attributes of the `<entry>` element. The actual message content is contained in the `textNode` inside the `<entry>` element. By placing the content in a child of the `<entry>` tag, you don't need to worry quite as much about the ugliness of a lot of data in an attribute or how attributes have stricter escaping rules for weird characters.

As more entries are added to the database, you just continue to add `<entry>` elements to the original `<msgBoard>` XML document, like so:

```
<msgBoard>
<entry name="Craig" title="Wish I had a cruller" date=
➥"2001-09-18 03:28:13">
    I'm all out and need inspiration! Can someone hook a brother up?
    <entry name="Gregg" title="Re: I wish I had a cruller" date=
➥"2001-09-18 03:44:17">
        Hahaha. Not me. Last time you gorged yourself and started dancing
➥to the sound of trucks reversing. Such a sad display - I will have no
➥part in it ;)
    </entry>
</entry>
</msgBoard>
```

Essentially, the structure is hierarchical. The message replies are included as children of the message. By looking at this XML, you should realize that you will have text fields in the movie, or in `movieClips` that correspond to these values. As a designer, you know you need to create containers somewhere in the movie for name, title, date, and the actual entry. Of course, as a programmer you know that you need to transport the data to and from the database by using these same descriptors.

Simple Database Schema

So let's fire up the database and begin working on a simple database schema. Pen and paper can be your best friend here. You know you will want to save the messages and the users in the database, so you start off with two tables: users and messages. Users will require a name and a password, so you'll need name and pass fields in that table. Messages will require a subject, a date, a sender, and, of course, some content. Therefore, the fields for each table look like this:

Table	Fields
users	name, pass
messages	subject, date, sender, content

If one message can reply to another message, how can you maintain this hierarchy, with the messages table being a simple flat table? Well, you add an ID to every message to give it a unique number, and then add a replyid field to hold the unique ID of whatever message you are replying to. If a message is *not* a reply, you'll set replyid equal to 0. However, if it *is* a reply, you'll get the ID from the message it's a reply for, and you'll put that ID in the this new reply's replyid field. The tables' structure now looks like this:

Table	Fields
users	name, pass
messages	id, subject, date, sender, content, replyid

For the sake of better organization, an ID is also added to the users table. This way, when you want to mark down the sender of a message in the messages table, you can simply record the ID of the user who is a sender. Here's the finished plan:

Table	Fields
users	id, name, pass
messages	id, subject, date, sender, content, replyid

Probably the simplest way to create this database is to install PHPmyAdmin (a free download from `https://sourceforge.net/projects/phpmyadmin/`) and enter the two tables through its nice, easy-to-use, Web-based interface. For those more comfortable with mySQL and SQL, here are the necessary SQL statements:

```
CREATE TABLE `users` (
  `id` int(11) NOT NULL auto_increment,
  `name` varchar(8) NOT NULL default '',
  `pass` varchar(8) NOT NULL default '',
  PRIMARY KEY  (`id`),
  UNIQUE KEY `id` (`id`,`name`),
  KEY `id_2` (`id`)
) TYPE=MyISAM;
```

```
CREATE TABLE `messages` (
  `id` int(11) NOT NULL auto_increment,
  `userid` int(11) NOT NULL default '0',
  `date` datetime NOT NULL default '0000-00-00 00:00:00',
  `subject` varchar(60) NOT NULL default '',
  `content` text NOT NULL,
  `replyid` int(11) NOT NULL default '0',
  PRIMARY KEY (`id`),
  UNIQUE KEY `id` (`id`),
  KEY `id_2` (`id`)
) TYPE=MyISAM;
```

Even the novice SQLer can pick the schema out of these statements. It's really
pretty simple. After you have that set up, you're ready to start building the application.

Included Database-Related Functions

One important piece of the server integration is the included db.inc.php file that
each of the PHP files accesses for backup. You'll want to make sure you set all
the variables at the top to the correct values, or you will be getting query errors
all over the place. We're assuming that your mySQL server is installed and configured correctly (and also that you know your name and password for it!).

```
<?
/*  =================== Database related - general ========================
This database stuff is pretty straightforward for a PHP programmer, but
it's useful to see the functions to understand how to use them.  */

// alter this information to reflect your own mySQL server!
$dbserver = "localhost";
$dbusername = "cainus_flash";
$dbpassword = "xml";
$dbname = "cainus_msgbrd";

function dbconnect() {
  // connect to the database using the above information
  global $dbserver, $dbusername, $dbpassword, $dbname;
  $db = mysql_connect($dbserver, $dbusername, $dbpassword) or die
  ("Database Error: ".mysql_error());
  mysql_select_db($dbname, $db) or die("Database Error: ".mysql_error());
  return $db;
}

function db_date () {
  // return a formatted date for the database
  return date('Y-m-d H:i');
}
```

```php
function count_rows($table, $where, $equals) {
   /* count the number of rows in a specified table that match the
      specified criteria */
   $sqlStr = "SELECT COUNT($where) AS somecount FROM ".$table." WHERE
   (".$where." = '".$equals."')";
   $result = mysql_query($sqlStr) or die("Database Error:
➥".mysql_error());
   return(mysql_result($result,somecount));
}

function add_user($name, $password){
    //add a user to the database, given her username and password...
    $sql = "INSERT INTO users (name, pass) VALUES ('$name', '$password')";
    $msgresult = mysql_query($sql) or die("Database Error:
➥".mysql_error());
}

function add_message($userid, $date, $subject, $content, $replyid){
    //add a message to the database
    $sql = "INSERT INTO messages (userid, date, subject, content, replyid)
➥ VALUES ('$userid', '$date', '$subject', '$content', '$replyid')";
    $msgresult = mysql_query($sql) or die("Database Error:
➥".mysql_error());
}

function lookup($needed, $tablename, $column, $value) {
  /*  This function returns a standard lookup value.  For instance, if you
want to know the name of a user from the users table who has an ID of 3,
you would say this inSQL:

     SELECT name FROM users WHERE id = 3.

     With this lookup function, you can get the result by simply calling:
     $returnval = lookup("name", "users", "id", 3);

     */
  $sql = "SELECT ".$needed." FROM ".$tablename." WHERE
➥ ".$column." = '".$value."'";
  $result = mysql_query($sql) or die ("\n<br>Invalid query: \n<br>".$sql);
  if (!(mysql_num_rows($result))) {
     $returnVal = "";
    } else {
     $returnVal = mysql_result($result,0);
    }
  return($returnVal);
}

?>
```

With all that primary stuff out of the way, you need to start working on the actual application. So let's jump into the Flash file so that you can begin understanding just how you'll do this.

Structuring the Flash File

Take a moment to open the msgBoard.FLA file on the Web site. You can find this file in the Chapter 7 directory inside the msgBoard folder.

First, take a look at the way we have arranged the timeline and layers. If you sneak a peek at Figure 7.1, you'll see the way the application has been laid out.

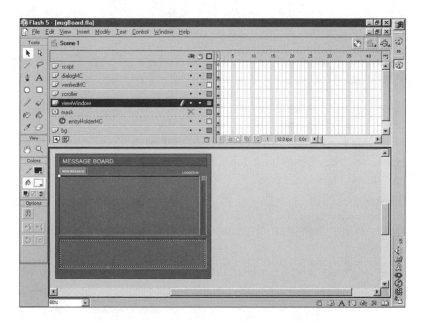

Figure 7.1   *The main timeline, layers, and components of the msgBoard.fla.*

As always, you have the script layer, which contains the functions used throughout this FLA. The dialogMC layer is used to display the dialog boxes used during login, registering, and posting and includes movieClips that are attached dynamically. The verifiedMC layer contains a movieClip with the same name, which is responsible for indicating to users whether they are logged into the board. The scroller layer contains the components used for the scroller. The postMsg layer contains the postBTN button, which is used to facilitate logging in to the board as well as posting or replying to threads. The mask layer is used to mask the stage for displaying the messages. You need to mask this area because all the posts are transferred from XML source to movieClips that represent the posts.

As in previous examples, you use attachMovieClip() to place these clip instances on stage. When you have more posts than will fit in the viewable area, you need the scroller—thus the need for the mask. The entryHolderMC layer is where you are attaching these clips. Because you will eventually have a long list of posts, you need to limit the viewable space and scroll through these clips, which is why you require the mask layer. The viewWindow layer is where the actual message content is displayed. Finally, the bg layer is where you place the graphical background elements that have no direct bearing on the file's interactivity.

Loading Message Board Content into Flash via PHP/ASP

When you first run the Flash file, the message board content is loaded via XML into Flash and then processed for display. As always, when importing XML into Flash, you need to establish a new XML object, load the content, and determine how to proceed after it's loaded with the onLoad() handler. You do this in the code found in the script layer:

```
linkdata = new XML();
linkdata.onLoad = linkdata_OnLoad;
linkdata.load("msgbrd.php?r="+(new Date().getTime().toString()));
```

Here you create linkdata, which is the XML object that you use to store the message board's content. You can see that the onLoad() handler is overridden with the custom function linkdata_OnLoad. This custom function lets you control what happens when the XML has finished loading and initiates display of the XML inside Flash, which we will cover shortly.

First, take a look at the load method in the preceding code:

```
linkdata.load("msgbrd.php?r="+(new Date().getTime().toString()));
```

Here you are loading a PHP script called msgbrd.php (note that you will need to alter the filename here to have an .asp extension, if you are using ASP), but you are also sending some additional information. In this instance, you are sending the variable r with a value equal to the Date.getTime() value. You do this to eliminate caching the XML document. Using the Date.getTime() value creates a "non-recurring" value to be appended to the PHP script. This value ensures that every time this file is hit, it is considered unique by the browser. This eliminates caching and makes the most recent content available at all times.

This PHP script is responsible for querying the database for entries in the message board, wrapping this data in XML and returning it to Flash to be processed and displayed to the user. This is the msgbrd.php script:

```php
<?
/* This file (msgbrd.php) shows the messages from the database
   in XML format.  Essentially you call a recursive function
   (replies2XML()) and it does the rest.
*/

function replies2XML($id) {
/* this function takes an $id number and spits out an XML document
   representing all the replies to that message, as well as all
   their replies (recursively) */
  $xOut = "";
  $sql = "SELECT id, userid, subject, date, content, replyid ";
  $sql .= "FROM messages WHERE replyid = $id";
  $results = mysql_query($sql)
                    or die("Database Error: ".mysql_error(). "\n" .
➥$sql);
    /* The above is standard communication of mySQL and PHP via SQL.
       Essentially, you're selectingall the relevant messages */
      if (mysql_num_rows($results) > 0){
          while ($row = mysql_fetch_array($results)){
          //for each row in the query result...
              $row["subject"] = str_replace ("'", "&apos;", $row
➥["subject"]);
              $row["content"] = str_replace ("'", "&apos;", $row
➥["content"]);
              $row["subject"] = str_replace ("\"", "&quot;", $row
➥["subject"]);
              $row["content"] = str_replace ("\"", "&quot;", $row
➥["content"]);
              $row["subject"] = str_replace (">", "&gt;", $row["subject"]);
              $row["content"] = str_replace (">", "&gt;", $row["content"]);
              $row["subject"] = str_replace ("<", "&lt;", $row["subject"]);
              $row["content"] = str_replace ("<", "&lt;", $row["content"]);
              /* in the above you replaced the special XML characters with
              their corresponding HTML entity */
              $xOut .= "<entry ";
              $xOut .= "name='".lookup("name", "users", "id",
➥$row["userid"]);
              $xOut .= "'title='".$row["subject"];
              /* check out "db.in.php" to see lookup().
              In the above usage, it is returning the result of a query like

              SELECT name FROM users WHERE id = $row["userid"]
```

```
          So... essentially it is finding a name that matches that
➥userid.
          */
          $xOut .= "' id='".$row["id"]."' date='".$row["date"];
          $xOut .= "'>";
          $xOut .= $row["content"];
          $xOut .= replies2XML($row["id"]);  // <--- recursive call!!
          $xOut .= "</entry>";
          /* above you output the XML document using a recursive call.
          You populate attributes with all the info, except for the
          'content', which is presented as a text node.  The replies
          to that node are included as a sibling to that text node, so
          that all replies are contained by the entry they are replying
          to.
          */
      }
  }
  return($xOut);
}

include("db.inc.php");  //include the necessary database libraries
dbconnect();            //connect to the database

/* below you create a root element called msgBoard and put all the
replies to id 0 in those tags.  Replies to id 0 are actually 'new'
messages, not replies at all. */
?><msgBoard><?=replies2XML(0)?></msgBoard>
```

After you run this script, it sends the XML to Flash for processing. This output will be handled initially by the custom `linkdata_OnLoad()` function, as shown here:

```
function linkdata_onLoad(success) {
    _root.nodeDepth = 0;
    for (var i = 0;i < _root.nodeNum+1;i++) {
        entryHolderMC["nodeMC"+i].removeMovieClip();
    }
    _root.nodeNum = 0;
    this.firstChild.expanded = true;
    this.firstChild.displayNodes();
}
```

Notice that you set the variables `nodeNum` and `nodeDepth` to 0. You may recall from earlier examples that you use these variables to track the number and depth of nodes in the XML object. You also erase all nodeMCs from the last XML representation. The nodeMCs are `movieClips` that represent each post in the message board. We used the same `movieClip` in the directory tree example, and will cover it again when we discuss the display function. This graphical display is handled by the custom function `displayNodes()`, which is the last action performed during the `onLoad()` event. It is here that you begin to use Flash for representing the XML data structure.

Displaying Message Board Entries in Flash

The `displayNodes()` function was created to handle displaying the XML content that is dynamically loaded into Flash from the PHP/ASP, which in turn received the data from the MySQL database. Let's take a peek at this function before dissecting it into its individual components and actions:

```
function XMLNode_displayNodes(){

  var nodeNum = _root.nodeNum++;

  if (this != linkdata.firstChild) {

      if (this.nodeType == 1) {
      var nodeNum = _root.nodeNum++;
      entryHolderMC.attachMovie("nodeMC", "nodeMC"+nodeNum, nodeNum);

        entryHolderMC["nodeMC"+nodeNum]._x = 200 + this.depth() * 18;

        entryHolderMC["nodeMC"+nodeNum]._y = 0 + nodeNum * 8;

        entryHolderMC["nodeMC"+nodeNum].nodePtr = this;


        entryHolderMC["nodeMC"+nodeNum].titlefield = this.attributes.name;
        entryHolderMC["nodeMC"+nodeNum].titlefield += " | ";
        entryHolderMC["nodeMC"+nodeNum].titlefield += this.attributes.date;
        entryHolderMC["nodeMC"+nodeNum].titlefield += " | ";
        entryHolderMC["nodeMC"+nodeNum].titlefield +=
➥this.attributes.title;
        entryHolderMC["nodeMC"+nodeNum].replyThread = this.attributes.id;
        entryHolderMC["nodeMC"+nodeNum].output = this.firstChild.nodeValue;

    }
    }
  if ((this.childNodes.length > 0) && (this.expanded)) {

    for (var i = 0; i < this.childnodes.length; i++) {
      if (this.childNodes[i].nodeType == 1)  {

        this.childnodes[i].displayNodes();  //    <-- notice the
➥recursion!
      }
    }
  }
}
```

This function is written to extend the XMLNode object with a new displayNodes() method. This method uses the MovieClip.attachMovieClip() method on a movie clip (that you link from the library) so that you can create graphics for each of the message board entries.

You create a new node graphic each time this function is run, position the graphic correctly on the screen, populate the text fields in it with the correct node information, and then do the same for all the XMLNode's children through a recursive call to displayNodes().

There are two main steps to this function. First, you determine whether there is an entry, which consists of an element node, and dynamically attach a movieClip to the stage to represent this entry. Second, you populate this attached movieClip with the data associated with this element.

The first thing you do when this function runs is increase the nodeNum value:

```
var nodeNum = _root.nodeNum++;
```

Because this function is recursive, you perform this action to track how many nodes you have. This function is called recursively until all nodes in the XML object have been examined. This value for nodeNum is helpful for always knowing how many nodes there are and for the proper visual display of the movieClips that represent the nodes. Because you are interested only in displaying the message board entries, it is unnecessary to process the root element or firstChild, as this is the <msgBoard> tag. You eliminate the firstChild with this line:

```
if (this != linkdata.firstChild) {
```

This ensures that the function runs through only children of <msgBoard>, which are the actual entries. These entries are represented as element nodes (<entry>), so you run through the XML checking for the nodeType. If it is equal to 1, meaning it's an element node, you attach a movieClip to represent this entry:

```
if (this.nodeType == 1) {
var nodeNum = _root.nodeNum++;
entryHolderMC.attachMovie("nodeMC", "nodeMC"+nodeNum, nodeNum);

  entryHolderMC["nodeMC"+nodeNum]._x = 200 + this.depth() * 18;

  entryHolderMC["nodeMC"+nodeNum]._y = 0 + nodeNum * 8;

  entryHolderMC["nodeMC"+nodeNum].nodePtr = this;
```

You represent this entry with the nodeMC `movieClip`, which is dynamically attached to the stage inside the entryHolderMC `movieClip`. If you recall, entryHolderMC is masked, allowing you to scroll through these nodeMCs when they extend past the visual area represented by the mask. Each nodcMC is numbered sequentially, matching the `nodeNum`. You can see why it is important to keep track of this `nodeNum` value. You use it to properly space and display the `movieClips` vertically with this line:

```
entryHolderMC["nodeMC"+nodeNum]._y = 0 + nodeNum * 8;
```

Finally, you create a new variable called `nodePtr`. Its value represents the `XMLNode` you are representing with the `movieClip`. This pointer will become useful later when you want to retrieve more information from this node.

Now that you have successfully found an `<entry>` element and represented it on stage as a `movieClip`, you want to populate this `movieClip` with the data contained in this element. Take a look at the nodeMC `movieClip` in Figure 7.2 to see how it is structured to contain this information.

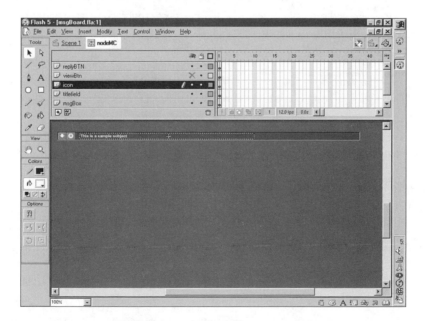

Figure 7.2 _The nodeMC_ `movieClip`, _which is used to display message board entries._

Right now, all you are interested in is the titlefield layer, where you have a text field with the same name. You use this text field to display information about the message board entry, not the entry itself. You can see by the following code from the displayNodes() function how you pass the name, date, and title attribute values to the text field labeled titlefield:

```
entryHolderMC["nodeMC"+nodeNum].titlefield = this.attributes.name;
entryHolderMC["nodeMC"+nodeNum].titlefield += " | ";
entryHolderMC["nodeMC"+nodeNum].titlefield +=
this.attributes.date; entryHolderMC["nodeMC"+nodeNum].titlefield += " | ";
entryHolderMC["nodeMC"+nodeNum].titlefield += this.attributes.title;
```

You also pass on additional information to this movieClip, but do not display it, as shown in these lines:

```
entryHolderMC["nodeMC"+nodeNum].replyThread = this.attributes.id;
entryHolderMC["nodeMC"+nodeNum].output = this.firstChild.nodeValue;
```

Here you assign the id attribute to a replyThread variable, which will be used later when replying to previous message board posts. You also pass on the nodeValue to a newly created output variable inside the movieClip. This nodeValue is the actual content of the user's post. You need to grab and transfer this information from the XMLNode to the movieClip, but it will not be accessible until later, when the user requests this information. We will discuss this procedure in the next section.

The rest of the displayNodes() function is the recursive call:

```
  if ((this.childNodes.length > 0) && (this.expanded)) {

    for (var i = 0; i < this.childnodes.length; i++) {
      if (this.childNodes[i].nodeType == 1)  {

        this.childnodes[i].displayNodes();  //    <-- notice the
➥recursion!
      }
    }
  }
```

Here you continue to drill down through the XML object. If the current node has its expanded property set to true, look for any other children that are element nodes (representing posts) and perform the displayNodes() function on them to graphically display them to the screen.

After this function call is finished, you will have the entire XML object, which was sent to Flash via PHP/ASP, represented visually onscreen. That means you can see all posts in the message board, as shown Figure 7.3.

Figure 7.3   *The message board with posts displayed.*

Right now you are displaying the name, date, and title of the posts. This is all fine and dandy, but what about the actual content of the post?

Displaying Message Board Content in Flash

The content of the posts are handled a little differently. If you recall from the earlier discussion on the XML structure, the content of the posts is contained in a textNode inside the <entry> element. So far, displayNodes() has successfully represented these posts and dynamically transferred the attribute values to the titlefield, but you can't view the content.

We've designed this board to be quick and easy to navigate. None of the actual posts are displayed unless the user requests them by clicking on the nodeMCs attached to the stage. If you refer to Figure 7.2, you'll notice a layer called viewBTN. This layer contains a transparent button that covers the entire movieClip. Attached to this button is the following action:

```
on(release){
  _parent._parent.viewWindow.message=this.output;
  _root.nodeMC_expand(this);
}
```

As mentioned, the nodeValue of the XMLNode is transferred to a variable called output in the attached nodeMC movieClip. Here you can see that you are accessing this content when the user releases the viewBTN inside the nodeMC. The viewBTN is an invisible button inside the nodeMC movieClip that drops the message content into the message text field, which is located in the viewWindow movieClip at the bottom of the stage.

You are outputting this data to a text field called message, which resides in the viewWindow movieClip. Because the nodeMC resides inside the emptyHolderMC layer, you need to target two parent levels up to reach the main timeline where the viewWindow exists. You can see what this looks like in Figure 7.4.

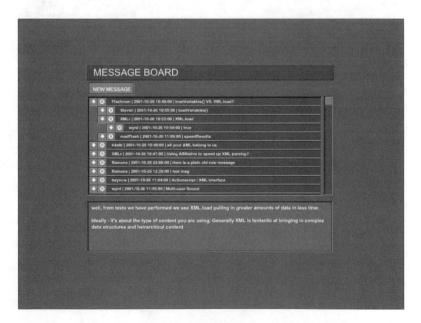

Figure 7.4   *The message board with a post selected, revealing replied threads.*

Navigating Message Replies

This viewBTN also calls the expand() function, which is used to collapse or expand the selected nodeMC. When you run the displayNodes() function, you perform an if statement that checks to see whether there are childNodes and, if so, that the node's expanded property is set to true. If the expanded property is set to true, you recursively add all childNodes of that node, as shown in the following code:

```
function nodeMC_expand(nodeMC){
    nodeMC.nodePtr.expanded = !nodeMC.nodePtr.expanded;
  for (var i = 0;i < _root.nodeNum+1;i++)
      entryHolderMC["nodeMC"+i].removeMovieClip();
  }
  _root.nodeNum = 0;
  _root.linkdata.firstChild.displayNodes();
}
```

You can see that when the displayNodes() function is called, you remove all movieClips from the stage and then call the displayNodes() function again. Basically, this function toggles the node's expanded property between true and false. Displaying replies to a message is solely dependent on this expanded property.

So far, we have discussed the process of importing and navigating through the message board, but have not discussed submitting posts to the board. This is a complicated process, as you must be a member before you can even post, so let's take a look at the Flash output side of this application.

Becoming a Member of a Message Board

In this message board, we have made being a member mandatory before you can post comments. Signing in and posting messages is possible by clicking the NEW MESSAGE button, as shown in Figure 7.5.

The code attached to this button is as follows:

```
on (release) {
    _root.replyThread = 0;
    showNewMsgWin();
}
```

You set replyThread to 0 to signify that you are not replying to a previous post, but creating a new post. As you've learned, replyThread is set based on the value of the id attribute of the <entry> element when the nodeMC clip is attached with the displayNodes() function. Each entry contains a replyBTN, represented by a small circle with an *R*, which is used to reply to existing posts and uses this value. Back to the login process!

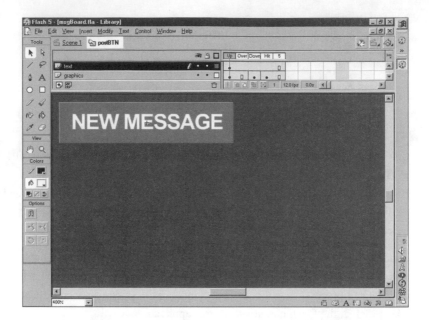

Figure 7.5 *The NEW MESSAGE button used to add entries to the message board.*

The first function that is called is showNewMsgWin(), which contains the following code:

```
function showNewMsgWin() {

    if (!_root.showingNewMsgWin){
        _root.showingNewMsgWin = true;

        if (_root.loggedIn == true){

        _root.dialognum++;
        _root.dialogMC.attachMovie("newMsgMC", "newMsgMC",
        _root.dialogNum);
        }

 else {
            if (!_root.showingLoginWin){
            _root.showingNewMsgWin = false;
            _root.showLoginWin();
        }
        }
    }
}
```

After setting _root.showingNewMsgWin to true, you check to see whether the user is logged in. Because you have not logged in nor even become a member yet, this value will be false. Instead of displaying a new message display box, you call the showLoginWin() function. This function basically attaches the loginMC to the stage as follows:

```
function showLoginWin(){
    _root.dialognum++;
    _root.showingLoginWin = true;
    _root.dialogMC.attachMovie("loginMC", "loginMC", _root.dialogNum);
}
```

It is inside the loginMC movieClip that you can either log in or create a new account, as you can see in Figure 7.6. In the following section, you'll step through the process of creating a new account because you cannot access the message board to post messages until you have an account.

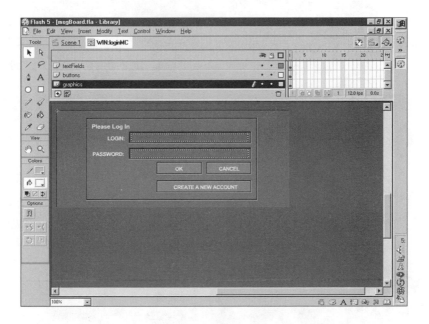

Figure 7.6   *The loginMC* movieClip *used to log in to the message board or become a member.*

Creating an Account

The code attached to the Create a New Account button in the loginMC clip calls the `createAccount()` function:

```
on (release){
  _root.createAccount();
}
```

This function's responsibility is to initiate removing the loginMC `movieClip` and attaching the accountMC `movieClip` to the stage, as shown here:

```
function createAccount(){
    cancelLogin();
    _root.dialognum++;
    _root.showingAccountWin = true;
    dialogMC.attachMovie("accountMC", "accountMC", _root.dialogNum);
}
```

There is no need to document the `cancelLogin()` function; it merely has a removeMovieClip that removes the loginMC clip. Now that you have accountMC attached on stage, take a closer look at it in Figure 7.7, as this is where the fun is!

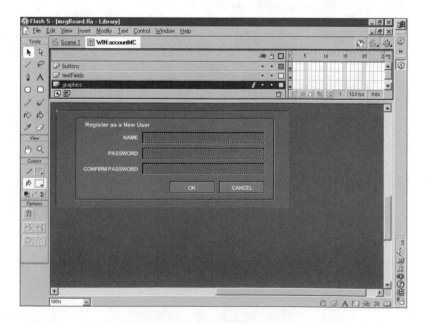

Figure 7.7 *The accountMC* movieClip *used to create a new message board account.*

In Figure 7.7, you can see that three fields are required to create an account: Name, Password, and Confirm Password. Users can take only two actions at this point. They can cancel the dialog box or click OK. Clicking the Cancel button calls a `cancelAccount()` function that removes the accountMC `movieClip`. Clicking OK, on the other hand, performs this action:

```
on (release) {
 _root.newUser(login, password, confirm);
}
```

In the preceding code, you gather the values from the three text fields and forward them to the `newUser()` function. It is in this function that you verify the users' information that has been submitted and send the data off to the PHP page to handle including the information in the database. Let's look at this `newUser()` function a little more closely:

```
function newUser(login, password, confirm){
  _root.postType = "newuser";
  _root.username = login;
  _root.userpass = password;
  _root.loader.name = _root.username;
  _root.loader.password = _root.userpass;

  if (confirm == password){
    _root.loader.loadVariables("newuser.php", "POST");
  } else {
    passwordError("Passwords did not match.");
  }
}
```

The main goal is to somehow send the login and password to the newuser.php script via `POST`. You could certainly send it as XML by using `XML.sendAndLoad()`, as you did in the previous chapter. For the amount of data here, though, it's not worth the trouble of creating a "new user" XML document to send and to be dealt with as XML on the server side. This is one of those situations in which `loadVariables()` excels. There is a tiny amount of data going from Flash to the server, and it's easily represented in name/value pairs. In this case, the loader `movieClip` in the FLA will be the `movieClip` used to call `loadVariables()`. It simply sits there and waits to be used for sending or receiving `loadVariables()` data. One thing you need to do is put the variables into the loader `movieClip`:

```
_root.loader.name = _root.username;
_root.loader.password = _root.userpass;
```

A simple call such as the following can send all that information to the
newuser.php script:

```
_root.loader.loadVariables("newuser.php", "POST");
```

You also set a variable called _root.postType to newuser so that the loader
movie will know it should expect a response from newuser.php. This variable is
used by the loaderDispatch() function, which handles all loadVariables()
data received by the loader movieClip, based on this postType value.

You also pass the login and password values that originated from accountMC to
the root variables username and pass with these lines:

```
_root.username = login;
_root.userpass = password;
```

By storing these values in the _root, you make them accessible for the user session. You do not need to constantly ask users to submit login and password information every time they submit a post. You merely grab that data from these root
values.

Before submitting login and password information to the server, an if statement
is run to check whether the user has entered the same password in both the
Password and Confirm Password fields. If they do not match, the
passwordError() function is called, which contains this code:

```
function passwordError(error){
    _root.dialognum++;
    _root.showingBadConfirmWin = true;
    dialogMC.accountMC._visible = false;
    dialogMC.attachMovie("badConfirmMC", "badConfirmMC", _root.dialogNum);
    dialogMC.badConfirmMC.passwordError = error;
}
```

Basically, this function attaches the badConfirmMC to the stage and passes the
value of error to the text field called passwordError.

If the confirm value is equal to the password value, the following script runs:

```
if (confirm == password){
    _root.loader.loadVariables("newuser.php", "POST");
}
```

Here you are loading variables from newuser.php into the loader `movieClip`, which is on the displayMC layer of the main timeline. This clip contains an `onClipEvent(data)` that is used to process all incoming variables, as shown here:

```
onClipEvent(data){
  _root.loaderDispatch()
}
```

The newuser.php script that will pass the variables contains the following code:

```
<?
/* This file (newuser.php) is used to post a message from Flash to the
   database.  */

$name = $HTTP_POST_VARS["name"];
$password = $HTTP_POST_VARS["password"];
/* the above lines get all the necessary information for adding
   a new user to the database */

include("db.inc.php");    //include the database libraries
dbconnect();              // connect to the database

$loggedIn = false;        // default to a false value for $loggedIn
if ((strlen($name) > 2) && (strlen($password) > 3)) {
//if the username and password are of acceptable length...
  if (count_rows("users", "name", $name) == 0) {
  //if there are users that match that username...
    add_user($name, $password);
                        /* add the user to the database (add_user()
                           is in db.inc.php if you want to see its
                           implementation). */
    $loggedIn = true;   // note that the user is logged in
  }
}

if ($loggedIn) {
   echo "loggedIn=true";
} else {
   echo "loggedIn=false";
}
/* In the above if-else blocks, you output the value of $loggedIn as text
   so that the loadVariables() call in Flash knows whether or not the
   user was accepted. */
?>
```

As soon as the variables from newuser.php are returned to the loader `movieClip`, the `loaderDispatch()` function is instantly called and performs the following:

```
function loaderDispatch(){
  if (_root.postType == "postmsg") {
    _root.linkdata.load("msgbrd.php?r="+(new
➡   Date().getTime().toString()));
  } else {
      if (_root.postType == "verify") {
      verify(_root.loader.loggedIn);
      } else {
      if (_root.postType == "newuser") {
         verify(_root.loader.loggedIn);
       } else {
       //nothing
       }
      }
  }
}
```

Because the `postType` variable was set to `newuser`, you send the `loggedIn` value to the `verify()` function, where it either reports an error or completes the successful login. We'll cover this `verify()` function a little more thoroughly in the following section.

Logging In to the Message Board as a Member

Now that you have covered the process to become a member, let's illustrate how a member logs in. Again, you'll refer to the loginMC `movieClip` that is attached to the stage when the member clicks the postBTN in the lower-left corner of the application. If you refer to Figure 7.6, you'll notice Login, Password, and Confirm Password fields that need to be filled in. After users fill them in, they click the OK button to submit this information. The code on this button calls a function to handle this process:

```
on (release) {
 _root.loginToSite(this.login, this.password);
}
```

You send the user-inputted login and password to the `loginToSite()` function, which takes care of processing the validity of the information. The code in this function is similar to the `newUser()` function you looked at earlier. Let's take a look at the differences:

```
function loginToSite(name, password){
    _root.postType = "verify";
    _root.loader.name = name;
    _root.loader.password = password;
    _root.username = name;
    _root.userpass = password;
    _root.loader.loadVariables("verify.php", "POST");
    cancelLogin();
}
```

The first line in the preceding code sets the postType value to verify, which is used in the loaderDispatch() function that's called when the variables are returned from the verify.php script loaded here. If you recall, these variables are loaded into the loader movieClip with an onClipEvent(data) event calling loaderDispatch().

You store the name and password again in the variables _root.username and _root.userpass so that they are available for the session and users need not enter this information every time they want to make a post. After the variables are loaded, you call cancelLogin(), which removes the loginMC from the stage.

Let's quickly take a look at the verify.php script to see what function it performs:

```
<?
/* This file (verify.php) is used to verify whether or not
   the user has provided a correct username/password.  */

$name = $HTTP_POST_VARS["name"];
$password = $HTTP_POST_VARS["password"];
// the above lines get all the necessary information name/pass check

include("db.inc.php");    //include the database libraries
dbconnect();              // connect to the database

$loggedIn = false;        // default to a false value for $loggedIn
if ((strlen($name) > 2) && (strlen($password) > 3)) {
//if the username and password are of acceptable length...
  if (count_rows("users", "name", $name) != 0) {
  //if there are users that match that username...
    if ($password == lookup("pass", "users", "name", $name)){
    /* if the provided password equals the one in the database...
    (see db.inc.php if you're wondering what lookup() is) */
        $loggedIn = true;   // note that the user is logged in
    }
  }
}
```

```
if ($loggedIn) {
   echo "loggedIn=true";
} else {
   echo "loggedIn=false";
}
/* In the above if-else blocks, you output the value of $loggedIn as text
   so that the loadVariables() call in Flash knows whether or not the
   user was accepted. */
?>
```

The PHP script returns the variable `loggedIn` to the loader `movieClip`, which then passes the variable off to `loaderDispatch()`. You can see how this is processed based on the `postType` value that was set. The `loaderDispatch()` function contains `if` statements for each possible `postType` value. Here is what you are concerned with:

```
if (_root.postType == "verify") {
     verify(_root.loader.loggedIn);
}
```

Although this `loggedIn` variable has just been echoed back to Flash, it has passed from the loader `movieClip` to the `loaderDispatch()` function and is then sent to be verified by the—you guessed it—`verify()` function. This is the final step in the verification process and is handled as such:

```
function verify(loggedIn){
    _root.loggedIn = (loggedIn == "true");
    if (!_root.loggedIn) {
        passwordError("Sorry. That login was rejected by the server.");
    } else {
        _root.verifiedMC._visible = true;
        cancelAccount();
    }
}
```

Here you have the function performing basically one of two actions. If the `loggedIn` value sent to the function is not equal to `true`, you call the `passwordError()` function with the argument `"Sorry. That login was rejected by the server."`. However, if the value is equal to `true`, you set the verifiedMC's `visible` property to `true`. This `movieClip` is located in the upper-right corner of the application and contains the static text LOGGED IN. Its purpose is to signal to users that they have successfully logged in.

Posting New Messages to the Message Board

Now that you have covered successful login to the message board as an existing member or by creating an account, you can finally explore the process of posting messages to the message board.

When a user clicks the postBTN and you call the showNewMsgWin() function, the loggedIn value will be set to true. Instead of being prompted with the loginMC, you will be prompted with the newMsgMC movieClip:

```
if (_root.loggedIn == true){
        _root.dialognum++;
        _root.dialogMC.attachMovie("newMsgMC", "newMsgMC",
➥       _root.dialogNum);
 }
```

This movieClip is used to submit posts to the message board and includes text fields for the user's subject and message, as you can see in Figure 7.8.

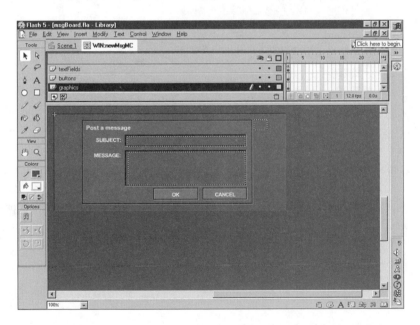

Figure 7.8 *The newMsgMC* movieClip *is responsible for submitting new messages to the board.*

This `movieClip` offers two options to the user: OK and Cancel. If the user chooses to click the Cancel button, you simply call the `cancelNewMsg()` function to remove the newMsgMC from the stage. However, if users do post messages, they will click the OK button, which contains the following action:

```
on (release) {
 _root.submit(subject, content, _root.replyThread);
}
```

Here you are sending along the user's `subject`, `content`, and `_root.replyThread` to the `submit()` function. If you recall, when you click the postBTN, it sets the `replyThread` value to `0` on `release()`, indicating that it is a new post. Now that you have finally submitted a new post, let's look at the meat of this operation in the `submit()` function:

```
function submit(subject, someContent, aReplyNumber) {
  _root.postType = "postmsg";
  _root.loader.name = _root.username;
  _root.loader.password = _root.userpass;
  _root.loader.subject = subject;
  _root.loader.content = someContent;
  _root.loader.replynumber = aReplyNumber;
  _root.loader.loadVariables("postmsg.php", "POST");
  cancelNewMsg();
}
```

This function basically stacks the loader `movieClip` with variables to be processed by the PHP script. You pass the `_root.username` and `_root.userpass` variables so that the script knows you are a member of the message board. You then transfer the `subject` and `content` variables to the loader as well. Also note that you have set the `postType` variable equal to `postmsg`, which will affect processing by `loaderDispatch()` when variables are returned from the PHP script.

So what does the postmsg.php script do with these variables? Let's take a look:

```
<?
/* This file (postmsg.php) is used to post a message from Flash to the
   database.  */

$name = $HTTP_POST_VARS["name"];
$password = $HTTP_POST_VARS["password"];
$subject = $HTTP_POST_VARS["subject"];
$content = $HTTP_POST_VARS["content"];
$replynumber = $HTTP_POST_VARS["replynumber"];
// the above lines get all the necessary information for the message
```

```
include("db.inc.php");    //include the database libraries
dbconnect();              // connect to the database

$loggedIn = false;        // default to a false value for $loggedIn
if ((strlen($name) > 2) && (strlen($password) > 3)) {
//if the username and password are of acceptable length...
  if (count_rows("users", "name", $name) != 0) {
  //if there are users that match that username...
    if ($password == lookup("pass", "users", "name", $name)){
    /* if the provided password equals the one in the database...
       (see db.inc.php if you're wondering what lookup() is) */
       $loggedIn = true;          // note that the user is logged in
       add_message(lookup("id", "users", "name", $name), db_date(),
                   $subject, $content, $replynumber);
       /* add the message to the database (db_date() is in db.inc.php
          if you want to see its implementation). */
    }
  }
}

if ($loggedIn) {
  echo "loggedIn=true";
} else {
  echo "loggedIn=false";
}
/* In the above if-else blocks, you output the value of $loggedIn as text
   so that the loadVariables() call in Flash knows whether or not the
   user was allowed to submit the message. */
?>
```

After the PHP script returns the variables to the loader movieClip, the loaderDispatch() function is automatically called. Because you set the postType variable to postmsg earlier, the following code runs from within loaderDispatch():

```
if (_root.postType == "postmsg") {
    _root.linkdata.load("msgbrd.php?r="+(new
    Date().getTime().toString()));
  }
```

This if statement, confirming postmsg, reloads the msgbrd.php script into the XML object. This script, covered previously in the "Loading Message Board Content into Flash via PHP/ASP" section, returns the posts in the message board as XML to the linkdata XML object. Of course, just like any XML.load(), you will have the custom onLoad() handler called that in turn calls the displayNodes() function and refreshes and redisplays all the posts.

There is still one other way to post messages—through a reply to a previously posted message.

Posting a Reply Message to the Message Board

When posting a reply, the only difference from submitting a new post is identifying the `replyThread` value. To post a reply, the user must click on the replyBTN button that is attached to every attached nodeMC `movieClip`, as shown in Figure 7.9.

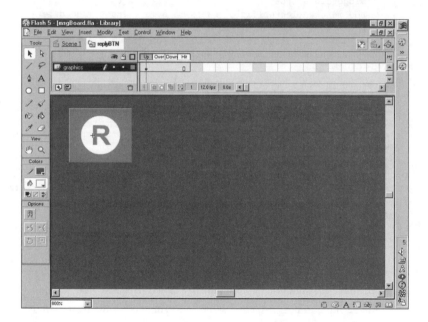

Figure 7.9   *The replyBTN is used to post replies to currently available threads on the message board.*

Clicking on this button will call the following actions:

```
on (release) {
    _root.replyThread = this.replyThread;
    _root.showNewMsgWin();
}
```

As you can see, you call the same function that the postBTN calls if you are logged in: showNewMsgWin(). However, you also set _root.replyThread equal to the value of the particular nodeMC's replyThread. If you remember, you set this dynamically when you perform the displayNodes() function:

```
entryHolderMC["nodeMC"+nodeNum].replyThread = this.attributes.id;
```

By using this replyThread value, you can use that information when you submit to the PHP script. The script will pass the value on to the database so that the newly inserted message has a reference to the message it is replying to. This is absolutely necessary to correctly create the XML from the database later because the childNodes of a given message are all the replied messages that have its id as their replyid.

Summary

Whew. You've just stepped through the most advanced example yet. You've incorporated a *lot* of stuff here. As complicated as this example may be, you'll see how we continue to use similar elements and functions from previous examples. The more you get accustomed to developing with XML, the more you will begin to see that it becomes more about the XML. Handling it inside Flash becomes somewhat rote. You'll find that a lot of the work goes into structuring your XML properly and spending time inside functions such as displayNodes(), which is responsible for passing the XML information into movieClips and controlling how these movieClips are laid out.

So What's Next?

Now that we've exhausted a whole host of examples and applications in Flash, it's time to tweak! We're talking performance issues and optimization. In the next chapter you are going to cover a number of methods and techniques to further speed up your XML processing. Flash is known for having a pig of a parser, and you're going to create some custom parsers to increase speed and performance in Flash. You'll test loadVariables() versus XML.load() in a speed-test cage match. You'll tackle the enemy whitespace by writing some custom ActionScript functions and explore server-side whitespace strippers that can greatly enhance performance. It's time to roll up your sleeves and get dirty!

{ Chapter 8 }

Performance and Optimization

As with everything else you do when building for the Web, you must optimize, optimize, optimize. Although we are all racing toward true global broadband, the reality is that it's just not here yet. There are many areas of the world (including parts of North America and most of Europe) where the Internet is not available with a connection faster than a 56KB modem. The last thing these users want is an excessive load or delay in their surfing experience, which makes optimization essential.

If you're familiar with Flash, you know all about optimization, from optimizing bitmap or vector art to the intelligent use and reuse of symbols to the streamlining of code. All these elements are part of the optimization process. However, in this chapter you are going to focus strictly on the optimization and performance of your XML. Whether you are pulling XML in or spitting it out, there are ways and techniques to maximize and streamline this process.

Performance Problems

Before we start digging into examples and speed tests between different processes, we'll discuss some of XML's inherent performance problems. These are inherent problems that we have no power against, but you should be aware of their effect on performance.

Bloated Tags

A general performance issue, slight as it may be, is that the tags are somewhat bloated. A simple XML structure might be as follows:

```
<book>
    <title>XML in Flash</title>
    <author>Gregg Caines</author>
    <author>Craig Swann</author>
    <publisher>Sams</publisher>
</book>
```

Although the XML specification for well-formedness states that you need to have proper closing tags, the same information could easily be conveyed without repeating the element names in the closing tag. The same document could also be displayed as shown here:

```
<book>
    <title>XML in Flash<//>
    <author>Gregg Caines<//>
    <author>Craig Swann<//>
    <publisher>Sams<//>
</>
```

We still have all the same information; all we have done is not include the element name in the closing tag. As minute as this might seem, in large XML documents, you could considerably reduce character count. This would result in smaller file sizes and ultimately quicker parsing. Although this is fantasyland and there is nothing we can do about the XML standard, it is one instance of an XML performance issue.

Another issue that could have been addressed in the XML specification to increase performance is the addition of lookup tables to handle similar element names. Longer element and attribute names slow down the parsing, even though it may be very slight. If you look at the following XML structure taken from slashdot.org, you can see how to cut down further on byte size by referencing a lookup table. Every <story> element has the same subelements, all of which take up byte size in the XML document:

```
<story>
  <title>How PDAs Intersect With School</title>
  <url>http://slashdot.org/article.pl?sid=01/08/23/2056230</url>
  <time>2001-08-23 20:58:41</time>
  <author>timothy</author>
  <department>from-a-special-correspondent</department>
```

```
    <topic>146</topic>
    <comments>25</comments>
    <section>articles</section>
    <image>topiced.gif</image>
</story>
```

Instead, with the use of a lookup table, you could create something like this:

```
Lookuptable:
1: story
2: title
3: url
4: time
5: author
6: department
7: topic
8: comments
9: section
10: image
```

The corresponding XML would look like this:

```
<1>
    <2>How PDAs Intersect With School</2>
    <3>http://slashdot.org/article.pl?sid=01/08/23/2056230</3>
    <4>2001-08-23 20:58:41</4>
    <5>timothy</5>
    <6>from-a-special-correspondent</6>
    <7>146</7>
    <8>25</8>
    <9>articles</9>
    <10>topiced.gif</10>
</1>
```

Again, although it might seem trivial, when using large documents, you would be reducing the document's file size and speeding up the parsing time needed to go through each element. Although there is nothing we can do to change the way XML is structured, it's worthwhile to acknowledge these setbacks.

Total Freeze

The number-one performance issue you run across when importing XML into Flash is narcolepsy of the playhead. When Flash begins to parse XML, the playhead stops, and your movie completely freezes. We're talking *total freeze* here. This means even if you have a looping animation `movieClip` on stage, it, too, will completely freeze until Flash is finished parsing the XML.

Playback freeze can be a big problem. If you do not explain to your users what's happening, they are likely to think there has been some sort of crash because the Flash movie is not responding to any interaction and all animations have ceased to run on stage. How do you get around this problem? Well, you could write a new parser, which would be spread out over frames. However, that still doesn't allow continuous interaction with the site because you're still parsing continuously—just in smaller chunks spread over frames. Another solution is sending the XML from the server side in smaller chunks if you are using an initially large XML document.

Being aware that Flash does in fact freeze when parsing through XML data means you can prepare your users for this problem. You can, for example, inform them with an onscreen message that information is being processed, or simply attach a `movieClip` to the stage before you call your XML and then remove it when the parsing is done by using `onLoad()`. For small XML documents, you probably will not notice the freeze, but it could be noticeable if the document is large or the user is on a particularly slow system.

`loadVariables()` Versus `XML.load()`: The Cage Match

Since version 4 of Flash has been on the shelves, we've all been using the `loadVariables()` method to draw data dynamically into our Flash applications and movies. With the advent of version 5, there has been much debate as to whether `loadVariables()` or `XML.load()` should be used. Generally, XML is most powerful when working with nested data or hierarchical/relational data structures. However, `XML.load()` still remains an excellent method for pulling in and sending out simpler data.

We'll attempt to destroy any myths about the most efficient way to bring data into the Flash environment. Each method has its place, and you can use either one, whichever is your preference. As you'll soon see, however, knowing is half the battle.

The `loadVariables()` Speed Test

First, let's begin with the standard `loadVariables()` command and import some dynamic data. It's time to crank open Flash and start plunking in some code.

You're going to create a movieClip that outputs the speed results to a dynamic text field on stage. First, select the first frame and open the Actions panel. Make sure you are in Expert mode by pressing Ctrl+E (Apple+E on a Macintosh). Insert the following code:

```
starttime=getTimer();
myMC.loadVariables("test.txt", this);
```

This code merely sets a beginning time value and then loads the test file into a movieClip named myMC. This file can be downloaded from http://www. xmlinflash.com, in the speedTest folder in the Chapter 8 directory. The test.txt. file you're using contains the following name/value pairs:

```
var1=value1&var2=value2&var3=value3&var4=value4&var5=value5&var6=value6&
➥var7=value7&var8=value8
```

Of course, now you'll need a myMC movieClip to do this loading, so create a simple movieClip somewhere on the stage (we used a simple blue box). Make sure you give your movieClip an instance name of "myMC" by filling in the name field on the instance palette. Now click on your newly created myMC, open the ActionScript window for it (Ctrl+Alt+A or Apple+Option+A), and insert the following code:

```
onClipEvent(data) {
    endtime = getTimer();
   trace(endtime - _root.starttime);
   trace("var1 is "+this.var1);
}
```

In this frame, you are creating an event handler that checks whether test.txt has fully been loaded. After the document has been successfully imported with the loadVariables() action, you perform your speed test by calculating totalTime: Subtract the starttime value from the current getTimer() value.

When you test the movie now, you'll see the time that loading takes to complete displayed in the Output window, along with a sample of the data it loaded in (var1, in this case). If you test a few more times, you'll see that the results fluctuate slightly. Used on a 600MHz PC machine, we got results of approximately 67ms to finish loading the text file. As we move on, you might want to jot down your results so that you can compare them to the rest of the tests we will run.

Keep in mind that you'll want to perform these tests on a local machine, not from a Web server over a network connection. A network connection is certainly closer to the reality of your Web applications, but network conditions can vary so much that testing would not be very useful.

So now that you have calculated the performance of the loadVariables() action, open a new file and get ready to knock out your first XML.load() test.

The XML.load() Speed Test

Before you insert any code, take a look at your source file for this performance test, which is in the same directory as the previous text file. The XML file testelem.xml contains the following data:

```
<data><var1>value1</var1><var2>value2</var2><var3>value3</var3>
➥<var4>value4</var4><var5>value5</var5><var6>value6</var6>
➥<var7>value7</var7><var8>value8</var8></data>
```

In your newly created Flash file, go to the Actions panel and insert the following code (which is also commented here to explain what is going on):

```
starttime=getTimer();            // store the startTime of your test
x = new xml();                   //create a new XML object named 'x'
x.onLoad = function(success) {
  /* create a custom callback handler to be called when the
     XML document is successfully imported into Flash */
  kidNum = this.firstChild.childNodes.length;
  /* set 'kidNum' to the number of childNodes in your
  XML document (children of <data> */
  for (var i = 0; i <  kidNum; i++) {
    _root[this.firstChild.childNodes[i].nodeName] =
➥this.firstChild.childNodes[i].firstChild.nodeValue;
    /* create variables named after childNode (element)
    names and set their values equal to their nodeValues */
  }
  endtime = getTimer();          //once loop is complete, get your
➥'endTime'
  trace(endtime-starttime);      //output time taken
  trace("var8 is "+_root.var8);  //output sample data
}

x.load("testelem.xml");          //load the XML
```

No movieClip is necessary with XML.load(), so you can simply drop this code into your first frame, and you'll be reading XML right away. With loadVariables(), this isn't possible. It's certainly possible to use

loadVariables() without an extra movieClip, but in that case you can't use
onClipEvent(data), so you are forced to use some kind of frame loop to keep
checking whether your variables are loaded. This is indeed possible, and many
people do it, but unless you have a high frame rate on your movie, frame loops
slow it down considerably. Ultimately, if you want to use loadVariables() and
have optimal performance from it, you'll need to create an extra movieClip for
the onClipEvent(data) action.

Now test your new XML.load() movie. Running on the same system as our previous example, we received speed values of approximately 94ms to import our data
via XML. This means our XML.load() action occurs in 1/10th of a second, only
30ms slower than the equivalent loadVariables() test. That's pretty darn
impressive!

Keep in mind that with this XML example, we can do everything in _root and
don't require the additional movieClip to control the loading, as we do with
loadVariables(). It's also somewhat of an unfair comparison to test name/value
pairs, as in the loadVariables() example, against the semi-nested data structures
of the XML.load() example. It seems, though, that loadVariables() is faster.

But wait...there's more! Information can be transferred via XML in a number of
ways, and one of the most effective ways is to use attributes as much as possible.
We've discovered that XML in Flash is handled much more quickly when access-
ing attribute values instead of elements, primarily because each element requires
Flash to create a new XMLNode, and the XMLNode constructor is one of the slowest.
So let's give this one more try by structuring the data in an attribute-based model.

The XML.load() Speed Test Using Attribute Values

Before you start coding this speed test, first take a look at a file, in the same
directory as the other data files, called testattr.xml:

```
<data var1='value1' var2='value2' var3='value3' var4='value4'
➥var5='value5' var6='value6' var7='value7' var8='value8' />
```

You can easily see that you still have the same eight variables matching your initial loadVariables() data, but notice the difference between this and the previous XML file. Here, instead of creating separate elements for each piece of data,
we are including them as attribute values inside one single-tagged, empty element named <data>.

Now let's set up some code to read this XML in and see what kind of speed you can get! In Frame 1 of a newly created Flash file, enter the following code in the Actions panel (keep in mind we are placing comments here for illustrative purposes; you can omit them in your file):

```
starttime=getTimer();      // set your 'startTime' value
x = new xml();             // extend the onLoad handler with custom func-
tion
x.onLoad = function(success) {
  /* create a loop to grab attribute values and place them into new
➥ variables */
  for (var i in this.firstChild.attributes) {
    _root[i] = this.firstChild.attributes[i];
  }

  endtime = getTimer();   // grab your endTime value
  trace(endtime-starttime);          //output time taken
  trace("var1 is "+_root.var1);      //output sample data
}

x.load("testattr.xml");   // load the XML!
```

After you have that script entered, you can test your movie and see what kind of speeds are generated.

Wow, 44ms! That's actually slightly faster than the loadVariables() example, contrary to popular belief.

If you take a look at Figure 8.1, you can see a chart displaying the load times using three different methods. Based on the chart, the most efficient way of importing this data is through the XML attributes method.

We've also included an additional test on the Web site that gives a nicely formatted version of the performance tests on loadVariables() and XML.load(). We won't go into describing it in detail here, but this test performs five tests on each method and provides the output in an easier-to-digest format. There are high, low, and mean average values for both methods, just to show how they compare. As you can see from the results in Figure 8.2, XML.load() came out on top in a sampling of five tests.

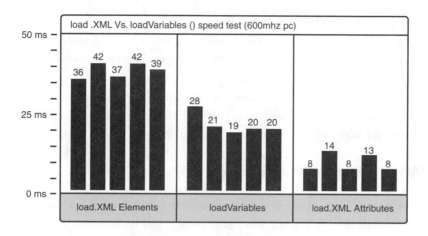

Figure 8.1   *The* loadVariables() *method versus XML elements versus XML attributes.*

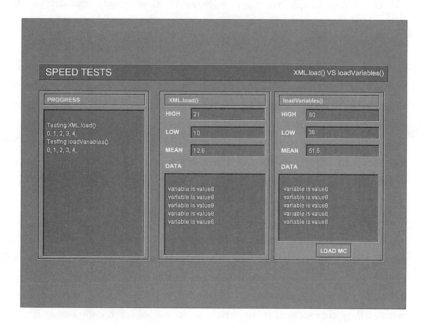

Figure 8.2   *The* loadVariables() *method versus* XML.load()*, with five tests each.*

A number of issues affect these results, so it's not really as cut-and-dried as it seems here. We've found that factors in the FLA, such as the graphical background and using dynamic text fields instead of trace(), have a strange adverse effect on the performance of loadVariables() (but not XML.load()!). Also, as you increase the number of tests, the mean average of loadVariables() gets faster. These are just details, but something to keep in mind. Normal server-side loading from a Flash movie would probably be necessary less than five times in a single load of an SWF. You might find you have more demanding needs, in which case loadVariables() could be better on average. In that case, it's probably best to do your own performance tests. Either way, grab the speedTest.fla from the Web site and see the results for yourself.

Whitespace Handling

One of the biggest barriers to XML efficiency when using Flash is our good old friend whitespace. You see, whitespace is our friend because with it we can lay out XML documents in a nice visual format that can be easily read and understood by us lowly humans. However, the Flash parser sees this whitespace a little differently. Until Flash player release 5.0r42, whitespace was dealt with awkwardly. With this release, though, came the ignoreWhite property, so we could happily chug along with our beautifully displayed XML documents.

Whitespace is a trade-off. Although you can strip or ignore whitespace from your XML documents, there is no denying that this process requires CPU cycles and will ultimately affect the performance of rendering your XML. However, without it, reading and comprehending the data structure is difficult. When dealing with programmers, producers, managers, and designers, it is important that your XML retain its readability to ensure open lines of communication between all team members.

Server-Side Whitespace Stripping

So, if you are going to create your XML documents using whitespace, there are several things you can do to make parsing more efficient in Flash. First, we will look at *server-side stripping*, which means passing off all whitespace removal to the server. Generally, server-side operations are quicker than client-side ones because they are executed more closely to the machine's real processor than client-side scripts are, which are executed through the browser. We are going to look at this technique using two of the most widely used middleware languages: PHP and ASP.

Before we just dump the code on you, though, it's probably best to describe the general algorithm in simple English. If you understand how it works, you'll be in a better position to read through the code and follow along with our comments.

You certainly don't need to understand these languages to use them, though. If your server supports ASP or PHP, you simply drop the appropriate script in your Flash directory and make all your `XML.load()` methods request your example.xml document, like this:

```
myXML.load("whiteout.php?filename=example.xml");
```

or

```
myXML.load("whiteout.asp?filename=example.xml");
```

It's that simple. Your whitespace-enhanced example.xml document will be automatically converted to a super-lean, whitespace-stripped version for Flash.

If you're interested, here's how it works:

1. Retrieve the filename from the query string. If a filename is specified, continue to step 2. Nothing happens if no filename is specified. Because there is no error-checking here, it's important that you make sure you are requesting a filename that exists, and the file is indeed available at the given path (if you've provided a path). You can verify this by opening your browser and entering the URL to the script with the same `filename` information appended in the query string, as shown here:

   ```
   http://www.yourdomain.com/exampledir/whiteout.php?filename=example.xml
   ```

   After the page loads, you should check it out by viewing the source. Verify that your document is indeed there, and it's stripped of whitespace as you would expect.

2. Read that file into a big string.

3. Strip the whitespace from the string, according to the rules of XML. This is a complicated process, but we'll explain it. It's important to understand that you can't just simply remove all the spaces, carriage returns, and so forth. These characters should only be removed between tags where no other character data exists. For now, just assume that you have such a function, and it works.

4. Return the string to the requesting browser. This is the easy part. You simply use `echo()` or `response.write()` with the string (depending on your language of choice).

As we said, the only non-trivial aspect of this algorithm is the `whiteOut()` function. If you want to understand its inner workings, you'll quickly see that we use a recursive algorithm, much as we did in ActionScript. The reason we use recursive algorithms is because they are a fairly intuitive and elegant way to deal with strings, too. There are limits to recursive algorithms, though, and in our development of these scripts, we saw those limits quite clearly. The problem is that when a function calls itself, and waits for input from itself, the computer must keep track of that waiting function. When the inner function call eventually returns, the computer must be able to continue with the original function call so that it can return to normal program execution. When a function calls itself eight or nine times, each of those function calls must reside in memory, waiting for the later one to return. This process is taxing on the system, whether it's Linux, Windows NT/2000, or some other platform. In our original attempts, neither PHP on Linux or ASP on Windows NT/2000 could handle a simple 25KB XML file. There were just too many recursive function calls.

The workaround was fairly simple, although perhaps more complex than we had hoped. Here's the basic algorithm for `whiteOut()`:

1. Take the string of XML and divide it into relatively equal portions (about 500 bytes each). The string is always divided by the next open bracket (<), rather than exactly on the 500th character, to make it easier to strip the whitespace later. It's important to make this distinction because you wouldn't want to strip the whitespace from a tag.

2. Add each 500-byte chunk to an array.

3. Go through and strip the whitespace from each element by using your `stripWhite()` function. This is another function call, and obviously it's not a trivial one. We'll get into that `stripWhite()` function next, but for now, just assume that it exists and does the job you need it to do.

4. Concatenate all the array elements into a large string of whitespace-stripped XML that represents your original document.

These 500-byte chunks are much easier on memory-hungry recursive functions. The only problem now is the `stripWhite()` function needed to strip the white-space correctly. Here's how it works: Take a string of characters that may or may not be a full XML document (remember, we're taking semi-random 500-byte chunks!), and test where the first open bracket (<) occurs.

If the location was the first character, you know you are starting with a tag. If not, you know this string starts with some kind of character data (maybe white-space, maybe not!).

From here, you must choose whether you continue with it as a tag or as text. We'll explain the steps for tags first:

1. Find the location of the closing bracket (>) for this tag. It's possible that the closing bracket is the next > in the string, but that's not necessarily the case. In DTDs or CDATA, multiple > characters can exist before the real closing bracket.

2. You know the starting and ending points for this tag, so you attempt to strip the whitespace from them. DTDs and CDATA are treated specially by leaving their internals completely intact. However, if it's just a regular node, replace all non-space whitespace characters with spaces. That way, line breaks in the middle of a tag are automatically fixed.

3. You have cleared that tag of all unnecessary whitespace, so you return it along with the result of `stripWhite()` on the text that exists after that tag. Yes, this is a recursive call. The remaining text will be put back through this same function.

If that remaining text is actual text data from a text node, it needs to be stripped in a different way. Here's the algorithm for text data:

1. If the first character is not an opening bracket, you know you are dealing with a text node; you just don't know whether it's all whitespace. So take that string, from the beginning to the first open bracket (<), and check to see whether it's all whitespace or not.

2. If it *is* all whitespace, you return the result of `stripWhite()` on the remaining text. If it isn't all whitespace, you return that text, concatenated with the result of `stripWhite()` on the remaining text. These are also recursive function calls, of course, and they both serve to further strip the unnecessary whitespace. If a string does not contain another open bracket for another tag, the recursion stops; this is your terminating condition. Eventually, every XML document will come to an empty string or a string of all whitespace at the end for which no further stripping is required.

So that's pretty much it. It is more complicated than we would like it to be, but it certainly makes whitespace stripping a lot easier, if your server supports one of these languages. For the most part, the two languages are fairly similar, although PHP seems to have better array support (there is a "push," just as in ActionScript) than VBScript. (If you're really keen, you can write up a JScript version for ASP, too. We'd certainly love to see it!) Feel free to peruse these two heavily commented pieces of code to see exactly how these algorithms are implemented in both PHP (Listing 8.1) and ASP (Listing 8.2).

Listing 8.1   PHP Stripper

```
<?
/* This script is written specifically for PHP 4.  PHP 3 and earlier do
   not access strings using PHP 4's curly brace syntax.
   There may be other issues as well.
```

Listing 8.1   continued

```
The XML has its whitespace stripped as a string.  Use it for whatever
purpose you see fit.
*/



function fileRead($filename) {
  /*This function takes a filename as input and returns the contents of it
    as a string */
  $fp = fopen($filename, "r");
  $contents = fread ($fp, filesize ($filename));
  fclose ($fp);
  return($contents);
}



function replaceCharAt($str, $i, $char) {
   //replace a character at specified index (i) with another character
   $str = substr ($str, 0, $i) . $char . substr ($str, $i+1,
➥strlen($str));
  return ($str);
}



function replaceChars($str, $inchar, $outchar) {
  //replaces all instance of $inchar with $outchar
  $found = true;
  while ($found) {
     $pos = strpos ($str, $inchar);
     if ($pos === false) {$found = false;}
        else {
            $str = replaceCharAt($str, $pos, $outchar);
            }
   }
  return($str);
}



  function killBaddies($s, $char){
    /*This function replaces all occurrences of carriage returns, line feeds,
     null characters, vertical tabs, and horizontal tabs (non-space
     whitespace) in the input string 's' with the character 'char'. */
    $s = replaceChars($s, "\n", $char); $s = replaceChars($s, "\r", $char);
    $s = replaceChars($s, "\v", $char); $s = replaceChars($s, "\0", $char);
    return($s);
  }
```

Listing 8.1   continued

```
function nextLT($str) {
  /*get the index of the next open bracket, "<", or return -1, if
    none exist in the string*/
  $retVal = -1;
  if (strlen($str) != 0) {
      for ($i = 0; $i < strlen($str);$i++) {
      if ($str{$i} == "<") {$retVal = $i;break;}
      }
  }
  return($retVal);
}
```

```
function getClosingBracket($str) {
  /*This function takes a string 'str' as input and finds the
    closing bracket '>' in the string.  What this means is
    that if you have a leading '<', you're looking for the '>'
    that closes it.  In most cases, it's a simple case of
    finding the NEXT '>', but in some cases, there are subsequent
    open brackets, which need a closing bracket before you search
    again for the closing bracket you need.

    The algorithm you use is simple.  For every occurrence of '<'
    in the string, you increment the count of '<' by one.  Right
    away, you should get an open bracket, and you loop through each
    character, incrementing the count for each open bracket and
    decrementing it for each closing bracket, until the count is
    back to 0, or the entire string has been cycled through.  The
    variable 'pos' hold your current position.  If the count returns
    to 0, then you know you have found the closing bracket, and you
    cut out of the loop automatically.  By cutting out of the loop
    automatically, the variable 'pos' holds the position of the
    closing bracket, so you return that value.  If, on the other
    hand, the closing bracket is not found, you return the value
    'null'*/

  $count = 0;                                   // set count to 0
  for ($pos = 0;$pos < strlen($str); $pos++){   /* go through the
                                                   string from the
                                                   first char to
                                                   the last */

    if ($str{$pos} == "<") { $count++; }        /* If you found a
                                                   '<', increment */

    if ($str{$pos} == ">") { $count--; }        /* If you found a
                                                   '>', increment */

    if ($count == 0) { break;  }                // If count is 0, exit
  }
```

Listing 8.1   continued

```
    if ($count == 0) {                      /* If you found a
                                               closing bracket, */
      return ($pos);                        // return its position
    } else {
      return (null);                        /* otherwise,
                                               return 'null' */

    }
  }




function stripWhite($aString) {
  /*This function uses a semi-complex algorithm to strip the
    whitespace from a string that may or may not be a complete
    XML document.  The string could start with character data
    or some other XML tag, and you have to strip the whitespace
    accordingly.  The input string is 'aString'. */
  $LTloc = nextLT($aString);                 /* Record the location of
                                                the first open bracket
                                                in the string */

  if (($LTloc==0) && (!($LTloc === false))) { /* If the location was the
                                                first character, you are
                                                starting with a tag */

    $index = getClosingBracket($aString);    /* Record the location of
                                                the closing bracket */
    if (substr($aString, 0, 2) == "<!") {    // if it's a DTD or CDATA...
      $aString = substr($aString, 0, $index+1).
➥stripWhite(substr($aString, $index+1, strlen($aString)));
          /*  you simply trim spaces off the front and back of the CDATA
              or DTD areas, and leave the internals completely intact.
              You then return that value with the white-stripped version
              of the remaining portion of the string.  This is a
              recursive call here because you are calling stripWhite()
              again. */
    } else {                                // otherwise, it's a regular tag...
      $aString = killBaddies(substr($aString, 0, $index+1), " ").
➥stripWhite(substr($aString, $index+1, strlen($aString)));
          /*  you replace all bad characters (carriage returns, line feeds,
              null characters, horizontal tabs, and vertical tabs) inside
              the tag itself with plain old spaces.  You return that new
              tag with the remainder of the string, white-stripped and
              concatenated onto the end.  This too is a recursive call
              because you are calling stripWhite() again.  */
    }
  } else {                                  /* if no opening bracket is found,
                                               it's text... */
    $aString = trim($aString);              /* strip off leading and trailing
                                               spaces */
```

Listing 8.1   continued

```
    if (strlen($aString) != 0) {    // if the string is still not empty....
        $ltpos = nextLT($aString);   /* find the location of the first open
                                        bracket */
        if ($ltpos == -1) {          // if no open bracket exists...
            $aString = trim(killBaddies($aString,""));
                /* trim the leading and trailing spaces off and remove all
                    the bad characters from thestring.  This is not a
                    recursive call because there is no further work to be
                    done.  Thisis what's called your terminating condition,
                    because eventually you will end up with a 'character data'
                    -only string (in the end, it will be an empty string), and
                    this will terminate the recursion.   */
        } else {                     //if there is an opening bracket...
            $parsed = trim(killBaddies(substr ($aString, 0, $ltpos),""));
                /* trim the leading and trailing spaces and remove all the
                    bad characters from the text portion of the string. */
            $toParse = stripWhite(substr($aString, $ltpos, strlen($aString)));
                /* Create a whitespace-stripped version of the rest of
                    the string (which  starts with your tag).  Again,
                    this is a recursive call for that portionof the string.
                    You can imagine that it will register as a tag and be
                    stripped that way in the next level of recursion. */
            $aString = $parsed.$toParse;
                // Concatenate the two strings and return the string's new value
        }
    } else {$aString = "";}
  }
  return($aString);
}




function whiteOut($str) {
/*  This function takes a string of XML and divides it into relatively
    equal portions (500 bytes each).  The string is always divided by
    the next open bracket '<', rather than exactly on the 500th
    character, because the whitespace stripper works only with strings
    started with text data or XML tags.  It's important to make this
    distinction because you wouldn't want to strip the whitespace out
    of a tag.  Each 500-byte chunk is added to an array, and later you
    go through the array and strip the whitespace from each element
    using your stripWhite() function.  The array elements are then
    concatenated into a large string of whitespace-stripped XML that
    represents your original document.  You strip using 500-byte chunks
    because large strings can quickly bog PHP down.  Because you use
    recursion, a lot of memory is used keeping track of each level of
    recursion until the terminating condition executes and the
    functions are all completed.  If you tried that on a huge string of
    XML, there would be so many functions running that you would get an
```

__Listing 8.1   continued__

```
    error from PHP.  Stripping 500 bytes at a time is much more
    economical on function call overhead, so you can process much
    larger XML files. */
$chunksize = 500;                            /* set the chunksize
                                                to 500 */

$finished = "";                              /* the finished
                                                string is
                                                currently empty */

$chunkArray = array();
if (strlen($str) > $chunksize) {             /* if the string is
                                                bigger than the
                                                chunksize... */

  $index = strpos($str, "<", $chunksize);    /* find the first
                                                open bracket */

} else {                                     /* otherwise, there
                                                is no need to
                                                break it up */

  $index = false;
}
if ($index === false) {$index = false;}
while ($index) {                             /* while you are
                                                breaking it
                                                up.... */

  array_push($chunkArray, substr($str, 0, $index)); /* put the new
                                                chunk into the
                                                new array
                                                position */

  $str = substr($str, $index, strlen($str)); /* put the unparsed
                                                portion of the
                                                string into
                                                str */

  if (strlen($str) > $chunksize) {           /* if you still
                                                need to break
                                                off 500-byte
                                                chunks... */

      $index = strpos($str, "<", $chunksize); /* find the next
                                                open bracket */

  } else {
      break;                                 /* otherwise, quit
                                                breaking up the
                                                string   */

  }
  if ($index === false) {break;}
}
array_push($chunkArray, $str);               /* add the last
                                                chunk to the
                                                array   */

for ($i = 0;$i < sizeOf($chunkArray);$i++) { /* cycle through
                                                the array */
```

Listing 8.1   continued

```
    $chunkArray[$i] = stripWhite($chunkArray[$i]);    /* strip the
                                                         whitespace off
                                                         each element
                                                         of the array */
    $finished .= $chunkArray[$i];                     /* concatenate
                                                         all the stripped
                                                         text into one
                                                         variable called
                                                         finished.*/

  }
  return($finished);
}




// ======================= M A I N   C O D E =========================
$filename = $HTTP_GET_VARS["filename"];    /* get the filename from
                                              the query string.  This
                                              means that you call this
                                              page as
                    www.yourdomain.com/whiteout.asp?filename=yourxml.xml */
if ($filename != "") {                      // If you supplied a filename...
  $xDoc = fileRead($filename);              // read the file
  $xDoc = whiteOut($xDoc);                  // strip its whitespace
  echo $xDoc;                               // write it to the browser
}
?>
```

Listing 8.2   ASP Stripper

```
<%
  ' This script is written to be usable without having to install
  ' MS XML on the server.  The XML has its whitespace stripped as
  ' a string.  Use it for whatever purpose you see fit.



  function fileRead(filename)
    'This function takes a filename as input and returns the
    'contents of it as a string
    Dim objFSO, fp
    Set objFSO = CreateObject("Scripting.FileSystemObject")
    set fp = objFSO.OpenTextFile(Server.MapPath(filename))
    do while not fp.atEndOfStream
      Dim contents = contents & fp.readline & vbcrlf
    loop
    fp.close
    set fp = nothing
```

Listing 8.2   continued

```
   set objFSO = nothing
   fileRead = contents
end Function
```

```
function killBaddies(str, char)
   'This function replaces all occurrences of carriage returns, line feeds,
   'null characters, vertical tabs, and horizontal tabs (non-space
   'whitespace) in the input string 'str' with the character 'char'.
   str = replace(str, chr(10), char)
   str = replace(str, chr(13), char)
   str = replace(str, chr(11), char)
   str = replace(str, chr(0), char)
   str = replace(str, chr(9), char)
   killBaddies = str
end Function
```

```
function getClosingBracket(str)
   'This function takes a string 'str' as input and finds the closing
   'bracket '>' in the string.  What this means is that if you have a
   'leading '<', you're looking for the '>' that closes it.  In most
   'cases, it's a simple case of finding the NEXT '>', but in some
   'cases, there are subsequent open brackets, which need a closing
   'bracket
   'before you search again for the closing bracket you need.

   'The algorithm you use is simple.  For every occurrence of '<' in
   'the string, you increment the count of '<' by one.  Right away,
   'you should get an open bracket and you loop through 'each character,
   'incrementing the count for each open bracket and decrementing it for
   'each closing bracket, until the count is back to 0, or the entire
   'string has been cycled through.  The variable 'pos' holds your
   'current position.  If the count returns to 0, then you know you have
   'found the closing bracket, and you cut out of the loop automatically.
   'By cutting out of the loop automatically, the variable 'pos' holds
   'the position of the closing bracket, so you return that value.  If,
   'on the other hand, the closing bracket is not found, you return the
   'value 'null'.
   dim Count, pos
   count = 0                                         ' set count to 0
   for pos = 1 to len(str)                 ' go through the string from
                                           ' the 1st char to the last
       if (Mid(str,pos,1) = "<") then count = count + 1     ' If you found
                                                            ' a '<' increment
       if (Mid(str,pos,1) = ">") then count = count - 1     ' If you found
                                                            ' a '>' increment
```

Listing 8.2   continued

```
      if (count = 0) then exit for        ' If count is 0,
                                          ' exit
   next
   if (count = 0) then                    ' If you found a
                                          ' closing bracket,
      getClosingBracket = pos             ' return its
                                          ' position
   else
      getClosingBracket = null            'otherwise,
                                          'return 'null'
   end if
end Function




function stripWhite(aString)
   'This function uses a semi-complex algorithm to strip the
   'whitespace from a string that may or may not be a
   'complete XML document.  The string could start with character
   'data or some other XML tag, and you have to strip the whitespace
   'accordingly.  The input string is 'aString'.

   dim index, LTloc, ltpos, parsed, toparse
   LTloc = inStr(aString, "<")            'Record the location of the
                                          'first open bracket in the string
   if (LTloc=1) then                      'If the location was the first
                                          'character, you are starting
                                          'with a tag.
      index = getClosingBracket(aString)  'Record the location of the
                                          'closing bracket
      if (isNull(index)) then index = 1   'If there is no closing bracket,
                                          'you note that it shouldn't be
                                          'stripped.
      if (Mid(aString, 1, 2) = "<!")  then 'If it's a DTD or CDATA...
         aString = trim(Mid(aString, 1, index+1)) &
➥ stripWhite(Mid(aString, index+1, Len(aString)))
                        'you simply trim spaces off the front and back of the
                        'CDATA or DTD areas, and leave the internals completely
                        'intact.  You then return that value with the
                        'white-stripped version of the remaining portion of the
                        'string.  This is a recursive call here because you are
                        'calling stripWhite() again.
      else                                 'otherwise, it's a regular tag...
         aString = killBaddies(Mid(aString, 1, index), " ") &
➥ stripWhite(Mid(aString, index+1, Len(aString)))
                        'you replace all bad characters (carriage returns, line
                        'feeds, null characters, horizontal tabs, and vertical
                        'tabs) inside the tag itself with plain old spaces.
                        'You return that new tag with the remainder of the
                        'string,
```

Listing 8.2   continued

```
                       'white-stripped and concatenated onto the end.  This
                       'too is a recursive call because you are calling
                       'stripWhite() again.
        end if
    else                                    'if no opening bracket is
                                            'found, it's text...
      aString = trim(aString)               'strip off leading and
                                            'trailing spaces
      if (Len(aString) <> 0) Then           'if the string is still
                                            'not empty....
        ltpos = inStr(aString, "<")         'find the location of the
                                            'first open bracket
        if (ltpos < 1) Then                 'if no open bracket exists...
          aString = trim(killBaddies(aString,""))
                                            'trim the leading and
                                            'trailing spaces off and
                                            'remove all the bad
                                            'characters from the string.
                                            'This is not a recursive call
                                            'because there is no further
                                            'work to be done.
                                            'This is what's called your
                                            'terminating condition,
                                            'because eventually you will
                                            'end up with a 'character
                                            'data'-only string (in the
                                            'end, it will be an empty
                                            'string), and this will
                                            'terminate the recursion.

    Else                                    'if there is an opening bracket...
          aString = trim(killBaddies(Mid (aString, 1, ltpos-1),"")) &
➥ stripWhite(Mid (aString, ltpos, Len(aString)))
                                            'trim the leading and trailing
                                            'spaces and remove all the bad
                                            'characters from the text
                                            'portion of the string.
                                            'Concatenate that with the
                                            'whitespace-stripped version of
                                            'the rest of the string (which
                                            'starts with your tag).  Again,
                                            'this is a recursive call for
                                            'that portion of the string.
                                            'You can imagine that it will
                                            'register as a tag and be
                                            'stripped that way in the next
                                            'level of recursion.

    end If
      end if
    end if
  stripwhite = aString                      'return the string's new value
end Function
```

Listing 8.2   continued

```
function whiteOut(str)
  'This function takes a string of XML and divides it into relatively
  'equal portions  (500 bytes each).  The string is always divided by
  'the next open bracket '<', rather than exactly on the 500th
  'character, because the whitespace stripper works only with strings
  'started with text data or XML tags.  It's important to make this
  'distinction because you wouldn't want to strip the whitespace out
  'of a tag.  Each 500-byte chunk is added to an array, and later you
  'go through the array and strip the whitespace from each element
  'using your stripWhite() function.  The array elements are then
  'concatenated into a large string of whitespace-stripped XML that
  'represents your original document.  You strip using 500-byte chunks
  'because large strings can quickly bog ASP down.  Because you use
  'recursion, a lot of memory is used keeping track of each level of
  'recursion until the terminating condition executes and the
  'functions are all completed.  If you tried that on a huge string
  'of XML, there would be so many functions running that you would get
  'an error from ASP.  Stripping 500 bytes at a time is much more
  'economical on function call overhead, so you can process much larger
  'XML files.
  dim chunksize, cALength, finished, index, chunkArray()
  chunksize = 500                              'set the chunksize to 500
  cALength = 0                                 'note that the
                                               'chunkArray's length
                                               'is 0

  finished = ""                                'the finished string
                                               'is currently empty

  if (Len(str) > chunksize) then               'if the string is
                                               'bigger than the
                                               'chunksize...

    index = inStr(chunksize, str, "<")         'find the first open
                                               'bracket

  else
    index = false                              'otherwise, there is
                                               'no need to break it up

  end if
  while (index)                                'while you are breaking
                                               'it up....

    cALength = cALength + 1                     'make the chunkArray
                                               'bigger to fit another
                                               '500 bytes

    ReDim Preserve chunkArray (cALength)
    chunkArray (cALength) = Mid(str, 1, index) 'put the new chunk into
                                               'the new array position
    str = Mid(str, index+1, Len(str))          'put the unparsed
                                               'portion of the string
                                               'into str

    if (Len(str) > chunksize) then             'if you still need to
                                               'break off 500-byte
                                               'chunks...
```

Listing 8.2   continued

```
      index = inStr(chunksize, str, "<")      'find the next open bracket
    else
      index = false                           'otherwise, quit breaking
                                              'up the string
    end if
  wend
  cALength = cALength + 1                      'add the last chunk to
                                              'the array
  ReDim Preserve chunkArray (cALength)
  chunkArray (cALength) = str
  for i = 0 to cALength                        'cycle through the array
    chunkArray(i) = stripWhite(chunkArray(i))  'strip the whitespace
                                              'off each element of the
                                              'array

    finished = finished & chunkArray(i)        'concatenate all the
                                              'stripped text into
                                              'one variable
                                              'called finished.

  next
  whiteout = finished
end Function




' =========================== M A I N   C O D E ===========================

filename = request.querystring("filename")   ' get the filename from the
                                             ' query string.  This means
                                             ' that you call this page as
                ' www.yourdomain.com/whiteout.asp?filename=yourxml.xml
if (filename <> "") Then                       'If you supplied a filename...
  xDoc = fileRead(filename)                    'read the file
  xDoc = whiteOut(xDoc)                        'strip its whitespace
  response.write xDoc                          'write it to the browser
end if
%>
```

Flash Stripper

Essentially, this is the whitespace stripper that you created in Chapter 4, "Using XML Data in Flash," included here just for completeness. It is probably the easiest and most popular method for whitespace stripping in Flash-bound XML documents, although it's not really the fastest, or the best. If you really need to do in-Flash stripping, check out our "ASNative Stripper" in the section that follows to see a new, bleeding-edge method.

```
XMLNode.prototype.stripWhite = function () {
  function whiteTest(str){
    var allWhite = true;
    var strLength = str.length;
    for (var i = 0; i < strLength; i++) {
      if (str.charCodeAt(i) > 32) {
        allWhite = false;
        break;
      }
    }
   return (allWhite);
  }

  if (this.nodetype == 1) {
      //it's a element; check its kids
      if (this.hasChildnodes) {
        var chlength = this.childNodes.length;
        for (var i=0;i < chlength; i++) {
          this.childnodes[i].stripWhite();
        }
      }
    } else {
      if (this.nodetype == 3) {
        //it's text; delete if whitespace
        if (whiteTest(this.nodeValue)) {
          this.nextSibling.stripWhite();
          this.removeNode();

        }
      }
    }
}
```

ASNative Stripper

ASNative is an undocumented and unsupported function in Flash that lets an ActionScript programmer tap into some of the inner workings of Flash's ActionScript interpreter. It's interesting in this context because it lets you interrupt XML processing at the stage between parsing and instantiating the objects that represent the XML document.

Before we continue, it's important to note that Macromedia can alter the way ASNative is implemented in future Flash player releases. Future releases might break the parser we have developed here. If you find any problems in the future when using the following pieces of code, check our site, xmlinflash.com, for updates and patches.

The function known as ASNative(300, 0) is the one responsible for XML parsing in Flash, but it does not return an object of type XML as the parseXML() method does. It does return a status as the XML.status property does, but it also creates an array of tags that it has parsed from the XML document. Here's a simplified example:

```
<example>simple</example>
```

This would parse out as the following array:

```
someArray[0].value = "example";
someArray[1].value = "simple";
someArray[2].value = "/example";
```

The translation to the array from the XML document is extremely efficient, so you only need to worry about optimizing the translation of the data from the array to the XML object.

The array is actually an array of objects, which have the important properties shown in Table 8.1.

Table 8.1   Properties of Objects in ASNative's XML Array

Property	Returns
type	Returns XML.nodeType
value	Returns XML.nodeValue if the nodeType is text; returns XML.nodeName if it's a regular element
attrs	Returns the XML.attributes associative array
empty	Returns true if the tag closes itself (such as <example />); returns false for two-tag elements (empty or otherwise)

The syntax of the function call is a little tricky because it depends on the version of Flash player that is playing the SWF. For minor version 30, the function call looks like this:

```
ASnative(300, 0)(aString, anArray);
```

ASNative is a function that returns another function. If you pass it the parameters 300 and 0, it returns a nifty "XMLstring to array" function. In some ways, it can be considered a "parser" because it does read the XML and stores it in a different format that can be manipulated, but we won't call it a parser here because it does only half the job of XML.parseXML(). Instead, we'll just call it xml2array() for lack of a better, more official name. When ASnative(300,0) returns xml2array(), you then pass the string and array parameters to xml2array(). The xml2array() method takes the string, which is an XML document, and puts that XML into the array in the format shown in the previous code snippet. Here's a quick example of retrieving one such array:

```
xml2array = ASnative(300, 0);
myXMLString = "<example>simple</example>";
myXMLArray = new Array();
theStatus = xml2array(myXMLString, myXMLArray);
```

The variable theStatus holds the same value that would be contained in XML.status. The array myXMLArray now holds the XML document in an array format like this:

```
someArray[0].value = "example";
someArray[1].value = "simple";
someArray[2].value = "/example";
```

Later versions of the Flash player have a slightly different syntax that looks like this:

```
ASnative(300, 0)(aString, anArray, aBoolean);
```

The Boolean is a value that declares whether whitespace should be ignored. The difference between the function call in each player is enough that you need to do some quick player version detection to use the function. You can quickly look up the minor version and define your xml2array() method accordingly:

```
var minorVersion = getVersion().split(",")[2];
if (minorVersion == "30") {
  xml2array = ASnative(300, 0);
} else {
  xml2array = ASnative(300, 0)(aString, anArray, true);
  // You set the Boolean to true to get rid of the whitespace, as is
  // necessary for most Flash-XML applications.
}
```

Now you're probably going to want to make this xml2array function a method of the XML object, but we've used it here as a function for the sake of simplicity. There are certainly advantages to extending the XML object with this new functionality, but you'll do that in the main application of xml2array(), which is a faster XML parser with automatic whitespace stripping in any Flash 5 player, regardless of the minor version. The steps you'll take are as follows:

1. Override the `XML.parseXML()` method to make it call `xml2array()` on your data.

2. Remove the empty nodes from the array (to get rid of whitespace).

3. Construct an XML document from the remaining elements.

That's really the main usage of `xml2array()`, and will essentially be the only thing you use it for in this book. Of course, you could always use ASNative's "xml array" as a data structure for storing your XML for longer term access. You might find that a simple linear array is easier to deal with than the XML tree created by the `XML` object, and you might appreciate the added efficiency. It's actually the instantiation of all the `XMLNodes` that really slows down Flash's stock XML parser, and you could, theoretically, skip that step.

Overriding the `onLoad()` event is mostly trivial now that you've learned how the `xml2array()` method works, so we'll continue the explanation with the actual XML tree building. We loop through the "xml array," looking at the type for each object in the array. The type is one of the five possibilities listed in Table 8.2.

Table 8.2   Object Types in the ASNative "xml Array"

Type Number	Type
1	tag (open, close, or empty)
3	text
4	docTypeDecl
5	xmlDecl
6	CDATA

The trickier types are the tags and the text (types 1 and 3). It's simple to add the `docTypeDecl` and the `xmlDecl` to the `XML` object after those types have been detected in the array. For type 6, CDATA, you simply add it as a text node with `createTextNode()`. Type 3, text, is not quite as simple as that because you want to ensure that you are stripping the whitespace. If a text element is composed only of spaces, carriage returns, tabs, and line feeds, you simply ignore it and continue traversing the array. You strip all the whitespace automatically here, without checking the `ignoreWhite` property.

It's conceivable that the function could be rewritten to check the `ignoreWhite` property first, but for the most part, XML applications do not require whitespace, so we've left it out for every case. This might not be a great thing if you are writing haikus in XML and want to maintain the formatting, but in that case, the formatting (that is, whitespace) can be added as CDATA. In that way, whitespace can be preserved for the small number of cases in which you would actually use it.

The tag processing is actually the most complex. If you think about it in a very simplified form, though, you can come up with an algorithm. If it's an empty, single-tag node (such as `<lemur name='ring-tailed' />`), you know to add it as a child and copy the `attrs` object over to the `attributes` object of the newly created child. If it's an open tag, you know that anything that follows it will be a child node or a closing tag. For that reason, you create an element to represent the open tag, you copy over the `attrs` object, and then you concentrate on the children of that node. You know that you can jump back to the node from any of its children using the `parentNode` property as soon as you encounter a closing tag (any tag starting with a /).

In this way, all the types are handled in each element of the array until the entire "xml array" is converted to an XML object. Here's the actual code:

```
//Flash XML parser rewrite
//clocked at 1000ms faster (1 second) than the standard
//XML parser on a 22KB document

//I don't strip \v (vertical tab) or \0 (null character)
  var minorVersion = getVersion().split(",")[2];
  if (minorVersion == "30") {
    XML.prototype.xml2array = ASnative(300, 0);
  } else {
    XML.prototype.xml2array = function (aString, anArray) {
        return(ASnative(300, 0)(aString, anArray, true))
    };
  }

XML.prototype.parseXML = function (aString) {
  var xArray = new Array();
  this.status = this.xml2array(aString, xArray);
  if (this.status != 0) {return(null);}
  var xArrayLength = xArray.length;
  var current = this;
  var i = 0;

  for (var i = 0; i < xArrayLength; i++){
    var theType = xArray[i].type;
    var theValue = xArray[i].value;

    if (theType == 1) {
      if (substring(theValue, 1, 1) eq "/") {
        current = current.parentNode;
```

```
      } else {
        var theObj = xArray[i];
        current.appendChild(this.createElement(theValue));
        current.lastChild.attributes = theObj.attrs;
        if (!theObj.empty) {current = current.lastChild;}
      }
      continue;
    }

    if (theType == 3) {
      var isEmpty = true;
      var contentsLength = theValue.length;
      for (var j = 0; j < contentsLength; j++){
        var hold = substring(theValue, j+1, 1);
        if ((hold ne " ")
         && (hold ne "\n")
         && (hold ne "\r")
         && (hold ne "\t")){
          isEmpty = false;
          break;
        }
      }
      if (!isEmpty) {current.appendChild(this.createTextNode(theValue));}
      continue;
    }

    if (theType == 6) {
        current.appendChild(this.createTextNode(theValue));
        continue;
    }

    if (theType == 4) {
      this.xmlDecl = theValue;
      continue;
    }

    if (theType == 5) {
      this.docTypeDecl = theValue;
      continue;
    }
  }
}
```

Summary

As you can see, there are many ways to go about incorporating XML into your project. We hope that after reading this chapter, you have a better understanding of when and where you should use different techniques. All the code used or mentioned in this chapter is available on the accompanying Web site, and we encourage you to use it and, if the opportunity arises, extend it. Every project presents new challenges, which could produce a new set of solutions.

So What's Next?

Now that you have spent considerable time developing Flash applications using XML and have a comprehensive understanding of the inner workings of Flash-XML integration, we're going to step it up a notch and delve into the wonderful world of the XML socket.

The addition of the XML socket to Flash 5 allows developers to create applications and games that run in real time. The XML socket enables you to connect directly to a socket server and share information with users who are also connected to the socket.

The XML socket opens up a whole new world of possible interactive projects—from whiteboards to communities to multiuser games. In the following chapter, we will cover the basics of the socket and the server before jumping head-first into the meat of the subject and some real-world examples.

{ Part III }

Flash and the XML Socket

{ Chapter 9 }

Introduction to the XML Socket

This chapter covers the true interactivity that XML now offers Flash developers—multiuser interactivity. You have stepped through the numerous examples that use the new XML object in Flash 5, but now you begin to explore the wonderful world of the XMLSocket object. This object is your tool for creating stunning multiuser applications and movies, including chat systems and multiuser games, and a wealth of push-technology applications limited only by your imagination.

Here you will realize the new ways in which developers can create truly engaging applications. Being able to communicate in real time with the server and ultimately other users puts you on a whole new level of development. As you explore the possibilities, allow yourself to dream of new ways of communicating and displaying information.

People are still just beginning to adopt and incorporate concepts of this new and exciting technology. It's a rapidly changing area of Flash development, with new uses constantly being developed. This chapter begins to unravel the mystery behind this powerful yet seldom used feature of Flash XML. Now that we've piqued your interest in this new technology, it's time for an in-depth look into the world of the XML socket.

The Purpose of the XML Socket

The primary purpose of the XML socket is to set up and maintain a continuous connection between the Flash movie and the server. When using `loadVariables()` or `XML.load()`, you were limited to using HTTP requests when communicating server side, so you had to make a round-trip call to the server every time a data request was made (Flash requests the data, the server sends it, and then the connection is dropped). Although HTTP communication did allow developers to create more dynamic applications with Flash, it can, in many cases, create unnecessary overhead in the communications between a Flash movie and a server. Figure 9.1 shows the path of information in HTTP's request-response style of communication. Flash initiates a data request that is sent to the server. After the request is received by the server, the data response is returned to Flash.

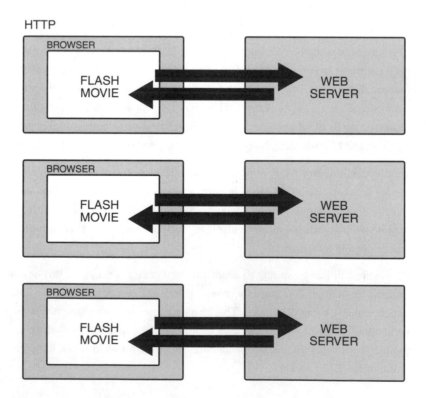

Figure 9.1   *The HTTP request-response model.*

Essentially, Figure 9.1 shows three separate request-response pairs between the Flash movie in the browser and the Web server. The timeline for one of these pairs is always the same:

1. The Flash movie connects to the Web server.

2. The Flash movie requests the document it wants (which should contain the information it wants).

3. The Web server responds with the document.

4. The Flash movie drops its connection to the server.

This is the same regardless of whether the Flash movie is sending data to the server, receiving data from it, or both. To send data, the Flash movie simply sends the data in its request. If the data is being sent via POST, that means the data is sent in the HTTP request header. If the data is being sent via GET, the data is being sent as part of the URL. Either way, the Web server can receive and process the information.

By examining the flow of information in Figure 9.1, you can easily see the over-head incurred when you need to repeatedly make requests to the server for infor-mation. Just to get information from the Web server by using HTTP, you need to open a connection to the server, request that information, wait to hear the result of your request, and then close the connection. There's no real problem with this method on its own, but the continual need for fresh data has the Flash movie repeating this procedure often.

In the next chapter, you'll be building a fake stock ticker in Flash that shows the ever-changing values of five different stocks. Constantly fresh data is important for that kind of application, so you need a fast communications protocol. Opening and closing the socket each time is the main overhead when using HTTP, but it's a waste to have to continually request the data you want. If the server could just send it to you without needing a request from you, you could update that data more often. This request-and-response communication is what we've been using all along, and it is an excellent method for those purposes. HTTP is probably the most popular communications protocol on the Internet for that reason. It's a simple protocol that is easy to work with, and it has all the fea-tures needed for client/server communication. Unfortunately, for keeping quickly changing data up-to-date, it's a little slow and cumbersome.

By using an XML server, you can sustain a continuous connection with the server, which instantly reduces the request overhead of working with dynamic server-side content via HTTP. The old method of "connect–get information–disconnect–repeat" is replaced by a new smoother method that connects and gets information constantly until no more data is (ever) needed, at which point the connection is closed. In addition to that optimization, there is no longer a need to make requests to the server. The server can send data whenever it deems necessary. In the stock market ticker example, the server could theoretically send new data whenever a stock's price has changed. If you were using HTTP for that, you'd need to call `XML.load()` or `loadVariables()` every five seconds to get remotely close to the kind of update speed the XML server can handle. Network traffic, CPU usage, bandwidth, and application performance would all be so adversely affected that using HTTP would have to be ruled out for this type of application. It is the XML server that enables you to streamline server communications and actually make these applications possible.

If you take a quick peek at Figure 9.2, you can see the direct interaction between Flash and the server to transfer information. This is the main advantage and overall purpose of setting up an XML server: fast and direct data exchange between client side and server side.

XML SERVER

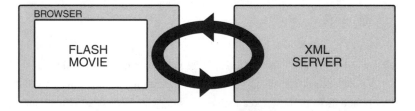

Figure 9.2   `XMLSocket`-*XML server communications.*

An XML server is actually quite a bit simpler than an HTTP (Web) server, as far as the style of communication. As shown in Figure 9.2, Flash connects to the server with a single persistent connection. Both the server and Flash can send information whenever they want; there is no request and response (unless you write it to do that). That means the server can simply send information whenever it deems necessary, and the Flash movie doesn't need to keep polling it, as it does with the HTTP method.

Let's explore some of the specific advantages that the XML socket offers to developers.

XML Socket Advantages

Now that you have a basic understanding of the role the XML socket plays, you might be thinking of specific examples or applications that this technology can make possible. One of the primary advantages of the XML server is the capability to create Web applications that are close to real time.

Real-Time Data Transfer

The continuous connection to the server means that your data basically "streams" back and forth between the Flash file and the server. You can access information quickly from the server because you do not need to establish a server connection every time you want to send a request to the server.

Web applications built with HTML as a front-end interface require a new page-load to pull in the information that was requested, creating long delays between requesting the information and actually viewing the data. A connection with the server must be opened first, and then an HTTP request is passed. Information is then transferred and placed dynamically in a new HTML page, which then needs to be reloaded in the user's browser.

This process is drastically streamlined when you use the Flash/XML server. As you know, by using Flash you can dynamically import data into your existing Flash movie without having to load any new files, so the information exchange is quick and seamless to the end user. Now this information can be passed back and forth almost instantly, which makes the socket an excellent candidate for creating Web-based applications.

Multiuser Environments

Another advantage of the XML socket is the ability to create multiuser applications or environments. Being able to access information directly from the server via the socket opens the door to transferring information not only between Flash and the server, but also between users.

Applications such as multiuser chat, whiteboard frameworks, and multiplayer games now become possible by incorporating the XML socket.

Push Technology

It's important to note that the socket doesn't need to be used just for user-to-user interaction or even for user requests, but can be used for what is called *push technology*. This means that as new information is placed in a database, it can immediately and instantly be transferred to all connected clients. For instance, you could have a Flash-based intranet or extranet that can send news updates to any connected client.

No longer does information need to be requested by the user. By merely being connected via the XML socket, information can be streamed to the user as the server receives it. The very second that content is updated on the server, it's immediately updated for all connected users. No need to refresh or request this information: The server automatically "pushes" it to the user.

This type of interaction is excellent for sites that offer constantly updated information. Whether it's stock-related information or updated news, it will be dynamically updated to users seamlessly without any interaction on their part.

XMLSocket **Difficulties**

Along with all the advantages of using an XML Server come a few difficulties. It's definitely a good idea to keep these things in mind, but don't let them stop you before you at least see the advantages of the XMLSocket in action. We will be showing two applications of Flash–to–XML server communications in the next two chapters, so you can see how we got around some of these problems.

Acquiring an XML Server

Use of Flash's XMLSocket with a server is currently very cutting-edge, so XML server products that support it are in their infancy. To be true, most actual uses of the XMLSocket with an XML server use a custom-programmed XML server for that particular application. There are certainly easier things to do than program a custom XML server, but that's the route most people have chosen to take so far. If you're not up to that task, you have a few options for using general-purpose XML servers. Check out some of the XML servers listed in Appendix D, "Resources." Whether you choose to write your own server or use a general-purpose one, you're going to have some learning ahead of you.

Hosting Issues

The XML server is not a program that runs on your Web server like the ASP and PHP scripts you've created earlier. It's a standalone piece of software that runs completely on its own. In most cases, it will run on the same machine as your Web server because Flash SWFs can connect to XML servers only on the same subdomain they are served from. Otherwise, the Web server and XML server have little to do with one another.

This creates a bit of a problem when you're looking for hosting for your Flash/XMLSocket application. Most Web hosts won't allow non–Web-based applications to run independently from the Web server in the background. Frequently, the only option is to host it yourself (including the SWF that makes the connection!) or get dedicated hosting that allows you to configure your own machine. Unfortunately, the latter option is relatively expensive compared to other hosting options.

For these reasons, you'll want to avoid the XML socket whenever near-real-time push technology is not necessary. It can be extremely invaluable for those purposes, though, so it's an important aspect of Flash to understand.

As powerful as an XML server can be, there are still a couple of key limitations you need to be aware of before working with the socket. One of the current difficulties of deciding to work with an XML server is identifying and finding a host that will allow you to run this type of server. To be able to function properly, the server needs to be custom configured—in this case, with Java. Many ISPs either do not allow this type of server or do not give you control to set up the server as required. This is the first hurdle you might face when beginning to develop with XML servers.

Limited Port Range

Another known limitation is the port number range available to the XML socket: You must use a port number higher than 1024. It can be any number higher than this, but cannot be lower. The reason for this restriction is that many server or network applications require a network connection in the 0–1024 range. This range of ports has been set aside for these network operations, leaving you with the range over 1024. This "limitation" really has little effect on you when developing; you just need to remember to make sure you have chosen a port higher than 1024 when you connect with the server.

Domain Issues

Last—and you might be familiar with this limitation—when loading movies or variables in Flash, you must ensure that your files reside on the same subdomain as the XML server when publishing online. Similarly, with the SWF that uses the XMLSocket, you must make sure it resides on the same domain as your SWF file. This security feature is part of the Flash architecture, and again, should not have any impact on your development; it's simply something to be aware of.

If you find that to be a problem and your hosting provider allows it, you can set up a domain alias to trick Flash into thinking the movie and the server are on the same domain. If you're hosting the server locally, this method can be very useful.

Summary

This chapter should have you primed for getting into the XML socket in more detail and inspired about the possibilities the socket opens for developers. Whether it's for push-technology content, multiuser games and environments, or real-time Web-based applications, the XML socket is the technology to use with Flash. The few limitations and restrictions on using the XML socket are far outweighed by its advantages.

So What's Next?

Now that you're stoked on creating dynamic applications with Flash and the XML socket, it's time to hook it all together. In the next chapter, you will be explicitly covering the setup of an XML server connection with Flash and XML. You'll learn how to set up a socket server using Java and how to read and display data through Flash!

To demonstrate this functionality, the example will be of a mock market ticker. This simulated stock updater will be used to dynamically display "real-time" stock information, including current values and changes in values. You'll carefully examine everything required to connect and receive XML data from the server.

{ Chapter 10 }

Socket to Me!

If you are interested in creating dynamic, real-time applications in Flash, this chapter is for you. It gives you the foundation in working with and communicating with a socket server with Flash. The information you learn in this chapter is fundamental to creating any sort of socket-related applications. We cover everything from connecting with the server to receiving XML content from the server. Until you have mastered the principles in this chapter, you can't move on to more sophisticated socket examples and applications.

This chapter is essentially a practical introduction to the XMLSocket object in Flash and the implementation of an XML socket server. We'll be covering most of the fundamentals here, and you should expect to have a basic knowledge of how all this works by the time you've completed this chapter and tried out the example.

Connecting to the Socket Server

The actual process of talking with the socket server is rather easy. Information gets sent in the form of an XML object to the Flash environment, and the socket server spits out XML objects. This process makes it incredibly easy to import and use XML in Flash. Before jumping into your first socket example, you should quickly go over the steps and methods for setting up communications with the server.

Before you have any hope of connecting to the server, you must first create a new XMLSocket object to store your data when it does arrive. You do this by using the following constructor:

```
rSocket = new XMLSocket();
```

After you have established your new XMLSocket object, you do the obvious: You make a connection with the server, and with no better method than the connect() method! This method takes two parameters: a URL (address) and a port number. To connect your newly created XMLSocket object, you would code the following:

```
rSocket.connect("127.0.0.1", 5555);
```

If you recall from Chapter 9, "Introduction to the XML Socket," you need to assign the port to a number higher than 1024 to avoid possible conflict with other network connections. So imagine that! With just two lines of code, you have created a connection with your server. Unfortunately, the server is useless to you at this point. You still need to handle the input and output of XML through the socket.

Socket Event Handlers

Like the XML object, the XMLSocket object uses event handlers. By themselves, however, the event handlers do you no good. Until you assign a custom callback handler to manage these events, you will not be informed when the server is passing XML to you. The three primary event handlers—onConnect(), onXml(), and onClose()—are explained in the following sections.

The onConnect() Event Handler

This handler operates in the same manner that the onLoad() handler worked with the XML object. This handler gets called when the connect operation is completed. You might customize this callback handler in a number of ways, but primarily it's used to handle the success or failure of your connection attempt.

The onConnect() method receives a Boolean value representing success or failure of the previous connect attempt. Based on this true or false value, you can write a custom callback handler.

For now, we'll demonstrate the onConnect() method by writing a custom function that merely traces whether you have made a connection. This is a useful function to include when handling socket connections to report the connection status to the user:

```
rSocket.onConnect = function () {
    if (success){
        trace ("successful Socket connection");
    } else {
        trace ("failure with Socket connection");
    }
}
```

Overriding this handler is important, as the onConnect() method is called not only when you have a successful connection with the server, but also when the attempt is completed. This function will indicate that status.

The onXML() Event Handler

The onXML() event handler is the one you should be most interested in, in terms of receiving XML from the server. This is the event handler that gets called when XML is sent to and received by Flash:

```
rsocket.onXML = function(theXML) {
  trace (theXML.toString());
}
```

This basic example will simply trace all XML that comes into Flash to your Output window. You could perform any number of operations here, depending on your intended use of the XML. In fact, this very handler could be written to determine what sort of XML is being received and then handle it appropriately.

The onClose() Event Handler

As the name suggests, the onClose() handler is called whenever the connection with the server is disconnected. This is not a result of the close method, but is determined by the server closing the connection. You could perform any number of actions when this event happens. You could program a custom alert window movieClip to appear or use some other method of modifying the display to get the message to the user. This simple example merely displays output, saying that there has been a disconnection with the socket server:

```
rSocket.onClose = function (){
    trace ("the server has disconnected");
}
```

You can close socket connections just as easily as you can make them. This one fragment of code completely terminates the socket connection:

```
rSocket.close();
```

As you can see, it takes only a few lines of code to make a socket connection and sustain it with custom-written event handlers. You can detect and output successful server connections, display all incoming XML, and update any disconnections with the server. Now it's merely a matter of customizing your Flash movie to manipulate this XML data stream from the socket server.

Creating a Simple XML Server

So now let's create a mock market ticker. It's a lot like stock market ticker applications that you might have already seen, but its stock prices are generated at random by a custom-built XML server. The XML server randomly changes the prices of a few imaginary "stocks" and supplies these quotes in real time via a socket. This example illustrates what's called *push technology*. The server supplies this new data to the user's Flash movie without its being requested, and it is automatically updated there. There is no constant monitoring or requesting of information from the server by the Flash client seeking new data. Data transfer is handled entirely by the server, eliminating the redundant and taxing process of constantly hitting the server and checking for content updates. For a number of reasons, this example is not quite as practical as other examples in this book. It's probably the lightest possible introduction to the XMLSocket, though, so it should prove useful to your overall understanding of how the XMLSocket works.

Before you get into the nitty-gritty of the Flash implementation, take a look at the XML structure being used to send the information to Flash:

```
<stocks>
<stock name='Microsoft (MSFT)' value='57.58' change='-2' />
<stock name='Macromedia (MACR)' value='13.74' change='+1.25' />
<stock name='SUN Microsystems (SUNW)' value='10.29' change='+1' />
<stock name='IBM (IBM)' value='96.47' change='-.85' />
<stock name='Apple Computers (AAPL)' value='17.37' change='+2' />
</stocks>
```

As you can see, the XML is pretty straightforward and completely readable. All stocks are placed inside —you guessed it—a `<stock>` element. As you learned in Chapter 8, "Performance and Optimization," Flash can parse through an XML document much faster if the content is structured with attributes instead of elements—as much as 20 times faster. Knowing this, you can speed up the real-time aspect of the socket server even more. You'll see later how these values are generated server-side, but for now it's useful to understand what the XML structure looks like so that you can follow the flow of the XML handling inside Flash.

The Flash File

Now that you've taken a peek at the XML structure, it's time to get busy inside the Flash environment. It's probably most useful to develop the server while you are developing the Flash side of things (that's how we did it). However, for the sake of simplicity, we're going to explain the Flash portion first, and then cover the server stuff. For this example, you are using the mockMarketTicker.fla file, located in the Chapter 11 directory of the source code from XMLinFlash.com.

After you have the file open, notice that the main timeline structure consists of three layers, shown in Figure 10.1. The xml layer contains a text field that displays the XML, the stocks layer contains the movie clips used to display the stock information, and the good old script layer is where all the action takes place.

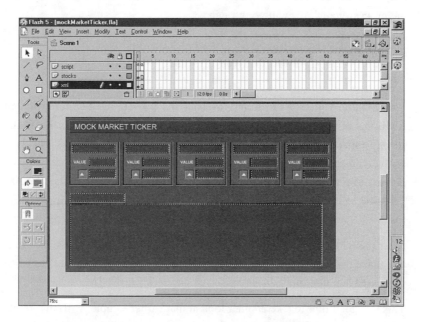

Figure 10.1   *The main timeline for mockMarketTicker.fla.*

The first thing you want to do is create a new socket connection with the server. You'll find the following code in the script layer in Frame 1:

```
mySock = new XMLSocket();
mySock.onConnect = function(success) {
  _root.status = "success is "+success;
}
```

This piece of code performs two main functions. First, it creates mySock to act as the new XMLSocket object for communicating with the server after you connect to it. Second, it creates a custom function to override the onConnect() method of the XMLSocket class. This function determines whether the socket connection attempt was successful and subsequently translates this success value to a variable in your movie defined as _root.status. This variable is displayed to the user onscreen through a dynamic text field on the stocks layer. It is helpful to test whether you are successfully getting XML content from the server.

The heart of the code in this example is the customized onXML() event handler. By creating this function, you determine how to handle XML that is passed to Flash. This is where you specify how the XML is to be manipulated and displayed to the user. Let's go through this function line by line to fully understand the process your XML will go through:

```
mySock.onXML = function(xObj) {
  _root.theXML = xObj.toString();
  _root.status = "status is "+xObj.status;
```

The first line declares a function to override the onXML() handler, referencing the XML that is passed from the server as xObj. The second line places the XML in string format into your dynamic text field (located on the xml layer). This is done so that you can see what XML content is passed and better understand the process of receiving content from the socket server. The third line modifies the _root.status value to reflect the status of the XML that has been imported into Flash.

After the XML is available to you in Flash, you can begin to analyze the content and make decisions in your code to determine how this information is to be processed and ultimately displayed to screen.

This is a good time to take another look at that earlier sample XML that represents the data Flash would receive. It will make it easier to understand how the rest of the onXML() handler processes the XML.

You can see how simply the XML is structured. The root element, or firstChild, is <stocks>, so you use the following line to create the stockArr object to hold the childNodes of the XML you have received:

```
var stockArr = xObj.firstChild.childNodes;
```

In this instance, the stockArr array will contain the five <stock> elements. You'll also notice that we have chosen to place all the content in attributes of elements. As you learned in Chapter 9, Flash parses through attributes many times faster than it does through elements, so this structure only increases the speed performance of your socket server, getting it as close to real time as possible.

Now that you have the information for your stocks in the stockArr array, you loop through them and assign the current data to the movieClip objects that represent the stocks in your Flash movie (see Figure 10.2).

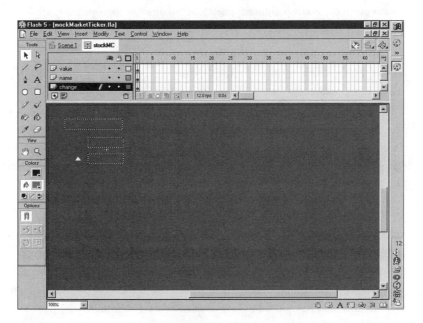

Figure 10.2 *The timeline for the* stockMC *clip.*

You'll notice in Figure 10.2 that the stockMC clip has layers containing text fields for each piece of information you are handling: name, value, and change. These movie clips are placed manually on stage and given unique identifiers, such as stockMC1, stockMC2, and so on, each representing a stock and containing the corresponding information from a <stock> element. So in the following code you

loop through these five clips, updating the content by placing it in these variable
containers:

```
for (var i=0;i<5;i++) {
  _root["stockMC"+(i+1)].name = stockArr[i].attributes["name"];
  _root["stockMC"+(i+1)].value = stockArr[i].attributes["value"];
  _root["stockMC"+(i+1)].change = stockArr[i].attributes["change"];
```

The `for` loop loops through the five stocks and places the `name`, `value`, and
`change` attribute values for each stock into the corresponding variables inside the
clips. At this point, the Flash file is updated as soon as this information is placed
in the `stockMC` variables.

Last, you perform a calculation to determine whether the change in the stock
value has increased or decreased. Based on this, you tell the `changeArrow` movie
clip to go to the corresponding frame that contains the appropriate graphic of an
up arrow or a down arrow:

```
if (stockArr[i].attributes["change"] < 0) {
 _root["stockMC"+(i+1)].changeArrow.gotoAndStop(2);
} else {
 _root["stockMC"+(i+1)].changeArrow.gotoAndStop(1);
}
```

That's all there is to it. This one function is all you need to dynamically update
this mockMarketTicker example. The only thing you have not done yet is actually connect to the server! You do this with the following line:

```
mySock.connect("127.0.0.1", 5555);
```

Here you are instructing the newly created `mySock` object to connect to the server
via the parameters you set as arguments. In this example, you are connecting to
the IP address 127.0.0.1 on your local machine via port 5555. Remember that
you must connect at a port higher than 1024. Any number will suffice, as long as
it is not currently being used by any other network operations.

Creating the Server in Java

We've chosen to write the server in the Java programming language for three
main reasons—Java has excellent socket support, it can run on multiple hardware
platforms and operating systems, and syntactically it's very close to ActionScript.
If you're an ActionScript-only programmer, maybe this can be a nice introduction to a new language. We certainly hope this example will at least get you

thinking about other possibilities you might want to try out. With Java's excellent built-in socket support (the `Socket` and `ServerSocket` classes), there's a good chance that you'll find basic network programming to be fairly simple and rewarding.

Running the TickerServ Server in Java

Java can run on almost any operating system or hardware platform, but the catch is that you need the Java runtime environment (JRE) installed. Because you'll actually be developing this server, not just running it, you'll want to download the entire Java Development Kit (JDK) from SUN at `http://java.sun.com`. Get the latest version of the JDK to ensure compatibility. It will contain the JRE you need to run this Java program, so don't worry about looking for it too.

If you're new to Java, the simplest method to get right into it is to download and install SUN's Forte for Java at `http://www.sun.com/forte/ffj/`. The Community Edition (CE) is free and fairly easy to install and use. Either way, we'll be assuming a near-intermediate level of competence when we explain this example. A complete beginner's tutorial on Java would be beyond the scope of this book.

The primary goal is to get the server actually running so that you can get an idea of what it does before we explain its inner workings. Even if you want to concentrate on the Flash side of things and don't care about how the server works, it's important to know what it does so that you can understand how Flash interacts with it. If you've never used Java before, this will definitely be something new, but it's a worthwhile experience. After you know how to run this Java program, you'll have the knowledge to run the program in the next chapter, too. Take it slow and make sure you follow the steps closely to ensure that Java is installed correctly. You don't want to waste any time getting to the fun stuff.

1. Download the Java Development Kit (JDK) from `http://java.sun.com/j2se/?frontpage-javaplatform`. You'll want to get latest non-beta SDK for your platform (which is the Java 2 SDK version 1.3.1 at the time of this writing).

2. Install the JDK. In Windows, you simply run the .EXE file, but every operating system is different (and Java runs on many other operating systems). There is installation documentation at `http://java.sun.com/j2se/1.3/install.html` that you should take a look at. In particular, you'll want to read about setting your Java path. That's essential, and probably the only semitricky part of it.

3. Copy the Java source file to your hard drive and open a console or command-prompt window (depending on your operating system; in Windows it is usually referred to as a DOS window). Navigate to the directory in which you copied the Java source file.

4. Compile it by typing **javac *Filename*.java**. Obviously, you'll want to replace *Filename*.java with the filename of the Java source you want to compile (in this case, it's TickerServ.java). The javac is the Java compiler; that's a program that makes Java class files from Java source files. If you have no errors and a new class file exists in the directory, you have it installed correctly. If not, check the documentation again. All the information you need should be there; just be patient and persistent.

5. Run it by typing **java *Filename***. Again, you'll want to replace *Filename* with the actual Java source or class filename (TickerServ, for this example). You're actually referring to the class file this time, but don't put .class on the end. The java part is the program that runs Java classes. Because of this, it's called a *virtual machine*. Anyway, it should now be running. Any time you want to run it again, just repeat this step (you need to compile only once, unless you've changed the source file).

The Importance of Testing

The most important thing to realize when writing your server is that testing is essential. Testing a networked system of software (like the one we aim to create between Flash and this server) is a fairly complex task. For debugging, you need to be able to pinpoint which component of the communication is failing before you make changes that you think might help. If you don't know where the trouble is, you can't effectively fix the problem. The key to testing and troubleshooting servers is using your favorite Telnet client program to connect to your server, and interacting with the server through the client. If your server isn't behaving as you would expect from Telnet, you can be sure that Flash won't have an easy time communicating with it either. In addition, if there are problems (either with the connection or with your protocol), Telnet will in many cases make them obvious.

Assuming that you have everything running, now is a great time to connect with Telnet and see just what this server does. We are going to cover this Telnet process from a Windows machine, so you Mac users out there will want to open your Telnet program. If you do not have one, you can download Better Telnet 2.0fc1 or Open SSH 2.5.2 from sites such as www.download.com to follow along.

You can access Telnet on Windows by going to your Start menu and choosing
Run to open the Run dialog box, as shown in Figure 10.3.

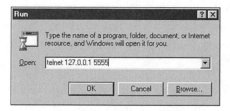

Figure 10.3   *The Run dialog box.*

After this dialog box is open, you need to type in the following command to connect to the server:

```
telnet 127.0.0.1 5555
```

{ Note }

In this example, we are using the localhost IP address 127.0.01, which
always refers to the computer you reference it from. If you have this
server on a remote host, make sure to use that remote IP address
instead to connect properly.

All we have done is request a Telnet connection to the preceding IP through port
5555. After you press Return, you should see the Telnet window appear. If everything has gone as it should, the Telnet window should be full of XML, as shown
in Figure 10.4.

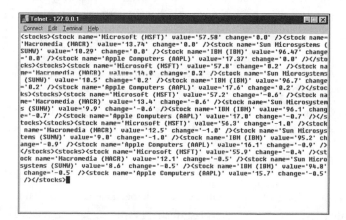

Figure 10.4   *The Windows Telnet window, full of XML.*

The Inner Workings of TickerServ

If you're interested in understanding how TickerServ works, this is the explanation. It's a good idea to refer to the source code as this explanation goes on because it will give you a more concrete idea of how TickerServ is implemented in Java. The source code can be found in the TickerServ.java file or in Listing 10.1 in this chapter.

In general, the Java server is made up of the main `TickerServ` class (Listing 10.1, lines 5–94) and two other supporting classes, `Stock` (lines 155–194) and `SendTask` (lines 115–154). `TickerServ` is, of course, the application class, and we'll discuss that last.

The `Stock` class (lines 155–194), when instantiated, represents a specific stock like one you would find on the NASDAQ or New York Stock Exchange. One of the first things you do in the `TickerServ` constructor is create an array of five stocks, complete with their names (Microsoft, Macromedia, SUN Microsystems, IBM, Apple Computers) and their corresponding trading values. If you take a look at the `Stock` class, you'll see the important `changeValue()` (lines 169–185) method that we've created. It's used to randomly change the stock's value, which can go up or down at any time by a fraction of a dollar. If we were really slick, we might hook the server up to a real stock feed, but for simplicity's sake, we're just using random numbers.

The `SendTask` class (lines 115–154) extends the standard Java `TimerTask` class, meaning it has a `run()` method that can be scheduled to execute at specific times on its own. It's important to take a look at the `run()` method (lines 127–153) because it's handling most of the network communications. It simply checks to see whether the socket is connected, and, if so, it sends off an XML document that describes the state of the five stocks. The document, as we said earlier, will look like this:

```
<stocks>
  <stock name='Microsoft (MSFT)' value='57.58' change='-0.2' />
  <stock name='Macromedia (MACR)' value='13.74' change='0.25' />
  <stock name='SUN Microsystems (SUNW)' value='10.29' change='1' />
  <stock name='IBM (IBM)' value='96.47' change='-0.85' />
  <stock name='Apple Computers (AAPL)' value='17.37' change='0.9' />
</stocks>
```

Of course, we won't add whitespace in the example because it's not much use to Flash, but otherwise, this data is very Flash-ready. Flash can parse it relatively quickly and put it to work.

TickerServ (Listing 10.1, lines 5–94), the application itself, works to orchestrate all these events and handle the client connection and disconnection. TickerServ first creates the five stocks and populates them with initialization data (their names and initial values; lines 24–32). Next, it creates a serverSocket on port 5555 and waits for clients to connect (lines 33–38). When a client connects, TickerServ creates a socket to talk with the client and accepts the connection (lines 37–38). It then creates a new Timer object and schedules it to execute SendTask's run() method every 1000 milliseconds (every second; lines 57–70). At that point, everything is set in motion until the client (your Flash movie) disconnects.

This is a simple, single-threaded, one-time-only server, intended to allow one Flash client to connect and stay connected for as long as it wants. When that client disconnects, the server finishes execution. It would be impossible at that point to reconnect (so don't bother clicking Refresh in your browser!). This is obviously a very simple and mostly impractical example of socket communications. If you're keen and capable, you might want to add a loop to get the socket to allow other connections later. You might even want to expand the example into a multithreaded version that can accept connections from multiple clients simultaneously. The next example in Chapter 11, "Creating a Multiuser Chat Application," will do just that. For now, peruse the source code in Listing 10.1, and try it out. Make that connection from Flash to the server, and you'll really get an understanding for how it works. Definitely try using Telnet, too, to help interpret the internal workings.

Listing 10.1   TickerServ.java, the XML Server for the Mock Market Ticker Example

```
1.    import java.net.*;
2.    import java.io.*;
3.    import java.lang.*;
4.    import java.util.*;  // Random, TimerTask, Timer

5.    public class TickerServ {
6.        /* TickerServ is your main, public class that creates a single-
7.        threaded server to serve XML to a single client, one time only.

8.        The XML will represent a list of 5 companies and their stock
9.        values, as well as changes from previous values.  These are
10.       really just random values, but this should be an example of how
11.       Flash and an XML server can cooperate.

12.       */
```

Listing 10.1   continued

```
13.     public Stock[] stocks;   // an array of type Stock, called 'stocks'
14.     public Timer timer;      /* a timer to make the server send the XML
15.                                 every second */
16.     public SendTask task;    /* a task to represent the task of sending
                                    XML */
17.     public boolean connected;// a Boolean to tell if a user is connected

18.     public static void main(String[] args) throws IOException {
19.         // your main() method simply instantiates a new TickerServ
20.         TickerServ myTickerserv = new TickerServ();
21.      }

22.     public TickerServ() throws IOException {
23.         connected = false;          //currently not connected
24.         stocks = new Stock[5];      //instantiate the stocks array

25.         /* Below you create the Stock objects and put them in the stocks
26.         array.  Take a look at the 'Stock' class definition later if you
27.         want to understand the Stock() constructor.  */

28.         stocks[0] = new Stock("Microsoft (MSFT)", 57.58);
29.         stocks[1] = new Stock("Macromedia (MACR)", 13.74);
30.         stocks[2] = new Stock("SUN Microsystems (SUNW)", 10.29);
31.         stocks[3] = new Stock("IBM (IBM)", 96.47);
32.         stocks[4] = new Stock("Apple Computers (AAPL)", 17.37);

33.         try {
34.           ServerSocket serverSocket = new ServerSocket(5555);
35.           // create and start the server on port 5555

36.           System.out.println("TickServ initiated and waiting.");

37.           Socket clientSocket = serverSocket.accept();
38.           // wait for a connection and then accept it

39.           PrintWriter out =
40.                       new PrintWriter(clientSocket.getOutputStream(),
41.                                           true);
42.           /* create a PrintWriter object called 'out' to allow
43.              writing information (the XML, in this case) to the
44.              socket.      */

45.           BufferedReader in =
46.                       new BufferedReader(
47.                         new InputStreamReader(
48.                           clientSocket.getInputStream()
49.                         )
50.                       );
51.           /* create a BufferedReader object called 'in' to enable
52.           the server to *read* from the socket.  You don't actually
53.           care about anything that Flash might send because this
```

Listing 10.1   continued

```
54.              socket is intended for output only, but it's useful to
55.              create this BufferedReader because you can use it to
56.              detect the client's disconnection. */

57.         timer = new Timer();              /* create a new timer so
58.                                              that you can send out
59.                                              the XML every 1 second
60.                                              (1000 milliseconds) */
61.         task = new SendTask(this, out);/* create a new SendTask
62.                                              and send it the
63.                                              TickerServ and
64.                                              PrintWriter objects to
65.                                              do its work. */
66.         timer.schedule(task,0,1000);     /* schedule the task to
67.                                              occur every 1000ms,
68.                                              and start the timer
69.                                              right away (after 0
70.                                              milliseconds)  */

71.         connected = true;                /* note that a client has
72.                                              connected */

73.         while (in.readLine() != null) {
74.           /*
75.              Make sure in.readLine() is not null.  It will be null
76.              when the client disconnects.  Stay in this empty loop
77.              while the client is connected.
78.           */
79.         }

80.         connected = false;               /* note that the client has
81.                                              disconnected */

82.         out.close();         // close the output buffer
83.         in.close();          // close the input buffer
84.         clientSocket.close();    // close the client socket
85.         serverSocket.close();    // close the server socket
86.         System.out.println("Client Disconnected.");
87.         System.exit(-1);         // exit the program

88.       } catch (IOException e) {  // simple error checking
89.          System.err.println("Server error");
90.          System.err.println(e);  // display the error
91.          System.exit(-1);        // exit the application
92.       }
93.     }
94.   }

95.   class SendTask extends TimerTask {
96.     /* SendTask is a helper class that extends Java's
97.        TimerTask to represent a task that the timer will
```

Listing 10.1   continued

```
98.        need to perform every second.  That task will be
99.        to randomly change the values on the stocks in a
100.       small way, and then send an XML document
101.       representing those stocks to the socket so that
102.       they can be ready by an XML client (in this case,
103.       Flash) */


104.   public TickerServ tsObj;    /* create a TickerServ
105.                                   object to represent the
106.                                   TickerServ (passed as a
107.                                   parameter to SendTask's
108.                                   constructor). */

109.   public PrintWriter output;  /* create a PrintWriter
110.                                   object to represent the
111.                                   socket's output buffer
112.                                   (passed as a parameter
113.                                   to SendTask's constructor).
114.                                   */

115.   public SendTask(TickerServ ts, PrintWriter op){
116.       /* This is the constructor for SendTask.  It takes 2
117.       parameters: a TickerServ (the main server object) and
118.       a PrintWriter (the output buffer used to write XML to
119.       the client's socket).  It creates itself as a TimerTask
120.       and stores the TickerServ and PrintWriter objects as
121.       members. */
122.
123.       super();      // TimerTask constructor
124.       tsObj = ts;   // store the TickerServ object
125.       output = op;  // store the PrintWriter object
126.   }

127.   public void run() {
128.       /* this is the run() method of the SendTask object.  When
129.        a Timer object tells a TimerTask (or in this case, a
130.        SendTask) to run, it executes this method.  In this
131.        method, it randomly changes the values on the stocks in
132.        a small way, and then sends representative XML to the
133.        socket. */

134.       if (tsObj.connected) {            // if it's connected
135.           output.print("<stocks>");     // open the root element
136.           for (int i = 0; i < tsObj.stocks.length; i++) {
137.               // for each stock...
138.               output.print(tsObj.stocks[i]);
139.                                          // output its info
140.               tsObj.stocks[i].changeValue();
141.                                          // change its value
142.           }
```

Listing 10.1   continued

```
143.                  output.print("</stocks>\0"); /* close the root
144.                                              element and add a
145.                                              null character so it
146.                                              will be Flash-readable */
147.             output.flush();            /* make sure everything in
148.                                              the Socket gets sent */
149.          System.out.println("sent to client");
150.       } else {                         // if it's not connected...
151.          System.out.println("listening...");
152.       }
153.     }
154.   }

155.   class Stock {
156.      /* Stock is another helper class designed to represent
157.      a company's name and stock value. */
158.      public String name;      // the name of the company
159.      public double value;     // the value of the stock
160.      public double change;    // the change since the last update

161.      public Stock(String str, double val) {
162.      /* This is the Stock() constructor.  It takes a String
163.         representing a company's name and a double to represent
164.         its value. */
165.         name = str;   // set the stock's name
166.         value = val;  // set the stock's value
167.         change = 0;   // set the stock's 'change' value
168.      }

169.      public void changeValue() {
170.         /* This method changes the value of an object of type Stock in
171.            a small, random way.  A Stock can go up or down in value by
172.            varying degrees. */
173.        Random rndm = new Random();        // create a random number
174.        double oldVal = value;             // record the value
175.        if (rndm.nextDouble() > 0.5) {     // if it's above 0.5...
176.          value += rndm.nextDouble();       // add a random number
177.          value = (Math.floor(value*10)/10);// round the value
178.        } else {                           // if it's <= 5...
179.          value -= rndm.nextDouble();       /* subtract a random number
180.                                              from value. */
181.          value = (Math.floor(value*10)/10);// round the value
182.        }
183.        change = value - oldVal;           // note the change
184.        change = (Math.floor(change*10)/10);// round the change
185.      }

186.      public String toString() {
187.         /* the toString() method for the Stock object is defined here. It
188.         is called implicitly when you print the object out the PrintWriter.
189.         As you can see, there is not much to it.  It simply outputs the
190.         Stock object's information as a single-tag XML node. */
```

Listing 10.1 continued

```
191.        return("<stock name='"+name+"' value='"+value+
192.                                "' change='"+change+"' />");
193.      }
194.   }
```

Putting It All Together

Well, assuming you have the XML server up and running correctly, and you've
verified this with Telnet, it's time to try connecting from the Flash file. As long
as the server is running, and you're not connected to it any other way, it should
be simple to get Flash to connect. Just test the movie in the Flash editing environment or in the browser, and you should see how this works. Figure 10.5
shows a snapshot of the action, but of course the Flash movie should have constantly changing information.

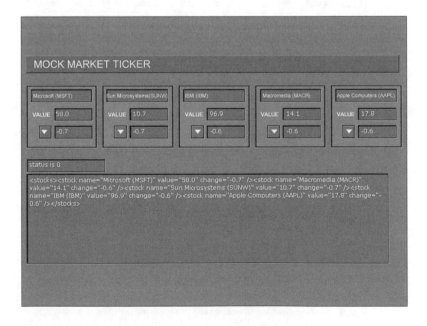

Figure 10.5 *This is the Mock Market Ticker example in action. (We're not responsible
for any financial decisions you make based on this information.)*

Summary

Although it takes some thought and determination to get your XML server up and running, after it is, you can begin to see how easily and efficiently you can push data to the Flash client. So far, you have covered only the passing of information from the server to the Flash client, but you now have a firm grasp of how to handle XML in and out of Flash. It's easy to see how you can extend this knowledge for use in many other applications.

So What's Next?

Now that you have dabbled with sending information by using the XML socket, it's time to get a useful and fun application of this new knowledge, a multiuser chat system in the style of IRC. You'll take a step farther into the world of the XML socket and begin passing information back to the server, but that's not all. You'll be coordinating this process with multiple Flash clients (theoretically, there is no limit to the number of users). You will learn how to send information to the server in much the same way you receive information. After we cover the two-way communication, you will begin to see the world of possibilities that exist when using the socket server, particularly in multiuser applications. Whether it's a dynamic whiteboard application, a game, or a robust chat application, the socket is the way to go and in the next chapter, we'll show you the way.

{ Chapter 11 }

Creating a Multiuser Chat Application

Now that we've covered the steps to set up and establish a socket server connection, it's time to dig in and get messy with multithreading capabilities with the socket server. Although the mock market ticker example from Chapter 10, "Socket to Me!," is valuable as a way to better understand the Flash/XMLSocket relationship, for the most part it doesn't showcase the true potential the XMLSocket object can offer to us Flash developers. You learned that you can create real-time communication between the socket server and Flash, but the example was restricted to just a single simultaneous connection.

In this chapter, you will build the socket much as you did in Chapter 10; however, you will make a number of fundamental changes to allow multithreading and enable you to create a true multiuser environment. In Chapter 10's example, the server was basically created for a single connection, and would wait until a connection was made and then close when there was a disconnection. Although this might not seem very practical, it was a good example to demonstrate the communication between the Flash client and the socket server. With the example in this chapter—multiuser chat—the server continues to exist even after users disconnect.

Beyond multithreading and the capability for multiple simultaneous users to connect, this chapter's example illustrates how you can send information from Flash back to the server and then "push" the information out to all connected Flash clients.

We've chosen to build a chat application, as it is perhaps the most practical multiuser application—allowing for the highest number of connected users. Although you can certainly build multiuser games by using a similar server configuration, you'll find that for high traffic and many continuous connections, you might be better off using a commercially available socket server. You can learn more about these options in Appendix D, "Resources," where we list a number of available servers to choose from, based on the needs and demands of your particular multiuser project.

Because this is a chat application, we have created it to be not only Flash-friendly, but also Telnet-friendly so that the application is much easier to debug. It also introduces you to another event handler accessed in the XMLSocket class in Flash: onData(). So before you get anywhere near Flash, first review the protocol we have developed to instigate communication between the client (Flash) and the Java socket server.

Establishing a Protocol: Let's Play Client and Server

When building network communications, *protocols* are defined as the rules determining the format and transmission of data between machines. A protocol implies some common message format and an accepted set of commands that all connected parties understand and that transactions among these parties follow predictable and logical sequences. As you most likely know, TCP/IP is the main protocol used throughout the Internet, including the Web and e-mail. The network communication in this chapter's example essentially uses TCP/IP, but we have created our own unique protocol to piggyback on TCP/IP for connecting between the Flash/Telnet client and the socket server. Any network communication requires a protocol, and our chat application is no exception. Because this book is about XML in Flash, it only makes sense that we base and structure a protocol on XML!

We'll use Telnet to dissect the way we have structured our protocol so that you can fully comprehend the communication between client and server. In Flash, although we are still using this protocol, it becomes invisible to users. They use the chat just as they would any other chat they're used to, without the need to format the content into the protocol. This is handled automatically through functions that we will create in Flash. So let's step into the wonderful text world of Telnet and take a peek into this custom protocol!

First, you need to establish a connection to your socket server. To do this, follow the same steps outlined in Chapter 10 (under the section "Creating the Server in Java") to set up the Java socket server on your local machine.

After you have the server configured, you'll need to open Telnet to go over the unique protocol for the chat application. We are going to cover this Telnet process from a Windows machine, so you Mac users out there should open your Telnet program. If you do not have one, you can download Better Telnet 2.0fc1 or Open SSH 2.5.2 from sites such as www.download.com to follow along.

Examining the Flash/Server Protocol Via a Telnet Connection

To examine this protocol, you must establish a Telnet connection to your socket server. You can access Telnet on Windows by choosing Start, Programs, MS-DOS Prompt to display the MS-DOS Prompt window, as shown in Figure 11.1.

Figure 11.1   *The MS-DOS Prompt window.*

After opening the MS-DOS Prompt window, you need to type in the following command to connect to the server:

```
C:\WINDOWS > telnet 127.0.0.1 5555
```

The chat application uses the IP of the localhost. Make sure to insert your local/remote IP address if it is different from this localhost address to properly secure a connection.

All we have done is request a Telnet connection to IP address 127.0.0.1 through port 5555. Press Enter to open the Windows Telnet window, shown in Figure 11.2.

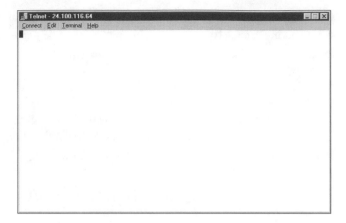

Figure 11.2   *The Windows Telnet window.*

You have now successfully connected to the server, but have yet to communicate with it. To do this, you need to understand the protocols used to log in, comment during chat, and log off. First things first—logging in to the chat.

Protocol for Logins

As mentioned earlier, the protocol for communicating with the server is structured entirely in XML. Also, as you discovered in Chapter 8, "Performance and Optimization," using attributes instead of elements reduces the overhead in Flash. For this reason, we have chosen to create simple data structures consisting of single elements with attributes. This structure is the basis for the login protocol. Take a second to look at the following code line for this protocol before entering it in your Telnet window:

```
<login name='Craig'/>
```

In this code line, we've gotten about as simple as we can get with XML. Notice that we have used a single empty element node, placing the content in an attribute instead of a text node inside the element. That's all there is to logging in to the chat via a client. If you return to your Telnet window, you can enter this command to see how the server responds. If it is not already set, you might want to turn on the Local Echo option under Terminal, Preferences on the Telnet menu to ensure that you can see what you are typing.

Currently Connected Users

If you type the login command, which is essentially the login protocol, into the Telnet prompt and press Enter, you will see the server respond with the following:

```
<list names='Craig'/>
```

The preceding piece of XML source code is the protocol used to transfer information about the current users who are logged in. Because you are testing it on your own at this time, your input will look like the preceding line. However, if you had several different users logged on, you might see something like the following line returned when connecting with your login protocol:

```
<list names='Craig, Gregg, Rob'/>
```

This `<list>` element is used to store and transfer all users who are logged in. Later you will see how this applies inside the Flash environment, but for now you just need to understand how we are establishing protocols for communicating this data to your clients. Next, turn your attention to the way messages are communicated through the chat application.

Message Sending

Now that you've seen how the previous protocols have been established, it's not too hard to see their common structure. Translating users' messages isn't much different. To successfully pass messages from the client to the chat server, you need to type the following into your Telnet window:

```
<msg content='this is a test'/>
```

Again, you are using a single empty element with attributes to pass your information; however, when you submit this command, you'll see the server return the following:

```
<msg content='this is a test' sender='Craig'/>
```

The Java-based server has been set up to automatically detect which user sends which message, so you don't need to transfer this information. Because the server handles this information, you are ultimately reducing the amount of data that needs to be sent from the client to the server. All users connected to the server will receive this same piece of XML. With all users receiving the `<msg/>` element with the appended `sender` attribute, all connected clients will be automatically updated with correct and complete information.

Disconnection Handling

Finally, there's the protocol for handling user disconnections. In the following line, you'll see that this command is structured exactly the same as the login XML, except that the element is named <disconnect>:

```
<disconnect name='Craig'/>
```

Because this chat application is a standalone application and is not currently integrated into a larger application, there is no actual disconnect button available to the user in the Flash front end. The act of merely closing the browser window or loading a new URL in the existing window causes a disconnection from the socket server. This disconnection is determined by the server, and the preceding command would be sent to all clients for updating their connected users list. When in Telnet, however, you can directly disconnect by using that command.

Now would be a great time to open multiple Telnet windows (by simply repeating the steps for opening one) and connect to the server simultaneously. If you try connecting and/or disconnecting, you can see what happens in the other Telnet windows when a single user connects or disconnects. There is theoretically no limit on the server as to how many people it can support at one time (we've had over 40 people in it at once), so feel free to try this with as many Telnet windows as you want.

You should be able to see at this point how simple and clean this protocol is. These simple lines of XML can be sent quickly and handled efficiently inside the Flash environment. If, however, you expected many individuals to connect to this chat application, you might consider creating even shorter element and attribute names. Ultimately, the application's efficiency is determined by how quickly information can be processed by the server and the client. For instance, you could simplify the disconnect protocol even further by structuring it as follows:

```
<dc n='Craig'/>
```

Although this isn't as readable as the current command, it is nearly half the byte size and would make a much bigger difference as more and more users are connected to the server. When programming, it is generally a good practice to use the smallest, yet most comprehensible, names for variables and elements to keep file size and data size for transferring down to a minimum.

You should now have a clear understanding of the protocols' formats and the reasons for their structure. You can close your Telnet window, and turn your attention to the inner workings of the Flash file to see how this protocol is applied and handled on the Flash client side.

Deconstructing the Flash Client

If you would like to follow along, open the multiUserChat.fla file in the multiUserChat directory in the Chapter 11 folder.

After opening the file, you can see the structure of the main timeline, shown in Figure 11.3. The main movie components are separated into five main layers: script, login, textFields, controllers, and bg, each of which consists of a single frame. Although this naming structure is rather straightforward, let's quickly outline the purpose of each layer and its components.

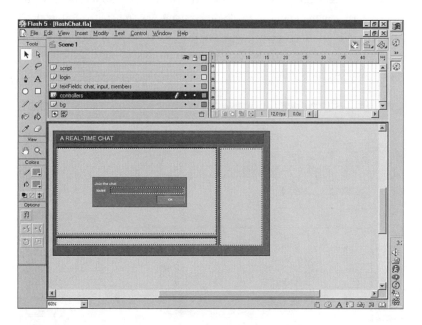

Figure 11.3   *The main timeline for multiUserChat.fla.*

The script layer, as in all the previous Flash examples, contains the movie's main code, including the functions and socket event handlers. The login layer contains the loginMC movieClip, which is responsible for handling the login interaction with the user. The textFields layer contains all the dynamic text fields, used to store and display the current chat log and currently logged in users, and an input text field for submitting messages to the chat. The controllers layer contains two movieClips that are responsible for monitoring keyPress events and the scroll status of the chat log text field. Finally, the bg layer is used to house all graphics-related elements for the chat application.

Now that you have a better understanding of the protocol you will be using and have had a good view of the lay of the land in the Flash file, it's time to start deconstructing the process and inner workings of the Flash file. We'll start where it all begins, with the login.

The Login Process

The login process begins with the login prompt box, which is labeled loginMC and resides in the login layer. You can view this movieClip in Figure 11.4. This is the first interaction your users will have with the chat application. As mentioned earlier with regards to the login protocol, you must also follow this same protocol in Flash to properly connect to the socket server. Fortunately, you don't need to make the users follow such stringent protocols, but can format their inputs with ActionScript to adhere to the protocols you have established.

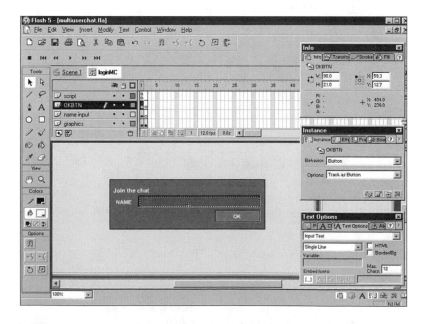

Figure 11.4 *The loginMC used to enter the multiuser chat.*

Let's take a closer look at the loginMC movieClip. You can see that this clip and its components are divided into four separate layers: script, OKBTN, name input,

and graphics. Although there is a script layer here, the only action it contains is a
`stop()` action. Primary handling of the login process is taken care of by functions in the script layer on the main timeline. The login process is triggered by an
`on(release)` action attached to the OK button. After users enter their login name
and click the OK button, the following actions take place:

```
on (release) {
 _root.login(this);}
```

The preceding code is attached to the OK button, and on release of the user's button click calls the `login()` function in the main timeline's script layer. When the
`login()` function is called, you pass along the variables, including `name`, to this
function when you set the argument to `(this)`. It is this function that begins the
connection with the server, as shown in the following code:

```
function login(loginMC){
  _root.name = loginMC.name;
  windowMC._visible = false;
  mySock.connect("127.0.0.1", 5555);
}
```

This function initiates server communications and performs several operations.
First, you pass the `name` value that the user submits in the loginMC to
`_root.name` in preparation for passing this data to the server for processing.
Because there is no need to log in to the chat more than once per session, you set
the visibility of the loginMC to `false` so that the user can no longer see it,
although technically it is still on stage. The call to `mySock.connect()` is then
made. In this case, we've used 127.0.0.1 for the IP address, assuming that you're
testing this from the same machine that is running your server. If that's not the
case, then put the IP address of the server in there instead. You'll definitely want
the server's address in there if you want people to be able to connect from different machines. Also, when testing, it's usually best to test in the browser instead
of simply using "Test Movie." The Flash player in the authoring environment can
be a little buggy for socket communications.

After creating the new `XMLSocket` object, as shown here,

```
mySock = new XMLSocket();
```

You make the call to connect with the server with this line:

```
mySock.connect("127.0.0.1", 5555);
```

After you have sent this connection request to the server, you await a response. As discussed earlier, the onConnect() event handler is triggered when the server responds to a connect request. We have created a custom function to handle the connection event as follows:

```
mySock.onConnect = function(success) {
  if (success) {
      mySock.send("<login name='"+escape(_root.name)+"' />\n");
      Selection.setFocus("_root.input");
  } else {
      loginMC.gotoandstop(2);
      loginMC._visible = true;
  }
}
```

The onConnect() event handler receives a Boolean success value, and you have built your function accordingly. Based on a successful connection with the server, the following actions are taken:

```
if (success) {
      mySock.send("<login name='"+escape(_root.name)+"' />\n");
      Selection.setFocus("_root.input");
  }
```

The second action is merely setting the focus of the cursor to the text field called _root.input so that the user can instantly enter the chat without having to click and make the text field active. However, as you can see, the first action is where you begin to communicate with the server by using the protocol discussed earlier.

Notice that you are taking the name value that was sent to the login() function and performing an escape() function on it. This function takes the name argument and encodes it in a URL-encoded format. This format enables users to include characters such as ' or / without causing any problems with the display. Because Flash is sending XML, you must encode any characters that are generally used with XML so that they are correctly displayed to the chat client. The reason you do this is because you are sending this information as attributes to increase Flash's efficiency in processing the XML. If you were sending this data by using text nodes inside elements, instead of empty elements, you would most likely be using CDATA to encapsulate the data being sent to ensure that characters would be received properly.

Basically, this XML string you are sending is identical to the protocol covered earlier via Telnet, with a couple of exceptions: sending the name attribute in

URL-encoded format, and including a `newline` character after closing the empty `<login>` element. It is important to understand that this XML still adheres to the protocol mentioned earlier. As explained, you need to URL-encode any data sent via XML to ensure that all characters are passed properly to the server.

If you recall from the discussion on the login protocol with Telnet, after the server received the login request, it returned the following:

```
<list names='Craig'/>
```

Of course, this is no different now, and this same information is being returned to Flash from the server. So let's take a look at how Flash handles receiving this XML data.

Receiving XML from the Socket Server: `onData()`

As discussed in the previous chapter, when receiving XML from the server, you use the `onXML()` event handler. Although this handler is used to receive and handle XML from the server, you can use another event handler to receive information from the server: `onData()`.

The `onData()` event handler is a somewhat undocumented handler of the `XMLSocket` class. It intercepts any data, including XML, before passing it on, by default, to the `onXML()` handler. Therefore, you can manipulate this content without the need for parsing.

The `onData()` handler basically constructs an `XML` object before sending it to `onXML()` where the XML is parsed. Like the `onConnect()` handler, you, too, can override the `onData()` handler and create a custom function to manually manipulate the data, thus improving performance over Flash's built-in XML parsing capabilities. Let's walk through the construction of the custom `onData()` handler:

```
mySock.onData = function(data) {
  var theStart = data.indexOf("<");
  var theEnd = data.indexOf(">");
  xObj.parseXML(data.substring(theStart, theEnd+1));
  inputHandler(xObj);
}
```

By constructing this custom function, the `onXML()` handler never receives the XML data; therefore, the data needs to be handled and parsed appropriately. The principle purpose of this function is to manually parse the XML and pass it off to the `inputHandler()` function. To do this, make sure to parse only the content between the < and >, which contains the element and attribute information.

Restricting parsing in this way eliminates any potential whitespace. All data sent to Flash from the socket server is followed by \0, so you need to remove this data extension before parsing. To do this, you use the substring() method to parse only the substring of data between the received XML element's opening and closing tags. The parseXML() method used to parse the XML is a default method of the XML object. After this XML source has been parsed, it is sent off to the inputHandler() function in the following form:

```
<login name='Craig'/>
```

Let's now explore the process of handling this server feed through custom functions created in Flash.

Input Handling of Data from the Socket Server

All XML content received from the socket is sent through the onData() handler. After it's parsed, it is then sent to the custom function inputHandler() for further handling. This function is responsible for communicating this data to users whether they are logging in, logging off, or submitting chat messages. First, you verify the status of this XML to determine whether there was an error during parsing:

```
function inputHandler(xObj) {
  if (xObj.status != 0) {trace("problem XML -->"+xObj.toString()+"<--");}
```

The XML sent from the onData() handler is received as xObj and instantly checked to see whether the status returns the value of 0. If it does not return with this value, you know you have received an error, and this xObj is then traced out with toString() to the Output window. This process is performed during the testing process merely to ensure that XML is being handled properly. Because the XML is as clean and simple as can be and is escaped as well as parsed, generally errors will not be returned; however, the inputHandler() function is there to catch any possible conflicts during the setup and configuration phase.

After the inputHandler() function receives the XML, you immediately create an input variable to contain the root element (or firstChild) of this XML:

```
var input = xObj.firstChild;
```

The input variable now contains the single element node that was sent to Flash. Based on the protocols discussed at the beginning of this chapter, you can receive one of four possible elements: <login>, <list>, <msg>, and <disconnect>. The inputHandler() function is set up to catch and process these possible elements.

If you recall, the server sends two streams of data to the Flash client when a user logs in, as follows:

```
<login name='Craig'/>
<list names='Craig'/>
```

Let's continue with the `<login>` element, which has so far been sent to the server by the user and subsequently returned to the Flash client.

```
if (input.nodeName=="login") {
    output("<font color='#734567'>*** "+input.attributes.name+
➥" joined the chat ***</font>");
    loginSound.start(0, 1);
  }
```

In this code, you are testing to see whether the name of the received XML element meets the `if` condition. When it is met, as it would be here, you perform two distinct actions. First, you send the following string to the `output()` function:

```
output("<font color='#734567'>*** "+input.attributes.name+
➥" joined the chat ***</font>");
```

This string is used to indicate that a user has joined the chat. You include `font` properties to alter the message's color so that it stands out from other users' chat messages. You then dynamically grab the value of the `name` attribute of the `<login>` element and send it to the `output()` function with the following string: `"joined the chat ***"`.

This `output()` function is used to place this string data into the text field on stage, as follows:

```
function output(str){
_root.chat += unescape(str) + "<br />";
}
```

The variable `_root.chat` represents the large text field on stage that is used to hold all the chat transmissions. You use the `unescape()` function to decode the string sent to the function from its URL-encoded format and place it in this text field accompanied with a line break (`\n`). The line break is added so that each message is placed on its own line, making for a clean display.

After completing this procedure, you return to the `inputHandler()` function to trigger a sound that indicates a user has logged on:

```
loginSound.start(0, 1);
```

This sound must first be initialized in the script layer actions, as follows:

```
loginSound = new Sound(loginSound);
loginSound.attachSound("loginSound");
```

Of course, sound isn't necessary; however, it is a good opportunity to illustrate that in any custom function you create, you can add any sort of interactive elements you are accustomed to using in your Flash projects.

This completes the actions carried out after receiving the `<login>` element from the socket. After this data has been sent to Flash, the server then sends an updated `<list>` element that represents logged-in users. This procedure is handled in the `inputHandler()` function, as shown here:

```
if (input.nodeName=="list") {
    list(input.attributes.names);
  }
```

When this `<list>` element is received, you instantly send the value of the `names` attribute to the custom `list()` function:

```
function list(str){
  str = (str.split(",")).join("\n");
  _root.members = str;
}
```

Here you are splitting the string value in the `names` attribute and adding line breaks between each split. For instance, if the following value for `names` was received

```
names="Craig,Gregg,Linda,John"
```

The `list()` function would translate this data to

```
Craig
Gregg
Linda
John
```

This newly constructed `str` value is then placed inside the member text field on stage, which represents the users logged in to the chat application.

Figure 11.5 shows what the chat application looks like after a user has logged in (being the only connected user at this time).

Figure 11.5   *The chat application after login.*

Transmitting Messages

At this point, you have covered everything involved with a successful login, but you still haven't used the chat application in terms of transmitting messages! These messages are sent by using a protocol similar to the ones for the login and the list() function, and are also handled in the inputHandler() function, as shown here:

```
if (input.nodeName=="msg") {
    var nameOut =
➡ "<font color='#000000'>&lt;"+input.attributes.sender+"&gt;</font>";
    var content = tagEncode(input.attributes.content);
    output(nameOut+content);
    contentSound.start(0, 1);
}
```

You can see from this code that messages are handled in much the same way; however, <msg> elements contain two attributes:—sender and content. For this reason, you need to handle each of these attributes separately.

The newly created nameOut variable takes the attribute value for sender and wraps it inside < and > to simulate most chat applications. You also set the font color for the sender as black (#000000) to stand out from the actual text in the content attribute of <msg>.

You then create a content variable that contains the value of the content attribute after it has been sent to the tagEncode() function. This function's responsibility is to run through the content attribute and create links from URLs that reside inside this attribute. If a chatter has typed in a URL (such as www. xmlinflash.com), the tagEncode() function finds the existence of a www. substring and creates a real HTML hyperlink for it, so other chatters can simply click on it and have the browser spawn a new window to load that URL. A simple anchor tag is wrapped around the URL so that it can be hyperlinked directly from the chat window. We won't go through this code here in detail because it's just an added feature, but we will display it for your review:

```
function tagEncode(str){
  str = unescape(str);

  // switch all ' to &apos;
  while (str.indexOf("'") != -1) {
    var ind = str.indexOf("'");
    str = str.substr(0, ind) + "&apos;" + str.substr(ind+1);
  }

  // switch all < to &lt;
  while (str.indexOf("<") != -1) {
    var ind = str.indexOf("<");
    str = str.substr(0, ind) + "&lt;" + str.substr(ind+1);
  }

  // switch all > to &gt;
  while (str.indexOf(">") != -1) {
    var ind = str.indexOf(">");
    str = str.substr(0, ind) + "&gt;" + str.substr(ind+1);
  }

  if (str.indexOf("www.") != -1) {
    var ind = str.indexOf("www.");
    var endpoint = str.indexOf("%20", ind);
    endpoint = (endpoint == -1) ? str.length : endpoint;
    var altern = str.indexOf(" ", ind);
    if ((altern < endpoint) && (altern != -1)){
      endpoint = altern;
    }
    var segment = str.substr(ind, endpoint-ind);
    var atag = "<a target='newone' href='http://";
    atag += escape(segment)+"'>"+segment+"</a>";
    str = str.substr(0, ind) + atag + str.substr(endpoint);
  }
  return(str);
}
```

After the `tagEncode()` function returns the new string to `inputHandler()`, you concatenate the `sender` and `content` data as follows and send it to the `output()` function, which as we've shown is responsible for displaying this data in the chat text field:

```
output(nameOut+content);
```

Again, as with the login process, a `contentSound` is triggered to signify that a user has submitted a message to the chat application. Figure 11.6 shows an example of a comment submitted by a user.

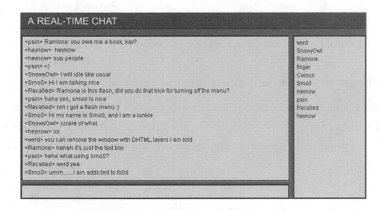

Figure 11.6 *User's comment in the chat application.*

Server Disconnection

The only remaining protocol we haven't covered is for disconnecting from the server. No user input is involved in this process. The server detects a disconnection when a user quits the browser or if there is some network breakdown and no connection can be made with the client. When this happens, much like the login process, the server sends a `<disconnect>` XML element to Flash, followed by an updated `<list>` element reflecting the recently disconnected user. This procedure is handled in Flash by the same `inputHandler()` function:

```
if (input.nodeName=="disconnect") {
    output("<font color='#734567'>*** "+input.attributes.name+
➥" quit the chat ***</font>");
    logOffSound.start(0, 1);
  }
```

Here you simply display text saying that a user has "quit the chat" in the chat text field. The value for this user is determined by the value for the name attribute. After this text is displayed, you trigger the logOffSound to signal to other connected users via audio that a user has disconnected. Flash would then receive a <list> element, just as it did when a user logged in, and process it exactly the same.

Meanwhile, on the Server Side...

By now you have the server running and are probably already asking "a/s/l?" from anyone you've persuaded to join the chat. If you're at all interested in what the server is doing, we'll be explaining that process now. If you don't care about these details, that's fine. They're essential only for programmers who want to customize the server to their liking.

As in the previous mock market ticker example, we've included all the classes in a single .java file. This isn't exactly great form (each class should be in its own .java file), but it keeps everything nice and neat. These are the three classes we're constructing:

- FCServer—the main, public class
- Client—a helper class to represent a single connected user
- Clients—another helper class, which is primarily an array of objects of type Client

FCServer, the main class, does most of the work. By running this class, the main() method is automatically invoked, and the program creates a network socket to listen for connections. When someone does connect, FCServer creates an instance of itself to manage that specific user so that it can go back to listening for other new users. The newly created instance is spawned as a new thread, meaning that it will manage itself and run at the same time as the main server. In that way, it can handle new connections and already connected users at the same time. The server can keep spawning these new threads as new users join the chat, so a theoretically limitless number of users can chat at the same time. Java runs quite a bit faster than ActionScript, too, so you can expect that very high user loads on your chat server will probably crash Flash long before they crash this server. We've tested it quite extensively, though, and haven't seen a limit on the number of users (yet).

It's also important to notice that FCServer contains a static member named clients, which is a *vector* (somewhat like an array in ActionScript, but a little more heavy-duty) of objects of type Client. It just keeps a bunch of those objects together for easy access.

The Client object that is held in the Clients object is meant to represent a user connected to the server via the network. When FCServer spawns an instance of itself (see the constructor for FCServer) as a new thread, that instance automatically creates a Client object to represent itself, and then it adds that object to Clients.

Communication between Client objects is pretty simple. When a client wants to say something, it loops through the entire Clients list, telling each client what it wants to say. This is mostly handled by the Clients.broadcast() method.

When the server receives a login XML document or notices a disconnection, it broadcasts that info to the clients; similarly, it also broadcasts a list XML document that keeps the users up to date on who is and is not still in the chat.

This is just a simple overview of what is going on, but if you want to know more about the details, check out the heavily commented source code in Listing 11.1 ("Use the source, Luke!").

Listing 11.1   FCServer.java, the Source Code for the Flash Chat Server

```
import java.net.*;
import java.io.*;
import java.util.*;  //for arraylist
public class FCServer implements Runnable {
    /*
    FCServer is a class to represent a Flash Chat Server, using our
    specific XML-based protocol.  It implements Runnable here so
    that multiple FCServers can exist concurrently, handling
    multiple connections from users (called 'clients' from here on).
    In this way, the multiple users can pass messages to one another
    in an IRC-style chatroom.

    At a transparent lower level, messages are sent using XML.  A
    user who wants to say 'hello' to the room would do so by logging
    in with <login name='Joey' /> and sending
    <msg content='hello' /> to the server.  The server would receive
    the login and send a new user's list to each person chatting with
    a format like this:

    <list names='Johnny,CJ,Marky,DeeDee,Joey' />
```

__Listing 11.1   continued__

```
In response to the 'msg' XML from the user, the server would
respond with <msg content'hello' sender='Joey' /> with the only
difference being the addition of a sender attribute.  In this way,
the server can broadcast to all connected clients that Joey has
said 'hello'.  This server is fully Telnet-capable, so feel free to
try it in Telnet as well as Flash.  It's certainly not as pretty
there, and you have to watch your XML syntax, but it should give
you a good understanding of how it works.

*/

Socket socket;       /* This socket object is used to manage network
            communications for a single client.  It is
            created in main(), but is passed on and exists
            for all clients in their respective threads. */
int ID;         //number to differentiate different clients
Client thisClient;  /* When an FCServer is instantiated (not
            static), this Client object represents a
            connected client.  The Client class definition
            is shown below the FCServer class in this file.*/
static Clients clients = new Clients(); /* Create a single new
                instance of Clients (class definition appears
                below the FCServer class). This class is a simple
                vector of Clients (also defined below
                FCServer).*/

public static void main(String[] arg){
    /* main() is the primary method and it is run when the
    application is started.  It exists as a single thread throughout
    the application's lifetime, despite the fact that this class is
    instantiated once for every user, because it is defined as
    'static'. */
    int port = 5555;     /*listen on port 5555.  (if you're
                planning on trying this with Telnet,
                remember to Telnet to your server through
                port 5555!) */
    try {
        ServerSocket s = new ServerSocket(port);
        /* The above line creates a new ServerSocket that will
        listen on the given port.  This is a special kind of socket
        used only for accepting connections from clients.  Once the
        connection is accepted, this socket can be used to create a
        Socket object that will handle the actual communications.
        */
        System.out.println("Waiting on port " + port);  /* a message
                to let you know that the server is running
                and listening on the given port. */
        while(true) {
        /* "while(true)" creates an infinite loop that will never
        terminate on its own.  This looping will continue until the
        application is closed.  In this way, the server is always
        listening.  */
```

Listing 11.1   continued

```
            Socket socket = s.accept();  /* s.accept() tells our
            ServerSocket (named 's') to wait until a client connects.
            When a client does connect, accept the connection, and
            pass it on as a socket called (interestingly enough)
            'socket'. */
            System.out.println("Connect! Number of users is now " +
                    clients.size() + "."); /* A message to
              let you know that a client has connected */
            FCServer fcserver = new FCServer(socket);
            /*  Here's where you create an instance of FCServer, by
            passing it a reference to the socket. */

            /* Below you create and start a new thread based on the
            newly created server. From here on, the server runs in
            its own thread and does not terminate until it terminates
            itself, or the entire application terminates. */
            Thread thread = new Thread(fcserver);
            thread.start();

            /* The "while(true)" loop continues at this point, so that
            the server may accept multiple connections at once. */
        }
    } catch (Exception e) {
        //Some simple error catching...
        System.err.println("Server error");
        System.err.println(e);
    }
}


FCServer(Socket socket) {
/* This is the constructor for an FCServer.  A Socket object is passed
   to it so that it can be put into a Client object for more permanent
   storage.
 */
    this.socket = socket;  /* put the socket into the FCServer's socket
                            member */

    try {
        OutputStream os = socket.getOutputStream();
        PrintWriter pw = new PrintWriter(os, true);
        /* Essentially, the two lines above create a PrintWriter object
          called pw from the socket.  The PrintWriter is all you need in
          order to talk through the socket.  You create a new Client
          object and passit the PrintWriter and the list of clients
          (called 'clients') */
        thisClient = new Client(pw, clients);
        clients.add(thisClient); /* add the new client to the the list of
                            'clients' */
    } catch (Exception e) {
        //Some simple error catching...
        System.out.println(e);
```

Listing 11.1   continued

```java
        }
}

public void run() {
    /* This method is called automatically when FCServer is started as a
       thread. */
    try {
        InputStream is = socket.getInputStream();
        InputStreamReader isr = new InputStreamReader(is);
        BufferedReader br = new BufferedReader(isr);
        /* What you've done above is created a BufferedReader from the
           socket.  The BufferReader object 'br' is all you need now
           to listen to incoming communications.
         */

        while (true) {
            /* here again you have an infinite loop that terminates only
             * when the thread dies or when the application itself
             terminates */
            String str = br.readLine();  /* wait until a carriage return
                        (\n) is received and put the entire string (up
                        until the carriage return) into a String called
                        str. */
            str = str.trim();  /*Trim off an extra whitespace (\0 an \n
                        are the main concerns). */

            // login stuff...
            if (str.substring(0,13).equals("<login name=\'")){
                //if it's a login...
                if (!thisClient.loggedIn){
                    //if the client is not already logged in...
                    System.out.println("logging in...");

                    /* below you extract the login name, and put it in
                     the 'name' member of the Client */
                    int aposInd = str.substring(13).indexOf('\'') + 13;
                    thisClient.name = str.substring(13,aposInd);

                    clients.listOut();  /* Call listOut() to let every
                                    client know the new updated
                                    client list.*/
                }
            }

            // message stuff...
            if (str.substring(0,14).equals("<msg content=\'")){
                //if it's a message...
                int aposInd = str.substring(14).indexOf('\'') + 14;
                str = "<msg content=\'"+str.substring(14,aposInd)+
                        "' sender='" + thisClient.name + "' />";
```

Listing 11.1   continued

```
                        /* The above lines extract the message's content and
                           rewrite the tag entirely, adding in the 'sender'
                           attribute, so all clients will know who the message
                           is from. */
                }

                // whether it's a login or a message...
                System.out.println("broadcasting: "+str);  /* show the string
                              going out in the console */
                clients.broadcast(str); // broadcast the string to all clients
            }
        } catch (Exception e) {
            /* Catch and display errors.  Here is where you catch a client
            disconnection.  A client disconnection generates an exception
            that breaks the while loop and enters these 'catch' and
             'finally' blocks. */
            System.err.println(e);
        } finally {
            System.out.println("Disconnect! Number of users is now " +
                        clients.size() + ".");
            clients.remove(thisClient);  /* Remove this client from the
                                      'clients' list. */
            clients.broadcast("<disconnect name='"+thisClient.name+"' />");
                /* let all the clients know that this client has
                   disconnected. */
            clients.listOut();  /* Call listOut() to let every client
                              know the new updated client list.*/

            try {
                socket.close();                    // close the socket
            } catch (Exception e) {
                /* you do nothing here; an error closing the socket means
                   the socket was already closed, so you don't care. */
            }
        }
    }
}
class Clients extends Vector{
    /* Clients is a class that extends Vector, intended for containing
    Client objects.  It adds the listOut() and broadcast() methods also.
    "broadcast()" takes a string and sends it out to each of the clients
    over their PrintWriter object, which represents the network socket.
    "listOut()" goes through the list and constructs an XML document
    representing the list of clients.  This list is then broadcast using
    broadcast().
    */

    public Clients(){
        super();  // use the standard Vector constructor;
    }
```

Listing 11.1   continued

```java
    public void listOut(){
        /* "listOut()" goes through the list and constructs an XML document
       representing the list of clients.  This list is then broadcast using
       broadcast(). */

        String cList = "<list names='";
        Iterator c = iterator();
        while (c.hasNext()) {
           cList += ((Client)c.next()).name +",";
        }
        cList += "' />";
        // above you create the XML document by looping through the clients

        System.out.println(cList);
        broadcast(cList);   //broadcast the XML document
    }

    public void broadcast(String str){
        /* "broadcast()" takes a string and sends it out to each of the
           clients over their PrintWriter object, which represents the
           network socket. */
        System.out.println(str);
        str = str.trim() + "\0"; //add the null character that Flash needs.

        Iterator writers = iterator();
        while (writers.hasNext()) {
          //loop through the clients, and for each...
          ((Client)writers.next()).hear(str); /* make them 'hear' what you're
                                                sending, the string. */
        }
    }
}
class Client {
    /* The Client class represents a client, which is a connected user.  */
    public PrintWriter ear;    /* PrintWriter output.  If you want to talk to
                                  the client, you do so through 'ear'. */
    public String name;        // the client's name
    boolean loggedIn = false;  /*status indicating whether or not they are
                                  logged in. Between connection and sending the
                                  actual login XML document, loggedIn is false.
                                  */
    Clients otherClients;      /* you keep a reference to the 'clients' list
                                  here too, so this Client can remove itself
                                  or broadcast() to the others. */
    public Client(PrintWriter prntwrtr, Clients clientsPtr ){
        /* This is the constructor for the Client class. It takes a
           PrintWriter and a Clients object (which is a list of Clients) */
        ear = prntwrtr;        // the PrintWriter is now the client's 'ear'
        otherClients = clientsPtr;  /* 'otherClients' will now point to
                                       the clients list. */
    }
```

Listing 11.1   continued

```
public void hear(String str){
   /* when you want the client to hear something (which means 'when you
   want to send something to a specific user connected via Flash'),
   you pass the string to this hear() method. */
   str = str.trim();      // cut out whitespace
   ear.println(str+"\0"); /* slap a null character on the end and send
                           it out! */
}

public void tell(String str){
   /* a client broadcasts to everyone when it has something to tell() */
   otherClients.broadcast(str);
}
}
```

If you have a little Java experience, you'll soon find that altering the protocol in this source file can be pretty simple, and you might even consider adding features such as private person-to-person messages or multiple chat rooms. If you don't have any Java experience, this might be a little inspiration to jump in and start learning. It's not the simplest language, but it does ensure that your XML server will run on many different hardware platforms and operating systems. We would certainly appreciate hearing about any modifications or improvements you make at www.xmlinflash.com.

Summary

You've covered a lot of ground here, moving from simple one-way socket communications to a full-on multiuser chat environment that can handle dozens of simultaneous connections. You learned how to create and establish protocols between the client and server and structure them in XML to support the XMLSocket class you have available at your disposal—and all of this with middleware scripts that allowed you to pull and push data to an database. From this example, you should be able to put to use what you've learned and begin to create your own applications, with your own Flash touch.

So What's Next?

Well, that's up to you! The tools are at your fingertips—it's all in the inspiration. Remember, XML is only a way to communicate data. Ultimately, when using Flash, it's what you do with that data that creates the first impression, that engaging interactive experience. It comes down to application. How can XML be used? How will XML be used? Share these questions with those you work with. Begin to visualize your content in these data structures. The more you do this, the more the rest of your development will adhere to this structure and streamline your XML production process.

In the pages that follow we've put together comprehensive appendixes covering all the methods and properties of both the XML and XMLSocket objects. A further resource appendix has dozens of links to Flash sites, XML sites, and XML-related sites based on both ASP and PHP. This book is meant to get you not only up on your feet, but also running. You should now be able, with this book, to tackle XML and begin to incorporate it into your projects, and we can't wait to see what develops!

We hope you'll share your insights and discoveries with us and others at the supporting www.xmlinflash.com site. We aim to make it a central resource for Flash developers interested in exploring the possibilities of XML in Flash. But first... Go outside. ☺

{ Part IV }

Appendixes

{ Appendix A }

The XML and XMLNode Objects

This appendix is intended as a reference for the methods and properties of the XML and XMLNode objects. Although the XMLNode object is not an officially documented object, it is actually more important than the XML object. Just as XML documents are made up of a hierarchy of elements, the representation of XML in Flash is made up of a number of XMLNode objects. The XML object is meant to hold a reference to the first XMLNode, which represents the root element. The XML object also has a few other properties used to describe the document as a whole, including the document type declaration (XML.docTypeDecl), and the XML declaration (XML.xmlDecl). Beyond these properties, the XML object is extremely close to being the same object as the XMLNode. It supports all the methods and properties that the XMLNode does, so this appendix discusses both objects at the same time.

Methods of the XML and XMLNode Objects

A *method* is a function that is logically tied to an object. Here's a brief look at the methods of the XML and XMLNode objects. Detailed descriptions of these methods are given later in this appendix.

```
XML.appendChild()
XML.cloneNode()
XML.createElement()
```

```
XML.createTextNode()

XML.hasChildNodes()

XML.insertBefore()

XML.load()

XML.onData()

XML.onLoad()

XML.parseXML()

XML.removeNode()

XML.send()

XML.sendAndLoad()

XML.toString()
```

Properties of the XML and XMLNode Objects

The *properties* of an object are its associated variables. All the properties of the
XML and XMLNode objects are readable, but some of them are not write properties,
meaning they cannot have values assigned to them. The following is a look at
these properties, but later in this appendix, detailed descriptions give information
about access restrictions.

```
XML.contentType

XML.docTypeDecl

XML.firstChild

XML.ignoreWhite

XML.lastChild

XML.loaded

XML.nextSibling

XML.nodeName

XML.nodeType

XML.nodeValue

XML.parentNode

XML.previousSibling

XML.status

XML.xmlDecl
```

Collections for the XML and XMLNode Objects

Collection is a loose term that describes data structures representing lists of data. The following is a listing of those collections for XML and XMLNode objects.

```
XML.attributes

XML.childNodes
```

XML() (Constructor for the XML Object Prototype)

The XML object constructor is used with the new keyword to create an XML object. Like all object constructors in ActionScript, it is a method carrying the same name as the object it constructs.

- **Type:** Constructor method
- **Syntax:**

```
new XML();
new XML(source);
```

- **Parameter:** source is a string representing an entire XML document to be parsed and used in creating the XML object.
- **Returns:** A reference to an XML object
- **Description:** This is the constructor function for the XML object and must be used (initialized) to access or manipulate any XML in Flash. No methods or properties of the XML object will be available until a new XML object instance is created.

  The XML object can be instantiated with or without a source XML document, as illustrated in the syntax. To create a simple empty XML object to populate and manipulate, you need only use new XML();.

  To alter an existing XML object in Flash, you need to set the argument for the XML source. This is in the form of a string.
- **Player Version:** 5.*
- **Examples:** The following line creates an empty XML object:

```
myXML= new XML();
```

The following code creates an XML object that contains the XML document specified in the source parameter of the XML object:

```
// create new XML doc as string
XMLstring = "<hello>there</hello>";
// create new object referencing XML doc that was placed in string
MyXML = new XML(XMLstring);
```

- **Notes:** This object represents the XML document, but it does not completely compose Flash's representation of that document. All the actual nodes of a document (from the root element to the leaf elements) are represented by the XMLNode object.

XML.appendChild (**also** XMLNode.appendChild)

The appendChild() method is used to add an XMLNode as the last child of another XMLNode in the object representation of an XML tree.

- **Type:** Method

- **Syntax:** XML.appendChild(childNode);

- **Parameter:** childNode specifies the child node to be added (appended) to the XML object's list of children.

- **Returns:** Nothing

- **Description:** This method is used to add childNodes to an existing XML object. When used, unless specified, it adds the childNode in the method's parameter to the end of the tree. This is actually a constructor for an XMLNode object, although it also attaches that XMLNode object to another XMLNode object or an XML object. The new child will be accessible as the lastChild of the XMLNode for which this method was called.

- **Player Version:** 5.*

- **Example:** The following example creates an XML object to represent the steps taken to wash your hair. In the beginning, the document is created with <lather /> and <rinse /> elements, but it is lacking the indispensable <repeat />. By using createElement(), the <repeat /> node is created. It is then appended to the firstChild of shampooAlgorithm (which is the root element). Because appendChild() appends to the end, calling trace() on the new shampooAlgorithm object reveals the steps in the correct order.

```
shampooAlgorithm = new XML("<sa><lather /><rinse /></sa>");
repeatNode = shampooAlgorithm.createElement("repeat");
shampooAlgorithm.firstChild.appendChild(repeatNode);
trace(shampooAlgorithm.toString());
```

XMLNode.attributes

The attributes array is an associative array representing the attributes of the XMLNode object.

- **Type:** Collection (associative array)

- **Syntax:** XML.attributes["varname"];

- **Description:** This object represents what is called a collection or *associative array* of attributes for a specified XMLNode. Unlike the arrays you might be accustomed to in Flash, which are numerical, this type of array uses literal indices. You cannot access attributes like this:

    ```
    myXML.firstchild.attributes[2];
    ```

    You must reference them literally:

    ```
    myXML.firstChild.attributes["name"]
    ```

    Essentially, you can think of this as an object, and each element is a read and write property of that object. For that reason, you can also access it like this:

    ```
    myXML.firstChild.attributes.name
    ```

- **Player Version:** 5.*

- **Example:** This example grabs the attribute value from a selected node:

    ```
    // create a simple XML doc
    Str = "<artist type="chill" albums="3">Tosca</artist>";
    // create a new XML object referencing the XML doc created
    myXML = new XML(str);
    // set value equal to the attribute "type"
    value = myXML.firstChild.attributes.type;
    //trace this 'value' to the output window
    trace (value);
    ```

    This code will trace chill into the Output window.

- **Notes:** Unlike the traditional arrays you might be used to in Flash, using attributes does not give you access to a length property. So to determine the number of attributes, you need a for loop that cycles through the attributes:

    ```
    counter = 1;
    // loop through each attribute of the firstChild
    for (var each in myXML.firstChild.attributes){
    // output attributes to output window
    trace ("Attribute # " + counter +" :  "  + each + " = "
    ➥+ myXML.firstChild.attributes[each]);
    counter++;
    }
    ```

This code will trace the following into the Output window:

```
Attribute # 1: type = chill
Attribute # 2: albums = 3
```

XML.childNodes (**also** XMLNode.childnodes)

The childNodes array represents the childNodes of the referenced XMLNode. (It can also be used for the XML object, but it has only one child, the root element.)

- **Type:** Collection (array)

- **Syntax:** MyXML.childnodes[i];

- **Description:** This property contains an array of elements in the XMLNode that is referenced. It can be used on any node in an XML object, not just the root element. This property is often used to pull data from XML documents by using recursive algorithms (see Chapter 4, "Using XML Data in Flash"). Unlike the associative array for .attributes, you can access the .length property of the childNodes array, which is helpful in directly pulling information from the XML document.

- **Player Version:** 5.*

- **Examples:** If you create a simple XML document as follows

```
str = "<artist><name>Tosca</name>";
str += "<genre>chill</genre><cd>Suzuki Dub</cd></artist>";
artistXML = new XML(str);
```

You can then access the child nodes (name, genre, cd) of <artist>, which is the firstChild of this XML document, by using the childNodes property like so:

```
for (i=0;i<artistXML.firstChild.childNodes.length; i++){
trace ("childNode # " + i + " is :  " +
                     artistXml.firstChild.childNodes[i]);
}
```

- **Notes:** MyXML.childnodes[0] refers to the root element of the XML document. You've also seen MyXML.firstChild refer to the root element of an XML document. Both syntaxes are valid and will work. It is often convenient to refer to the root element as firstChild to differentiate the subelements of an XML document from the root element. Similarly, these other equalities can be useful:

```
XMLNode.childnodes[XMLNode.childNodes.length] == XMLNode.lastChild
XMLNode.childnodes[2] == XMLNode.childnodes[1].nextSibling
```

```
XMLNode.childnodes[1] == XMLNode.childnodes[2].previousSibling
(XMLNode.childnodes.length > 0) == (XMLNode.hasChildnodes())
```

XML.cloneNode() **(also** XMLNode.cloneNode()**)**

The cloneNode() method is used to make a copy of an XMLNode object.

- **Type:** Method

- **Syntax:** XML.cloneNode(deep)

- **Parameter:** (deep) is a Boolean value used to determine whether to clone all childNodes of the node being cloned. If set to true, it includes all recursive childNodes; if set to false, it copies only the referenced node and its attribute values.

- **Returns:** Nothing

- **Description:** This method is used to clone or duplicate XML nodes from an XML hierarchy. As mentioned, the parameter (deep) is used to determine whether to recursively clone all children of the node or just the node that is referenced.

- **Player Version:** 5.*

- **Examples:** This example clones a node from one XML document and places it inside the variable newNode:

```
// here you define the XML document
Str = "<artist><name>tosca</name><genre>chill</genre></artist>";
// here you create the XML object using the document you defined
MyXml = new XML(str);
// here you clone the node and place it in 'newNode'
NewNode = MyXML.firstChild.cloneNode(true);
```

  Now you can easily modify the contents of this clone and add it back to the original XML document:

```
// modify the <name> element value
newNode.firstChild.firstChild.nodeValue = "Ramones";
// modify the <genre> element value
newNode.firstChild.nextSibling.firstChild.nodeValue = "punk";
```

  So newNode has been completely altered from the original cloned node. This makes it easy to add it back to the XML object:

```
// add the cloned node to the myXML object
myXML.appendChild(newNode);
```

If you perform a `trace()` action on the entire XML object, you now get this:

```
<artist><name>tosca</name><genre>chill</genre></artist><artist>
➥<name>Ramones</name><genre>punk</genre></artist>
```

You have successfully cloned the original node, modified it with new content, and added it back to the XML object.

- **Notes:** The Boolean value that determines whether `childNodes` are included in the cloning can be hard-coded or set dynamically. You can place `true` or `false` as the parameter to hard-code this method:

```
MyXML.cloneNode(true);
```

Or you can set the value of the `deep` parameter to be `true` or `false` so that you can set the value dynamically based on other events in your Flash application:

```
deep = true;
MyXML.cloneNode(deep);
```

XML.contentType

The `contentType` property is used to read or set the content type of the XML object (only revision 41 and later).

- **Type:** Property
- **Syntax:** `XML.contentType;`
- **Description:** This property, added in build 5.0.41 of the Flash player, is used to reference the MIME type sent to the server when using `myXML.send` or `myXML.sendAndLoad`. The default for the `contentType` property is `application/x-www-urlform-encoded`. This property can be modified for individual XML objects or changed globally for all XML objects via the `prototype` method.
- **Player Version:** 5.0.41 and later
- **Examples:**

```
trace("The content type for this document is" + myXML.contentType);
```

XML.createElement (also XMLNode.createElement)

The createElement() method is used to create a nontext XMLNode.

- **Type:** Method
- **Syntax:** XML.createElement(name);
- **Parameter:** name is a string representing the new element's nodeName.
- **Returns:** A reference to a new XMLNode object representing a node of type 1 (an element node).
- **Description:** This method is essentially an XMLNode constructor used to create a new XML element node with the name specified in the argument (name). When created, this XMLNode will contain no parent or children nodes.
- **Player Version:** Flash 5.*
- **Examples:** The following example adds a new element to an empty XML object:

```
myXML = new XML();
newElement = myXML.createElement("artist");
myXML.appendChild(newElement);
trace (myXML);
```

This code sends the following to the Output window:

```
<artist/>
```

As you may recall, that is the way empty elements are displayed. You can also reduce the code by placing the newElement reference to the argument of the createElement method, like so:

```
myXML = new XML();
myXML.appendChild(myXML.createElement("artist"));
trace (myXML);
```

- **Notes:** This method cannot create text nodes; to do this, you need to use the createTextNode method.

XML.createTextNode (also XMLNode.createTextNode)

The createTextNode() method is used to create a text XMLNode.

- **Type:** Method

- **Syntax:** XML.createTextNode(text);

- **Parameter:** (text) defines the text to be used in the new text node that is created.

- **Returns:** A reference to a new XMLNode object representing a node of type 3 (a text node).

- **Description:** This method is responsible for creating new text nodes in an XML object. Like createElement(), this method creates an XMLNode. However, this XMLNode represents character data. If you are not referring to a variable containing the text, you must encapsulate the text string in quotes.

- **Player Version:** 5.*

- **Examples:** Taken from the createElement example, you have this code:

```
myXML = new XML();
myXML.appendChild(myXML.createElement("artist"));
trace (myXML);
```

All you've done here is create a new element: <artist>. A call to trace() displays the following in the Output window:

```
<artist/>
```

Now add a text node to this element:

```
newTextNode = myXML.createTextNode("Tosca");
myXML.firstChild.appendChild(newTextNode);
trace (myXML);
```

When you issue a trace() statement, you will see the following in the Output window:

```
<artist>Tosca</artist>
```

XML.docTypeDecl

The docTypeDecl property is used to read or set the document type declaration of the XML object.

- **Type:** Property

- **Syntax:** XML.docTypeDecl

- **Parameters:** None

- **Returns:** This property returns the DocType declaration of the XML object.

- **Description:** This property is used to read or manipulate the XML document's DocType declaration. Although Flash's XML parser does not validate the XML or reference any DTDs during parsing, you might still need the DocType declaration in your XML for any server-side parsing of the XML or to describe the XML document's content.

  This information is stored in the docTypeDecl property of the XML object so that it can be accessed later, if necessary. Note that this data is represented as string data, not as an XMLNode object.

  The doctypeDecl property returns as undefined following Flash parsing if it is not found in the XML document. If, during parsing, the docTypeDecl is detected, Flash places it immediately after the document's XML declaration.

- **Player Version:** 5.*

- **Examples:** The following example sets the DocType declaration for a newly created XML object:

```
MyXML = new XML();
MyXML.docTypeDecl = "<!DOCTYPE newsContent SOURCE \"newsXML.dtd\">";
```

- **Notes:** The docTypeDecl of the XML object always immediately follows the xmlDecl of the XML document. Both declarations are not XMLNode objects, but rather string representations. Although Flash records this information, it does not use it in any way. Flash's XML parser is a non-validating parser.

XML.firstChild (also XMLNode.firstChild)

The firstChild property is used to get the first child node of the referenced XML or XMLNode object.

- **Type:** Property (read-only)

- **Syntax:**

```
XML.firstChild
XMLNode.firstChild;
```

- **Returns:** The first child in the parent node's list of children

- **Description:** This property is used only to identify the first `childNode` in a parent's list of child nodes. This property is read-only and cannot be used to set the actual first child node of the `XMLNode` object. If the `XMLNode` contains no children, this property returns `null`. The same child is also accessible as follows:

  ```
  XMLNode.childnodes[0];
  ```

- **Player Version:** 5.*

- **Examples:** The following example demonstrates how to access nodes by using this property:

  ```
  // create an XML doc to be used to populate your XML object
  str = "<artist><name>Tosca<genre>chill</genre></name></artist>";
  // create new XML object and populate it with 'str'
  myXML = new XML(str);
  ```

  Now the root element in this XML document is <artist>. Inside <artist> is a child node called <name>, which contains another child node with the <name> value Tosca. You can access or reference these nodes as follows:

  ```
  // access the firstChild of the XML doc <artist>
  trace (myXML.firstChild);
  // access the firstChild of <artist> which is <name>
  trace (myXML.firstChild.firstChild);
  ```

- **Notes:** The `firstChild` property is identical to using the `childNodes` array. You can reference the same node by using `firstChild` or `childNodes[0]`. Both properties return the same value, as shown here:

  ```
  // the following trace() statements will produce the same result
  trace (myXML.firstChild.firstChild);
  trace (myXML.firstChild.childNodes[0]);
  ```

  These `trace()` statements both return the `myXML.firstChild.firstChild` element to the Output window.

XML.ignoreWhite

The `ignoreWhite` property is used to toggle the flag that determines whether the XML object should ignore whitespace when parsing (only revision 41 and later).

- **Type:** Property

- **Syntax:** `XML.ignoreWhite;`

- **Returns:** A Boolean value indicating whether whitespace should be ignored for this particular XML object for subsequent calls to XML.parseXML().

- **Description:** This property, added in build 41 of the Flash 5 player, was intended to ease parsing of XML documents by ignoring whitespace. Whitespace is the carriage returns, tabs, and so forth used for easy human readability when creating XML documents. Before this property was available, you had to manually "strip" whitespace from the XML object after the XML had been parsed.

  Based on a Boolean value, ignoreWhite either discards or includes whitespace in an XML document. By default Flash sets ignoreWhite to false, so you need to set it to true if you want to discard empty nodes that have been created as a result of your formatting.

- **Player Version:** 5.0.41 or later

- **Examples:** The following example sets the ignoreWhite property to true, discarding all text nodes that contain whitespace only:

```
XML.ignoreWhite= true;
```

- **Notes:** This property can be applied to all XML objects by setting the value in the XML object's prototype, or it can be applied only to specific documents by setting it for that particular instantiation of the XML object. It cannot be used on individual XMLNodes because it is a property of the XML object, not the XMLNode object. You must also set this property before the actual parsing of your XML document.

XML.hasChildNodes() (also XMLNode.hasChildNodes())

The hasChildNodes() method is used to determine whether an XMLNode has child nodes.

- **Type:** Method

- **Syntax:** XML.hasChildNodes();

- **Parameters:** None

- **Returns:** true if the specified XML object contains child nodes

- **Description:** This property determines whether the specified XML or XMLNode object contains any childNode objects. This is a particularly helpful method when performing any recursive functions, such as writing a whitespace stripper or parsing XML objects into Flash.

- **Player Version:** 5.*

- **Examples:** The following example detects whether an `<artist>` node contains any children. If so, it calls a function to further work with the information:

```
str = "<artist><name>tosca<genre>chill</genre></name></artist>";
myXML = new XML(str);
If (XML.firstChild.hasChildNodes()){
ArtistFunction(XML.firstChild);
}
```

This script simply determines whether there are `childNodes` in the `<artist>` element. If so, the `ArtistFunction` gets called, sending the `<artist>` element as an argument. It could be used to further manipulate the particular data in the `childNode` object.

- **Notes:** This method is essentially the same as
  `(this.childNodes.length > 0)`.

XML.insertBefore() (also XMLNode.insertBefore())

The `insertBefore()` method is used to append a child node, but it allows you to insert that node before other siblings if you are concerned about their order.

- **Type:** Method
- **Syntax:** `XML.insertBefore(newNode, beforeNode)`
- **Parameters:** `newNode` is a reference to an existing `XMLNode` object that you want to insert into an `XML` object.

  `beforeNode` specifies which node you would like to insert the `newNode` before.

- **Description:** Like the `appendChild()` method, this method is used to insert `XMLNode` objects into an existing `XML` object hierarchy. However, this method holds a little more power because you can control where you want to place the `XMLNode`. Unlike `appendChild()`, which merely adds it to the bottom of the hierarchy, `insertBefore()` enables you to insert it anywhere in an XML document by simply specifying in the parameters which node you would like it placed before.

- **Player Version:** 5.*
- **Example:** The following example creates a short two-node list of favorite foods. Right away, create the list with one node in it.

```
var str = "";
str = "<favorite_foods><food name='chicken pitas'
/></favorite_foods>";
foodsXML = new XML(str);
```

Unfortunately, it's missing the best food there is, so create a node to hold it by using createNode():

```
pizzaNode = foodsXML.createElement("food");
pizzaNode.attributes.name = "pizza";
```

Do a few calls to trace() to make sure you know what the XML currently looks like:

```
trace("pizzaNode: " + pizzaNode);
trace("foodsXML: " + foodsXML);
trace("");
```

This list of favorite foods should be in order of most to least favorite, so use insertBefore() to insert pizza in its rightful place (before chicken pitas):

```
trace("inserting "+pizzaNode.attributes.name
            +" before
"+foodsXML.firstChild.firstChild.attributes.name);
```

Here's the actual call to insertBefore():

```
var thePita = foodsXML.firstChild.firstChild;
foodsXML.firstChild.insertBefore(pizzaNode, thePita);
```

Then show the final XML in all its glory:

```
trace("");
trace("after: "+foodsXML);
```

XML.lastChild (**also** XMLNode.lastChild)

The lastChild property is used to get the last child node of the referenced XML or XMLNode object.

- **Type:** Property
- **Syntax:** XML.lastChild;
- **Returns:** The lastChild node of the referenced XMLnode
- **Description:** Like firstChild, this property is read-only and cannot be used to set the first child node of an XMLNode. This property simply returns a reference to the node that is the last child of the referenced node object. If there are no children, the property returns null.
- **Player Version:** 5.*

- **Example:** This example traces the value of `lastChild` to the Output window:

```
ArtistXML = new XML("<music><artist>Jazzanova</artist>
➥<artist>Kraftwerk</artist><artist>Tosca</artist></music>");
```

To access the `<artist>` elements and particularly the `lastChild`, you need to reference the `<music>` element (which is your root element and `firstChild` of the XML object) as the parent:

```
trace(artistXML.firstChild.lastChild);
```

This line sends the following to the Output window:

```
<artist>Tosca</artist>
```

- **Notes:** This property is similar to using `childNode[childNodes.length-1]`, as it returns the last child of the parent node object. Using `lastchild` is usually a more elegant way to access the same node object.

XML.load()

The `load()` method is used to load an XML document into an XML object tree. It can be used for loading XML from a Web server or from the local hard drive.

- **Type:** Method

- **Syntax:** `XML.load(location);`

- **Parameters:** `location` is the location where the XML document is loaded from. It's a string that can specify a relative or an absolute path.

- **Description:** This method is responsible for loading an XML document from an external location into the Flash environment. Once imported, the XML document is parsed and placed in the specified `XML` object. Like the `onData()` handler you may be familiar with in ActionScript, the `XML.load()` method is asynchronous and can work with the `XML.onLoad()` event handler.

- **Player Version:** 5.*

- **Examples:** You can load the XML document in by using a relative path:

```
MyXML = new XML();
MyXML.load ("myXML.xml");
```

Or you can load it in by targeting an absolute path:

```
MyXML = new XML();
MyXML.load ("http://www.yourDomain.com/xml/myXML.xml");
```

- **Notes:** There are several things to note here. First, like loadVariables(), all XML documents specified in the XML.load() method must reside on the same server as the Flash movie that calls it. There are ways around this through the use of middleware; however, generally files must reside on the same server.

  Although this method is responsible for loading XML content, you must still ensure that this information was imported and parsed properly inside Flash. To do this, you must either test the XML.loaded property or set a callback handler by using XML.onLoad(). The XML.status property can give you information about the success of the actual parsing.

XML.loaded

The loaded property is used to determine whether the XML document has finished its loading process, assuming load() was called at some time. It's probably more useful to override onLoad() if you really want to know whether loading has finished.

- **Type:** Property (read-only)

- **Syntax:** XML.loaded;

- **Parameters:** None

- **Returns:** true if the document has been loaded and false if it has not

- **Description:** This property is used with the XML.load() method. The purpose of this property is to test whether the document has been properly and fully loaded into the XML object hierarchy. If the file has been successfully parsed into Flash, it returns true; if a failure occurs during the load, it returns false.

- **Player Version:** 5.*

- **Example:** The following example loads in an XML document from the server and, using the XML.loaded property, forwards the movie to the appropriate area:

```
// create XML object
MyXML = new XML();
// load XML doc into newly created XML object
MyXML.load ("http://www.yourDomain.com/XML/myXML.xml");
// test to see if XML is loaded
if (MyXML.loaded){
// if it is go to frame label named 'initialize'
 gotoAndPlay("initialize")
}
```

- **Notes:** Along with using the `XML.loaded` property, you can also use the `XML.onLoad()` handler for setting actions to perform after the XML has been successfully parsed and placed in an `XML` object.

XMLNode.nextSibling

The `nextSibling` property is used to get the next sibling node of the referenced `XMLNode` object.

- **Type:** Property (read-only)
- **Syntax:** `XML.nextSibling;`
- **Parameters:** None
- **Returns:** `null` if no sibling exists; otherwise, it returns the `next sibling` node.
- **Description:** This read-only property is used to reference an `XMLNode`'s next sibling under its parent node. If there are siblings, this property returns the `nextSibling` in the parent node's child list. Using this property is useful for traversing through nodes in an `XML` object.
- **Player Version:** 5.*
- **Example:**

```
myXML = new XML("<bands><band name='The BeeGees' />
➥<band name='Screeching Weasal' /></bands>");
trace("The good band is
➥"+myXML.firstChild.firstChild.nextSibling.nodeName);
```

XMLNode.nodeName

The `nodeName` property is used to read or set the name of the referenced `XMLNode` object, assuming it's a regular, nontext element.

- **Type:** Property
- **Syntax:** `XML.nodeName;`
- **Returns:** The name of the element that the node represents
- **Description:** This property is used to access the node name of an `XMLNode` object; in particular, it accesses the node name of element nodes. If, however, the `XMLNode` is a `textNode`, this property returns `null`.
- **Player Version:** 5.*

- **Example:** This example searches through an XML object hierarchy and counts the number of <news> items you have, based on the name of the element tags:

```
// create simple XML doc
str= "<newsList><news>story#1</news><news>story#2</news>
➥<news>story#3</news></newsList>";
//create new XML object with newly created 'str'
newsXML = new XML(str);
// set news story counter to 0
counter = 0;
// loop through all childNodes of <newsList>
for(i=0; i < newsXML.firstChild.childNodes.length; i++){
    // check if nodeName of childNode is equal to "news"
    if (newsXML.firstChild.childNodes[i].nodeName == "news"){
    // increase counter if string matches
counter ++;
    }
}
// output to Output window the number of <news> stories
trace ("there are " + counter + " news stories in this xml docu-
ment");
```

XMLNode.nodeType

The nodeType property is used to get the type of the referenced XMLNode object. The value will be 3 for text nodes or 1 for nontext (element) nodes.

- **Type:** Property (read-only)

- **Syntax:** XMLNode.nodeType;

- **Returns:** 1 to denote an element node, or 3 to denote a text node

- **Description:** This property is used to determine the nodeType value of a given node. Unlike the full DOM specification for node types, which includes 12 different kinds, in Flash there are really only two nodeTypes you work with: element and node. An XML element is given the nodeType of 1, and all textNodes are given the nodeType of 3.

- **Player Version:** 5.*

- **Example:** The following example extracts the nodeTypes from the most basic XML structure:

```
// create XML doc
myXML = new XML("<artist>Tosca</artist>");
// determine nodeType of firstChild <artist>
trace("The node type is : " + myXML.firstChild.nodeType);
// determine nodeType of firstChild.firstChild
trace("The node type is : " + myXML.firstChild.firstChild.nodeType);
```

XMLNode.nodeValue

The nodeValue property is used to read or set the value of the referenced XMLNode object, assuming it's a text element.

- **Type:** Property

- **Syntax:** XML.nodeValue;

- **Parameters:** None

- **Returns:** The text of an XMLNode representing a text element

- **Description:** The nodeValue represents the string value of a text node. This property is used for extracting string information from textNodes (with a nodeType of 3) only. If the nodeValue is used with an element node, it returns a null nodeValue. It can be used to not only read or access nodeValues, but also to set or manipulate them.

- **Player Version:** 5.*

- **Example:** The following example first tests the value of a node and then manipulates that information by using nodeValue:

```
// construct new XML object
myXML = new XML("<artist>Dave Matthews Band</artist>
➥<albumTitle>Under the Table</albumTitle>");
// set variable to hold nodeValue
valueOfNode = myXML.firstChild.nextSibling.firstChild.nodeValue;
trace(valueOfNode);
```

The preceding trace() statement returns "Under the Table" to the Output window. However, the correct title is "Under the Table and Dreaming." Now that you've seen how to access the textual nodeValue of an XML element, you can modify the title to correct it:

```
// change and set the nodeValue of <albumTitle>
MyXML.firstChild.nextSibling.firstChild.nodeValue =
➥"Under the Table and Dreaming";
```

XML.onData()

The onData() method is useful for intercepting XML before the parsing is complete. It's an event handler that executes when Flash has received the XML data. If overridden, onData() lets you access that XML data before it is parsed.

- **Type:** Event handler

- **Syntax:** XML.onData(XMLsrc);

- **Parameters:** XMLsrc, a string of unparsed XML

- **Description:** The onData() event handler is the intermediary step between loading the XML document into Flash and parsing it. If the XML source has been loaded into Flash successfully, by default, onData() passes it on for parsing. As it does this, the loaded property is set to true and onLoad() is passed the success argument of true. If the XML document does not load successfully, onData() sets the success parameter for onLoad() to false.

  The onData() handler is particularly interesting if you do not want to leave the parsing to Flash's native parser. You can manipulate and perform your own parsing by assigning these functions to the XML.onData() event handler.

- **Player Version:** 5.*

- **Example:** The following example demonstrates how to override the native Flash player by assigning a function call to the onData() event handler:

```
myXML = new XML();
myXML.onData = function (data){trace(data);}
```

  The last line of the preceding code is all you need to redirect the raw XML that is loaded into your custom-built function. It is particularly useful if manipulating the XML directly is more efficient than passing it on to the native Flash parser. We do something similar with an alternative XML parser in Chapter 8, "Performance and Optimization."

XML.onLoad()

The onLoad() method is an event handler that is executed automatically when a loaded XML document has been completely parsed and distributed into an XML object tree. It does nothing by default, but is overridden in most Flash-XML applications because it's an excellent way to determine when the XML object is ready to be accessed.

- **Type:** Method

- **Syntax:** XML.onLoad(success);

- **Parameters:** success is a Boolean true or false value indicating whether the XML has successfully loaded with a load() or sendAndLoad() method.

- **Description:** The onLoad() method is basically a function with a parameter for successful loading—set with a Boolean value. After an XML document is loaded into Flash, the onLoad() method is called. The purpose of this method is to communicate when it is safe to work with the imported

XML document. Unlike the loading of SWFs, which might require pre-loaders, you can simply rely on this method to be called when it is successfully loaded.

Generally, as stated, calling this method means passing a success value, but the power lies in creating a custom function in place of the onLoad() method—and thus extending its functionality.

- **Player Version:** 5.*

- **Example:** The following example overrides the default onLoad() method by setting it to a custom function that will handle further processing or display of the XML content:

```
// create XML object
myXML= new XML();
// define your custom function statements
customFunction (success){
// perform the following actions ....
}
// set the onLoad method to your 'customFunction'
myXML.onLoad = customFunction;
// load XML
myXML.load ("myXML.xml");
```

Because the new customFunction() will receive the Boolean success value, you can also customize the function to handle loading failures by using an if statement to handle the true or false values.

XMLNode.parentNode

The parentNode property is used to get the parent node of the referenced XMLNode object.

- **Type:** Property (read-only)

- **Syntax:** XMLnode.parentNode;

- **Returns:** The parent node of the referenced node

- **Description:** Like the childNode property, you cannot use this property to set an XMLNode's parent node. This property simply returns the parentNode of the specified XMLNode object. If the specified node does not have a parent, a null value is returned.

- **Player Version:** 5.*

- **Examples:** In the following string of XML source code, the <mymusic> node (element) is the parentNode of the <artist> node/element:

```
<mymusic><artist>Tosca</artist></mymusic>
```

To verify this in Flash, you can do the following:

```
// create XML object and populate
myXML = new XML("<mymusic><artist>Tosca</artist></mymusic>");
// check to see what <artist> parentNode is
trace (myXML.firstChild.firstChild.parentNode);
```

The preceding code will produce the <mymusic> node object in the Output window because it is the parent of <artist>.

XML.parseXML()

The parseXML() method parses a given string of XML and returns an XML object representing it. It's called implicitly by both the XML object constructor and the onData() handler, so most times it's not needed.

- **Type:** Method
- **Syntax:** XML.parseXML(source);
- **Parameters:** source specifies the XML source code to parse into an XML object
- **Description:** This property is used to parse strings of XML data into an XML object.
- **Player Version:** 5.*
- **Examples:** A good example of using parseXML() is when transferring small pieces of information gathered from strings or input fields into an XML object for further use.

For instance, you can easily pass information about a membership submission process to an XML object. Assume that the following variables have been captured in the Flash movie:

Name = john smith;

Age = 35;

Occupation = programmer;

You can easily store this information in an XML object by parsing it into the object as follows:

```
// create new XML object
membershipXML = new XML();
// place variable information in XML source code
XMLToParse = "<member><name>" + name + "</name><age>" + age
        + "</age><occupation>" + occupation + "</occupation>
➥</member>";
```

```
// parse this XML string into the created XML object
membershipXML.parseXML(XMLToParse);
//trace resulting XML to the Output window
trace(membershipXML);
```

The Output window will now contain the following:

```
"<member><name>John Smith</name><age>35</age>
➥<occupation>programmer</occupation></member>"
```

XMLNode.previousSibling

The `previousSibling` property is used to get the sibling node that exists before the referenced `XMLNode` object.

- **Type:** Property (read-only)

- **Syntax:** `XMLnode.previousSibling;`

- **Returns:** Returns the previous child in the `childNodes` array of the parent of the referenced node

- **Description:** This property references the specified `XMLNode` and checks to see whether there is a `previousSibling` in the parent node's child list. It returns the node that precedes the specified `XMLNode`. Because this property is read-only, it is not possible to set an `XMLNode`'s previous sibling directly with the `previousSibling` property. It is meant only to provide a reference to the existing `XMLNode`.

- **Player Version:** 5.*

- **Example:**

```
// create new XML object
xStr =
"<music><artist>Tosca</artist><artist>Jazzanova</artist></music>";
myXML = new XML(xStr);
// output the lastChild of <music> hierarchy
trace(myXML.firstChild.lastChild);
// output the previousSibling to lastchild
trace(myXML.firstChild.lastChild.previousSibling);
```

XMLNode.removeNode()

The `removeNode()` method removes the referenced `XMLNode` from its parent node.

- **Type:** Method

- **Syntax:** `XMLnode.removeNode;`

- **Parameters:** None

- **Description:** As the name implies, this method is responsible for removing or deleting the specified node from the XML object hierarchy. The node object that is referenced will be deleted as well as all subsequent children of this node. After the node object has been removed from the XML object, the parent nodes' childNodes properties will automatically be updated.

- **Player Version:** 5.*

- **Example:** The following example simply removes the specified node:

```
// create new XML object
xStr =
"<music><artist>Tosca</artist><artist>Jazzanova</artist></music>";
myXML = new XML(xStr);
// output the number of childNodes in <music>
trace(myXML.firstChild.childNodes.length);
```

This code will display "2" in the Output window:

```
// remove the lastChild node of <music>
myXML.firstChild.lastChild.removeNode();
// output the number of childNodes in <music>
trace(myXML.firstChild.childNodes.length);
```

This code will display "1" in the Output window, so you have successfully removed the node.

```
// output entire XML to illustrate the node removal
trace (myXML);
```

Last, you just use trace() on the entire XML object to ensure that the node has been successfully removed.

XML.send()

The send() method sends the XML to a server-side script via HTTP.

- **Type:** Method

- **Syntax:**

```
myXML.send(url, window);
```

- **Parameters:**

  url   Specifies the destination URL to send the XML object to.

  window   Specifies the browser window or frame that the server will return data to. It can be a custom name of a frame or one of the following four presets:

  > _self   The current frame in the current window

  > _blank   A new browser window that does not yet exist

  > _parent   Represents the parent window of the current frame

  > _top   Identifies the top-level frame of the current window

- **Description:** This method is used to transfer XML objects from within the Flash environment to an external URL by using the POST method unless it is from a standalone application, in which case it uses the GET method.

  Generally, this XML will be sent to a server-side script or application for further processing, manipulation, or storing of the XML data. The window parameter is used to determine where the server-side script or application will return results from the send. This method is used for HTML output.

- **Player Version:** 5.*

- **Example:** The following is a simple example of sending an XML document you already have—ourXML—to a server-side script:

  ```
  ourXML.send("http://www.yourdomain.com/processXML.php", _blank);
  ```

  The preceding code sends your XML to the referenced URL, which contains a PHP script. This PHP script could do any number of things, including passing this data to a database or using it to perform further calculations. Anything that this script returns to the client will be placed in a new browser window, specified with the _blank parameter.

- **Notes:** If you want to have the server return information to the Flash movie, you need to use the sendAndLoad() method. That method is used for receiving and returning data via HTTP.

XML.sendAndLoad()

The sendAndLoad() method is essentially a combination of the send() and load() methods. After sending the XML to the server-side script, the script's response is read as XML.

- **Type:** Method

- **Syntax:** XML.sendAndLoad(url, targetXML);

- **Parameters:**

  url Sets the URL destination where the XML will be transferred to and must reside on the same subdomain as the location of the Flash movie requesting the sendAndLoad().

  targetXML This parameter holds information about the XML object that will receive the return information from the server-side script or application.

- **Description:** The XML.sendAndLoad() method is used to transfer information stored as an XML object in Flash to a server-side script or application through a URL location. This method translates the Flash XML object into an XML document and then sends it to the location specified in the method's url parameter.

  This method also needs to specify an XML object that's used to receive and store the results from the send operation as specified with targetXML. This XML object handles all returning data that will be structured as an XML document.

- **Player Version:** 5.*

- **Examples:** This example demonstrates sending and loading XML in and out of Flash, including the creation of a targetXML object for handling information returned from the server. We'll use a login process to demonstrate and assume that you have the following two variables entered by a user:

  Name = user27;

  Pass = sesame;

```
// create loginXML object to store user/pass info
xStr = "<login><name>user27</name><pass>sesame</pass></login>";
loginXML = new XML(xStr);
// create XML object to receive reply from server
loginStatus = new XML();
/* send this information to a server-side PHP script to verify
password information in database */
loginXML.sendAndLoad("/scripts/login.php", loginStatus);
```

Finally, you can add a custom onLoad() handler to the loginStatus XML to handle the reply and advance accordingly. (Note: Here we're not covering the function that handles the reply; we're merely illustrating it.)

```
VerifyLogin(){
/* here your code to handle the server's response
would go in the form of an if statement based on success
of login entry. */
...
}
loginStatus.onLoad = verifyLogin;
```

By adding this last line of code, you can have Flash immediately process the `verifyLogin` function after the XML returned from the server is successfully loaded.

- **Notes:** This method is used when you want to have results sent back to the Flash environment. If you want to have information returned to a browser window, you must use the `XML.send()` method.

  Because returned information from the server is placed in `targetXML`, you will need to check the `loaded` property of `targetXML` to ensure that the XML has successfully and completely been loaded before accessing the data.

XML.status

The `status` property is used to get a numerical value representing how successfully the XML was parsed into the referenced `XML` object. A value of `0` denotes a "no error" status.

- **Type:** Property

- **Syntax:** `XML.status;`

- **Returns:** The status returned by the XML parser

- **Description:** This property is used to determine whether an XML document has been successfully parsed by Flash into an `XML` object. If the document was parsed successfully, it returns a value of `0`; otherwise, it returns one of many negative values based on the reported error.

  Below is a full list of the status codes:

0	Success; the document was parsed without errors
-2	A CDATA section was not properly terminated
-3	The XML declaration was not properly terminated
-4	The DocType declaration was not properly terminated
-5	A comment was not properly terminated
-6	An XML element was malformed
-7	Out of memory
-8	An attribute value was not properly terminated
-9	A start tag was not matched with an end tag
-10	An end tag was encountered without a matching start tag

- **Player Version:** 5.*

- **Example:**

```
myXML = new XML("<example bad tag />");
trace(myXML.status);
```

- **Notes:** It's important to note that once an error has been found, all parsing stops, so you may in fact have further errors, but they will not be reported. It is also best to ensure that you have already tested the loaded property to make sure it has finished before checking the status.

XML.toString() (also XMLNode.toString())

The toString() method is the string representation of the XML object and/or XMLNode object, and all related child nodes. It is called implicitly any time you try to use an XML object or XMLNode object as a string.

- **Type:** Method

- **Syntax:** XML.toString();

- **Parameters:** None

- **Returns:** A string of XML representing the XML or XMLNode object that is specified

- **Description:** The XML.toString() method is used to translate data stored as XML objects into a string representation, which is basically XML markup. If it is an XML object, both the XML and DocType declarations are also included in this outputted string unless they are undefined. The method goes through and textually represents the complete XMLNode hierarchy of the calling object (whether it's an XML or XMLNode object).

- **Player Version:** 5.*

- **Example:**

```
myXML = new XML("<?xml version ='1.0'?><example>simple!</example>");
trace(myXML.toString());
trace(myXML.firstChild.toString());
trace(myXML);  // toString() is actually called here, implicitly.
```

- **Notes:** It's interesting to note that if you use the toString() method when the ignoreWhite method is set to false, the string will contain all white-space, just as when the document was originally created. If you want to get the information in a node but you don't know whether it's an element or text, try toString() instead of nodeName or nodeValue.

XML.xmlDecl

The xmlDecl property is used to read or set the XML declaration of the XML object.

- **Type:** Property

- **Syntax:** XML.xmlDecl;

- **Returns:** The XML declaration of the XML document

- **Description:** This property is used to store the document's XML declaration upon parsing. After parsing is completed, the property is set based on the XML declaration in the source XML document. If there is no declaration in the original XML document, this property is set to undefined. Although Flash records this information, it does not use it in any way.

- **Player Version:** 5.*

- **Examples:** If no XML declaration was set in the source XML document, it can still be set in Flash by using this property:

```
myXML.xmlDecl = "<?xml version=\"1.0\"?>";
```

{ Appendix B }

The XMLSocket Object

The XMLSocket object is a full-duplex network socket capable of communicating with a server specifically designed to serve XML content. The connection is a persistent one, unlike HTTP, allowing new levels of server-side interactivity that were previously not possible.

Methods and Properties of XMLSocket

XMLSocket()—constructor

XMLSocket.close()—close the socket

XMLSocket.connect()—connect to a server

XMLSocket.onClose()—handle the closing of a socket

XMLSocket.onConnect()—handle the connection of a socket

XMLSocket.onXML()—handle the arrival of XML

XMLSocket.onData()—handle the arrival of data in general (delimited by \0)

XMLSocket.send()—send information to the server

XMLSocket() **(Constructor, Not Object)**

- **Type:** Method (constructor)

- **Syntax:** `new XMLSocket();`

- **Parameters:** None

- **Returns:** Object of type `XMLSocket`

- **Description:** This is the constructor function for the XML socket object. It's used to connect via a raw TCP/IP socket to a server at a specified IP and port.

- **Example:**

  `MySock = new XMLSocket();`

- **Notes:** Port must be greater than 1024.

  `XMLSocket` can connect only to servers on the same subdomain where the SWF containing the `XMLSocket` originated.

XMLSocket.close()

- **Type:** Method

- **Syntax:** `MySock.close();`

- **Parameters:** None

- **Returns:** Nothing

- **Description:** This method closes the socket connection, if one exists.

- **Example:**

  `MySock.close();`

- **Notes:** None

XMLSocket.connect()

- **Type:** Method

- **Syntax:** `MySock.connect(host, port);`

- **Parameters:**

  `host` An IP address, or domain name

  `port` An integer higher than 1024 matching the server's listening port

- **Returns:** Boolean, indicating success of connection (true/false).

- **Description:** This method attempts to connect the Flash SWF to a server at a specified domain (or IP address) and port.

- **Examples:**

```
MySock.connect("192.168.0.1", 1025);

MySock.connect("www.somedomain.com", 2500);
```

- **Notes:** Port must be greater than 1024.

  XMLSocket can connect only to servers on the same subdomain where the SWF containing the XMLSocket originated.

XMLSocket.onClose()

- **Type:** Method (event handler)

- **Syntax:** MySock.onClose();

- **Parameters:** None

- **Returns:** Nothing

- **Description:** This function does nothing by default and should be overridden to be useful. It is a callback function that is called automatically when the server socket or client socket closes.

- **Example:**

```
MySock.onClose = function () {
  Trace("socket closed!");
}
```

- **Notes:** None

XMLSocket.onConnect()

- **Type:** Method (event handler)

- **Syntax:** MySock.onConnect(success)

- **Parameters:** A Boolean value, specifying whether the connection was a success.

- **Returns:** Nothing

- **Description:** This function does nothing by default and should be overridden to be useful. It is a callback function that is called automatically when the client socket finishes its initial connection attempt to the server socket. It gets passed a Boolean value indicated whether the connection was a success. The value, therefore, will be true or false, and should be useful information for overriding this method.

- **Example:**

```
MySock.onConnect = function (success) {
  If (success) {
    Trace("Socket connected!");
  } else {
    trace("Sorry.  Not connected.")
  }
}
```

- **Notes:** You can use whatever variable name you want to store the Boolean value that is passed. We use success just because it seems like a fitting name.

XMLSocket.onXML()

- **Type:** Method (event handler)

- **Syntax:** MySock.onXML(XML object);

- **Parameters:** An XML object, automatically passed from the XML parser.

- **Returns:** Nothing

- **Description:** This function does nothing by default and should be overridden to be useful. It is a callback function that is called automatically when the Flash parser finishes parsing new XML received from the server socket. It gets passed an XML object containing the parsed XML data received from the socket.

- **Example:**

```
MySock.onXML = function (xObj) {
    Trace("received: "+xObj.toString());
}
```

- **Notes:** None

XMLSocket.onData()

- **Type:** Method (event handler)

- **Syntax:** MySock.onData(someData);

- **Parameters:** A string of data, usually XML

- **Returns:** Nothing

- **Description:** By default, this function parses a received XML document from the client socket and returns an XML object by passing it as a parameter to onXML(). It can be overridden for other purposes, though, including receiving non-XML data. It is a callback function that is called automatically when new XML is received from the server socket (and *before* the XML parser parses it). It gets passed a null-terminated string of data as collected from the client socket.

- **Example:**

```
MySock.onData = function (xObj) {
    Trace("received: "+xObj.toString());
}
```

- **Notes:** If you don't need XML data, but you still want the power of the socket, this method can be overridden to provide a faster, non-XML connection with the server.

XMLSocket.send()

- **Type:** Method

- **Syntax:** `MySock.send(someData);`

- **Parameters:** Mixed data, usually an XML object, to be sent to the server socket as a string

- **Returns:** Nothing

- **Description:** This method is used to send information from your Flash movie/application to the socket that you connected to via the `MySock.connect` method. If the `MySock` object is not connected to the server, this method will be inoperable and fail in its attempt to pass information to the server.

  Basically, `MySock.send(myXMLObject)` sends information in the form of a string to the server. The information passed to the server "should" be in the form of an XML object; however, you can also pass along string data. Upon execution, the method's object parameter is converted into a string and sent to the server, followed by a zero byte (null).

  The `MySock.send` method does not return a success value to determine whether the information was sent successfully to the server.

- **Examples:**

```
myXML = new XML("<someXML>example</someXML>");
MySock.send(myXML);
MySock.send("<someXML>example</somexml>\0");
MySock.send("not XML!!\0");
```

- **Notes:** None

{ Appendix C }

FAQ

Here we have collected a number of frequently asked questions that come up when working with XML in Flash. Many of the common pitfalls we have addressed and covered throughout the book, so these examples are common problems that developers often run into when beginning to use XML in Flash.

What's the difference between POST and GET?

POST and GET are both methods to send variables to a Web server. Everyone's seen GET; it's the method used when you see the question mark in the URL, such as

```
www.asdf.com/asdf.asp?variable=value&meaningoflife=42
```

It's easy to see that variables and values are being sent to the script asdf.asp. POST is a little more elusive, though, because it is actually being sent in a less obvious place: the HTTP Request Header. That's a chunk of information sent to the server when you request a Web page, and it all happens behind the scenes.

Typically, GET is used in hyperlinks, and POST is used in HTML forms. If you have a choice (as you do with Flash's getURL() and loadVariables() methods), POST is usually the better choice because it is not restricted to 255kbps of information, as the query string of getURL() is. It's also done behind the scenes, saving you from ugly long URLs that everyone can see.

If you want your HTML pages to be more easily bookmarkable, GET can be easier.

Why is my `XML.sendAndLoad()` getting called with GET instead of POST?

Flash always uses the GET method when executed from the Flash application or from a standalone projector. POST is used with Flash files in an online environment free from standalones.

Why won't my movie work when it is uploaded to my Web server?

This problem could be a result of the security features built into the Flash player. Flash will not import or export information to a server other than the one hosting the original Flash file. Although from standalone projectors *or* from the Flash environment, you can retrieve information from any source (such as `slashdot.org`), this doesn't work when placed on a Web server.

The simplest way to subvert this "security" is to have redirect scripts that simply redirect a request to the other server. You put these scripts on the same domain as the SWF, so Flash treats them as local, despite the fact that they can redirect the script to an external document. Here are examples in ASP and PHP:

ASP:

```
<% response.redirect("http://www.somedomain.com/somexml.xml") %>
```

PHP:

```
<?
header("Location: " . "http://www.somedomain.com/somexml.xml");
?>
```

How can I prevent my XML files from being cached by the browser?

This is an issue for not only XML files, but also many sorts of files that can pull in dynamic content. When the browser caches the file, every hit to this file after it's loaded will pull up its first instance. To avoid this, you must make the file unique in some way. The simplest method is to dynamically append a name/value pair at the end of the file. When you do this, it makes no difference to the server, but the browser sees this file as unique and thus will hit the server for this file instead of pulling it from the cache. Let's quickly demonstrate this.

The following is how you might normally load in a file:

```
http://www.xmlinflash.com/content.xml
```

By simply modifying the URL for this file load, you can set it to be unique by attaching a random value at the end. First, inside Flash, you will want to create a variable "container" to store the value before loading the XML file:

```
dontCache = random(100000);
```

You have set the `random` variable equal to a value between 0 and 100,000. Now you concatenate it to your URL:

```
http://www.xmlinflash.com/content.xml?randomdontCache=54897
```

By adding this unique value to your URL, your browser will not cache the document and it will be refreshed from the server each time.

However, this method doesn't 100% guarantee that you won't receive a duplicate return when you use `random()`. Another common method that we used in some of our own examples is to append a time value.

We could have used the following, which will always return a new value that will be 100% unique, as it is linear based:

```
dontCache = getTimer();
```

Then we just simply add this value (represented in milliseconds) as we did in our random example:

```
http://www.xmlinflash.com/content.xml?dontCache=3478
```

How can I import HTML (1.0) into Flash via XML?

To import any sort of characters that XML might use itself, such as <, >, &, ', and so forth, you need to use what is called CDATA. It is particularly useful when you want to bring in HTML data, as it allows you to bring in CDATA content as is, without worrying about HTML tags affecting your XML structure. The following example demonstrates how easy this is; you simply need to place your HTML content inside the XML by using CDATA:

```
myXML - new XML("For further information <![CDATA[<a href-
➥'http://www.xmlinflash.com'><b><u>
<font color='#CC55CC'>check out</font></u></b></a>]]> our
➥companion site XML in Flash");
_root.textBox = myXML;
```

This example requires that you have a dynamic text field on stage called textBox and that you select the HTML option. This text field will display all the HTML contained in the preceding line, including the text formatting and anchor link.

As an aside, remember that to include <b> for your text, you must ensure that you have that font embedded in your FLA as well as the non-bold format.

How do I delete an attribute in my XML?

Unlike nodes (whether element nodes or text nodes), you cannot access attributes through any sort of numerical index array, such as `childNodes`. To delete an attribute, unfortunately you need to know its correct name. The following code is a simple example illustrating the deletion of an attribute.

First, create a simple XML document with one element named <musicArtist> containing the attributes `name` and `album`:

```
str= "<musicArtist name='Pink Floyd' album='Dark Side of The moon'/>";
myXML = new XML(str);
```

If you wanted to delete the `album` attribute, you could do so like this:

```
delete myXML.firstChild.attributes.album;
```

or

```
delete myXML.firstChild.attributes["album"];
```

If you wanted to delete all the attributes in an element, you can do this easily with one line of code:

```
delete myXML.firstChild.attributes;
```

What is CDATA for?

You'll definitely want to read up on CDATA in Chapter 2, "The Details of XML." Essentially, it is a different kind of node that contains information such as a text node. Here's a quick example:

```
<!CDATA[ blah blah blah ]]>
```

The purpose of CDATA is to safely store characters such as <, >, and / because they mess up an XML parser if they are in a text node. Flash is capable of parsing CDATA, but it stores it as a text node after it is parsed. This allows you to embed HTML tags, for instance, without having them "break" the XML structure.

How do I get the text from an element?

This is a common problem for newbies. For example, say you have the following node:

```
<ournode>here's some text</ournode>
```

You really have two nodes: one is <ournode> and the other is its child, a text node. Yes, that's right. Text is stored in its own node. If ourNode.nodeName is ournode, then ourNode.firstChild.nodeValue is here's some text. If you read that again carefully, you'll notice that you get the value of text from a text node by using nodeValue, and you retrieve the name of an element node by using nodeName. Take a look at Chapter 3, "Getting Your Feet Wet," if you want to read more about this topic.

What is the proper way to escape characters in Flash when using XML?

It's important to realize that you need to "escape," or encode, certain characters when placing them in your XML. As you've seen already, you can use CDATA to pull this string data in directly, or you can avoid that by using charCodes. These are strings that represent characters and follow the format of < (this would display the < character).

You can determine the proper charCode for any symbol or letter (especially useful for foreign letters and symbols) by using the following code:

```
charTest = "<";
trace (chartest.charCodeAt(0));
```

This will output the value 60, so the entire charCode for the character < would be <. If you wanted to place this character inside an XML element without using the CDATA tag, you would do so like this :

```
myXml = new XML("<DATA>expenses &#60; profit</DATA>");
trace (myXML);
```

The preceding code will output the following:

```
<DATA>expenses < profit</DATA>
```

Why is my XML not working from the standalone player?

This is most likely a result of using XML features enabled in versions r41 and r42 of the Flash player. This includes XML.contentType and XML.ignoreWhite. These two particular properties were added after r30 of the Flash player. You can use these new additions only in the browser environment, as Macromedia updates the browser plug-in but not the standalone version. Therefore, if you are using XML.ignoreWhite, it will not work in the standalone environment.

If you need to strip whitespace from your XML in a standalone environment, you might want to consider using our custom-built whitespace strippers, which are covered in Chapter 8, "Performance and Optimization."

Why do I have nodes without node names?

This is a common error when first working with XML in Flash, and it happens as a result of whitespace. Whitespace includes characters such as spaces, tabs, and line feeds. They are often used to format the XML display so that's it more readable for humans. However, Flash interprets these characters as nodes, and thus destroys the XML structure.

You can avoid this problem by setting the `ignoreWhite` property of your XML to `true`. This method will work in r41+ versions of the Flash player. You can set this line like this:

```
MyXML.ignoreWhite = true;
```

For more sophisticated stripping of whitespace, refer to Chapter 8, where we cover Flash-based strippers as well as server-side (PHP/ASP) versions in which we handle the removal of whitespace.

{ Appendix D }

Resources

Development communities are often one of the best ways to not only get inspired, but to find answers to questions you are having trouble with. In this appendix, we have attempted to provide you with a number of resources to aid in the development of your Flash and XML projects. We've divided the resources into Flash, XML, XML and ASP, XML and PHP, and finally XML socket servers.

There is a wealth of information to be found through these links. Whether you are a Flash developer, a database designer, or a PHP head, you'll find everything you need to know to assist you in creating powerful Flash-based applications.

Flash Resources

We begin with a list of Flash resources. The following URLs will take you to some of the most well-visited Flash-based resource sites on the Net. Many of them have been built around the notion of a community and offer the trials and tribulations of developers who have gone before you. As a Flash developer, most of them should be familiar, but we hope we've added some resources that will inspire and guide you as you tackle your own personal Flash and XML projects.

I-Technica

http://www.i-technica.com/whitestuff/index.asp

This is an excellent Flash 5 resource site that offers a wealth of information. Particularly of note is the Flash Q & A Archive, where you will find a large number of questions and answers, completely searchable, that have been culled from the many great minds that contribute to the Flash Coders list.

Layer51

http://www.layer51.com/proto

This site is aimed at intermediate to advanced Flash developers. It offers a wide range of prototypes, submitted by developers, to assist in Flash 5 development. The site offers custom prototypes for the XML and XMLSocket classes as well as all other Flash 5 objects.

Moock

http://www.moock.org/webdesign/flash/

Long a staple of the Flash community, Moock has contributed to the Flash scene in numerous ways and has made his discoveries available on his site. From the Moock fps speedometer to tips on programmatic motion, check out his code depot for many downloadable examples and FLAs.

Ultrashock

http://www.ultrashock.com

As one of the slicker Flash community sites and with more Flash heads than you can shake a stick at, Ultrashock is a must resource for all Flash developers. Featuring downloadable FLAs, tutorials from some of the best Flashers on the planet, and more than 10 forums dedicated to Flash, you'll find enough information and inspiration to keep you up really, really late.

Flashkit

http://www.flashkit.com

One of the long-standing pillars of the Flash community, Flashkit now has its own Flash developer conference! The site offers FLAs, tutorials, and frequently visited forums on every aspect of Flash development. You'll also find a host of supporting elements from soundFx to textFx for use in your Flash projects.

Were-here

http://www.were-here.com

This is another well-visited site with an active message board, including an XML board. Other than informative message boards, you can search through plenty of downloadable FLAs and tutorials by top Flashers.

Flashmagazine

http://www.flashmagazine.com

Although this is not specifically a Flash resource site, it is an excellent site for keeping up to date on the Flash scene. Covering the latest news in the Flash world, articles, tutorials, book and software reviews, Flashmagazine is a one-stop site for what's happening in the world of Flash.

Flashcoders List

http://chattyfig.figleaf.com/

If being on the pulse of Flash development is what you are after, look no farther than the Flashcoders list. This Flash mailing list is run by and subscribed to by some of the best and brightest in the field. Drop by and join the list, and begin to get some of the greatest Flash insights in your mailbox daily.

XML Resources

In this section you will find a host of resources aimed at XML development. From learning the basics of XML, following the standards that are being created, or covering the more complicated intricacies of XML and server-side languages, here you have some of the most popular XML resource sites available, with detailed descriptions on how each one can benefit you.

ProjectCool XML Zone

http://www.projectcool.com/developer/xmlz/index.html

A great beginner and intermediate site, Project Cool takes the user through why, how, and when to use XML successfully. The many references, tutorials, and concepts will get beginners well on their way to deciding whether XML is right for the project at hand.

eXtensible Markup Language (XML) from W3C

http://www.w3c.org/XML/

This site for the advanced developer wanting to keep abreast of the evolving world of XML offers a lot of news and includes changes/revisions to XML by date and XML standards from the guys who make them. A must bookmark.

Visualbuilder.com—XML

http://www.visualbuilder.com/article/index.asp?id=7

Visualbuilder.com regards itself as a "community for multi-skilled developers." The XML section of the site includes a forum, various articles, and reviews of other related Web sites, not to mention source code. The site also delivers content on many other programming languages, including ASP, VB, JScript, Java, and PHP/Perl, among many others.

Web Developer's Virtual Library—XML

http://wdvl.com/Authoring/Languages/XML/

A truly great Web developer's site, offering many XML references, FAQs, tutorials, scripts, and more, ranging from the most basic to advanced. A great reference site.

Webmonkey—Authoring XML

http://hotwired.lycos.com/webmonkey/authoring/xml/index.html

This site expands on the introduction of XML and includes an overview of the other XML-ish languages, including but not limited to XHTML, WML (wireless device programming), and XSLT. Also introduced is Synchronized Multimedia Interface Language (SMIL).

What Is XML?

http://www.builder.com/Authoring/Xml20/

This site's goal is to introduce the beginning developer to the world of XML. Topics include answers to questions such as How are SGML, HTML, and XML related? Who should learn XML? And what is the future of XML? A quick read of this site will help the developer figure out whether XML is a good technology to embrace for a particular project.

XML101.com

http://www.xml101.com/

As you might have guessed, this site deals again with the basics of designing XML-driven Web sites. Topics include XML basics, XML DOM, XML DTD, and XML XSL. The site also provides XML examples. Furthering those topics, the site focuses on the use of ASP and XML together. This is a must visit for ASP programmers looking to include XML technologies into their core development languages.

XMLhack

http://xmlhack.com/

The XMLhack Web site is geared toward the more advanced XML programmer. It delves into the use of XML alongside many OSD (open source development) tools and includes a huge searchable archive. We've just added this site to our IE link bar.

XML Resources

http://www.xmlresources.com

As you might have guessed by the site's name, you'll get many links to all sorts of XML-related content. Among other features, this site includes a section of reviews of various XML publications and lists XML-related Web sites, newsgroups and forums, and software. This site also provides links to documentation, whitepapers, and APIs.

DevShed XML Basics

http://www.devshed.com/Server_Side/XML/

This is truly one of the best developer sites. The XML portion of the site has many basic and more advanced tutorials and covers topics such as PHP and XML, WML and WAP, DTD design, and the introduction of Xlink. A must visit for any developer interested in client- or server-side technologies, this is a comprehensive site with an active community and a great newsletter.

XML.com

`http://www.xml.com/`

Another great starting site to get the feel for the scope of XML programming. Sections of this site include definitions of XML, XSLT, Xlink, XML Schema, and more. The reference section of this site includes information on Schemas, Mobile, Style, and Web. Other sections of the site are Columns, Guides, Toolbox, and a searchable archive.

W3Schools.com—XML Examples

`http://www.w3schools.com/xml/`

This site provides all the benefits of school without the tuition. It is divided into beginner and advanced sections: XML School explains the difference between XML and HTML, XML Examples teaches the user how to use XML by example, and XML Quiz provides a place to test your newly learned skills. The advanced section contains topics such as XML Server, XML technologies, XML CDATA, and many more.

XML FAQ

`http://www.jguru.com/faq/XML`

The purpose of this site/organization is to provide a place for developers to discuss and promote industry standards. The idea is to remain community minded, ensuring the open design and development of XML. Sections include FAQs, forums, articles, peerscope, learn, and news.

XMLpitstop.com

`http://www.xmlpitstop.com/`

The idea behind this Web site is to provide a place for developers to learn about XML, easily find XML resources, and interact with other developers. On this site you will find many working demos and their source code. Some sections of the site are resources, tutorials, examples, books, and user groups.

XML Scripts and Programs

`http://www.hotscripts.com/XML/Scripts_and_Programs/`

A portal Web site, Hotscripts is a one-stop shop for many diverse scripts in several different programming languages. The XML section of the site includes scripts on topics such as authoring tools, databases, discussion boards, e-commerce, and processors.

XML-Zone.com

http://www.xml-zone.com/

Another great developer site, with a huge searchable archive on XML topics. The site also encompasses all other programming languages. Go here to find information on any facet of programming.

XMLTimes

http://www.xmltimes.com

The main focus of this site is to provide timely news articles pertaining to XML technologies from many different news sites, including but not limited to ZDNet, CNET, XML Magazine, and traditional newspapers such as the *Washington Post*. Also included are an introduction to XML and a daily newsletter.

PerfectXML

http://www.perfectxml.com

This site includes a huge collection of references on many different aspects of XML technologies. Too much information to review in this short paragraph. A very cleanly organized site.

Microsoft Developers Network (MSDN)—XML

http://msdn.microsoft.com/xml/default.asp

Microsoft's review of the XML revolution, focusing on the use of XML along with various Microsoft technologies. This site is the XML side of the MSDN Web site.

Apache—XML

http://xml.apache.org

This site focuses on the contributions to and technologies of the open source XML revolution by the Apache Organization. Its goal is to provide commercial-quality solutions developed in an open-source fashion.

Projects include

- Xerces—XML parsers in Java and C++ (with Perl and COM bindings)
- Xalan—XSLT stylesheet processors in Java and C++
- FOP—XSL formatting objects in Java
- Xang—Rapid development of dynamic server pages in JavaScript

- SOAP—Simple Object Access Protocol
- Batik—A Java-based toolkit for Scalable Vector Graphics (SVG)
- Crimson—A Java XML parser derived from the Sun Project X Parser

XMLSpy

http://www.xmlspy.com

XMLSpy is designed to be a comprehensive and commercial development tool to facilitate advanced XML application development. The site also contains various references and resources.

XML Tools

http://www.garshol.priv.no/download/xmltools/cat_ix.html

This Web site offers information on hundreds of XML tools. A must-see site for any XML developer.

ASP/XML: Resources

If you choose to structure your server-side processing by using ASP, these resources are for you. Here we have gathered some excellent resources as they pertain to development of ASP using XML, including Microsoft-related resources.

4GuysFromRolla.com ASP and XML Articles

http://www.4guysfromrolla.com/webtech/xml.shtml

This page contains a list of XML resources that are helpful for both the beginning and veteran XML student. Sections include Introducing XML, XML in Practice, In-Depth XML, and XML Article Collections. ASP programming also heavily influences the site.

DevGuru.com XML-DOM Quick Reference

http://www.devguru.com/Technologies/xmldom/quickref/xmldom_intro.html

This site is another great starting point for the new XML developer. Included for a nominal fee is a valuable 239-page reference detailing all the interfaces that the W3C deems basic to any DOM implementation.

DevGuru.com Intro to XSLT in ASP

`http://www.devguru.com/Technologies/xslt/quickref/xslt_intro.html`

This site is geared toward combining XSLT and ASP technologies. Included in this section of the site—again, for a nominal fee—is a comprehensive 101-page reference source for all the elements and functions that compose the eXtensible Stylesheet Language Transformation (XSLT) version 1.0. This quick reference features real working code examples that were tested using the Microsoft XML parser version 3.0.

Intro to Creating Dynamic Web Pages with XML/ASP & XML Format

`http://www.vbxml.com/xsl/articles/dynamic/dynamic.asp`

This section of the site provides a useful introduction to creating Web pages using ASP and VB scripts with XML. The site also includes a code library, discussion lounge, and tools section.

ASP-XML Demos from Microsoft

`http://msdn.microsoft.com/downloads/samples/internet/default.asp?url=/`
`Downloads/samples/Internet/xml/asp_samples/Default.asp`

This section of the MSDN site gives a downloadable example of a server-side XML (ASP) demo and includes a description of the demo's function and various links to XML sections of the MSDN Web site.

PHP/XML Resources

For you "open-source" developers out there who are using PHP to interface between the client and server side, here you will find some tasty links to PHP-specific resources. From the basics of PHP/XML development to a custom-written xPath parser for PHP, these links should get you past any obstacles you might encounter.

DOM XML Functions

`http://www.php.net/manual/en/ref.domxml.php`

This site is part of the PHP Manual and contains information on how to use the DOM API in a PHP/XML document. Also included are notes provided by the PHP community about the DOM.

Gnome XML Library

http://www.xmlsoft.org/

This site describes in great detail the XML C library, libxml (for Gnome). The site is organized into the following components: Introduction, Documentation, Reporting Bugs, Getting Help, Downloads and News, XML, XSLT, The Tree Output, The SAX Interface, XML Library Interfaces, Namespaces, Validation, and DOM Principles. Also included is a well-documented real example.

PHP-DOM

http://devil.medialab.at/phpdom.php

This site explains how to use the phpdom class library, based on the DOM/XML library of PHP 4. There is a comprehensive documentation section of this site that includes a demo, as well as sections on API-Doc, usage, and features.

James Clark's Expat

http://www.jclark.com/xml/

James Clark has put together another XML reference site that focuses on various tools and parsers, including Expat, a library for XML parsing written in C. The site also includes test cases for testing XML parsers.

PHP XML Parser Functions

http://www.php.net/manual/en/ref.xml.php

This section of the PHP.net site contains information on XML parser functions. One of the sections is on building Expat. Other sections include case folding, error codes, character encoding, and some interesting examples. Also included are user comments about the examples.

Zend on PHP and XML

http://www.zend.com/zend/art/parsing.php

This site is intended for the experienced PHP programmer, interested in writing applications using XML. The focus of this section of the site introduces Expat, an XML parsing example with a sample script. However, the site also contains tutorials, columns, technical articles, and book reviews.

phpXML: XPath Parser Written in PHP

http://www.phpxml.org/

Xpath is an open source project still in the alpha stage that provides a PHP class for handling XML databases. An XML database contains one or more tables that can each contain records. Suitable for small to medium databases, in which SQL database hosting is not viable. It does not require DOM, and is built on the PhpXML class.

PHP-DOM Tutorial at PHPBuilder.com

http://www.phpbuilder.com/columns/matt20001228.php3

This section of the PHPBuilder Web site shows the XML developer an alternative to Expat using DOM. Sections include configuring the Apache Web server to use DOM and explanations of how DOM structures XML, the objects used in DOM, and examples using DOM, as well as references. The PHPBuilder Web site has many sections, some of which are a code library, a forum, and a searchable mail archive.

Socket Servers

Setting up a robust socket server for multiuser games and environments is no easy task. Although we have covered the fundamentals of establishing connections and passing information between user-to-socket and socket-to-user, you might find it worthwhile to look at some of the current open source and commercially available socket servers. More often than not, they will give your multiuser project a big boost in server performance and cut project development times.

The following is a list of XML socket–compatible servers.

Enhydra

http://enhydra.enhydra.org

The Enhydra project is an open source Java/XML server. Although enterprise Java standards such as Servlet 2.2 and JSP 1.1 are used to support presentation logic, Enhydra contains additional functionality to build dynamic Web applications, including an XML engine (Enhydra XMLC), database connection pooling, object-to-relational mapping tools, and more.

FD Server

`http://www.media-style.com/FDServer/Html_e/fdservindex_e.htm`

FD is a Flash 5 XML/Java server that works on Linux, Intel, and Sun Solaris platforms.

Flash Nexus

`http://www.flashnexus.com/download/`

Unlike other servers, the Flash Nexus was designed to be easily administered and incredibly easy to set up! Using a full GUI, you can easily see who is registered, who is currently online, and in what group he resides. Also, functions such as the ability to ban a user and disconnect a user are built-in to the interface. They've also added the ability for you to store and retrieve XML documents on the server from a Flash client. This allows you to save room and user preferences, room moderators for chat rooms, and many more uses. It currently runs on Windows machines/servers, but will be working on a Linux version in the future.

FlashNow

`http://www.nowcentral.com`

FlashNow is a server package available for Linux and Windows that's designed to support live Flash multiuser applications. With it, you can easily create flexible, extensible, visually arresting multiuser environments! Create games, chats, whiteboards,instant messaging, even whole collaborative Web systems. FlashNow enables live, two-way synchronous interaction.

Fortress

`http://www.xadra.com/`

The Fortress Interactive Entertainment Platform is a comprehensive solution for the rapid development, deployment, and management of single and multiplayer games, accessible by Web and wireless devices.

Fortress applications operate across heterogeneous networks and interface with phones, PDAs, game consoles, set-top boxes, and PCs by using industry-leading tools, including Macromedia Flash and Shockwave, Java, J2ME, BREW, and any other XML-capable environment.

LoserSoft

http://www.losersoft.de/eng/proj_flashserver.shtml

This TCP/IP socket server for Flash 5 clients is a cross-platform server based on Java technology. It offers XML communication server-clients and client-clients, hosting of unlimited groups and users (depending on the license), and a configurable database back end to support dynamic Flash content.

Swocket

http://sourceforge.net/projects/swocket/

Swocket is a cross-platform modular XML socket server framework implemented in Python with the intention of being used to communicate with Macromedia Flash 5 content, but can easily be used with other platforms that support the same flavor of XML sockets.

TextXML

http://www.ixiasoft.com/downloads/downloads.asp

TEXTML Server is a native XML database for dynamically storing, indexing, and retrieving XML content. In sharp contrast to most XML repositories that decompose the instance file into element content objects and store the markup as metadata in a relational or object-oriented database, TEXTML Server doesn't touch the native XML instance. Instead, TEXTML parses it and builds indexes based on markup.

XFactor

http://oc.xfactorstudio.com/

XServer is a pure Java server designed specifically for the Flash XML socket connection. It was created to give Flash designers the missing link to using the XMLSocket object in Flash. It is easy to configure, provides a simple API, and is flexible enough to be both a chat server and a multiplayer game server.

{ Index }

SYMBOLS

A